CASENOTE® Legal Briefs®

CIVIL PROCEDURE

Keyed to Courses Using

Subrin, Minow, Brodin, Main, and Lahav's
Civil Procedure: Doctrine, Practice, and Context
Seventh Edition

Authored by: Publisher's Editorial Staff

ASPEN PUBLISHING

To contact Customer Service, e-mail customer.service@aspenpublishing.com, call 1-800-950-5259, or mail correspondence to:

Aspen Publishing
Attn: Order Department
1 Wall Street
Burlington, MA 01803

Printed in the United States of America.

1 2 3 4 5 6 7 8 9 0

ISBN 979-8-8890-6958-4

SUSTAINABLE FORESTRY INITIATIVE Certified Sourcing www.forests.org SFI-00756

PRE-TRIAL PROCEDURE/ DISPOSITIONS

VOLUNTARY AND INVOLUNTARY DISMISSALS

1. Voluntary dismissal. (FRCP 41(a)). *McCants v. Ford Motor Co.*, 781 F. 2d 855 (1986).
   a. Without prejudice: plaintiff may reinstate action, within limitations period.
   b. With prejudice:
      i. Court order required.
      ii. Second voluntary dismissal.
      iii. Court or parties do not specify otherwise.
2. Involuntary dismissal. (FRCP 41(b)). *Link v. Wabash R.R.*, 370 U.S. 626 (1962).
   a. Defendant may seek for action or any claim, alleging:
      i. Failure to prosecute.
      ii. Failure to comply with federal rules.
      iii. Failure to comply with court order.
   b. Presumptively, with prejudice:
      i. Constitutes adjudication on merits.
      ii. Bars plaintiff, triggers *res judicata*.
   c. Exceptions:
      i. Lack of jurisdiction.
      ii. Improper venue.
      iii. Failure to join party. (FRCP 19)

PRETRIAL CONFERENCES OR ORDERS

Judge brings parties together to do the following:

1. Resolve procedural and discovery matters.
2. Schedule pretrial matters and conferences.
3. Consider settlement or other early disposition.
4. Simplify legal and factual issues for trial. *Sanders v. Union Pacific RR. Co.*, 154 F. 3d 1037 (9th Cir. 1998); *McKey v. Fairbairn*, 345 F. 2d 739 (D.C. Cir. 1965).
   a. Pretrial conferences (FRCP 16) to:
      i. expedite litigation;
      ii. control the case;
      iii. streamline pretrial activities;
      iv. encourage preparation for trial; and
      v. encourage settlement
   b. Discovery planning meeting (FRCP 26(f)) must be held and discovery plan submitted. District court then issues scheduling order that limits time in which:
      i. pleadings may be amended;
      ii. parties may be joined;
      iii. motions may be filed; and
      iv. discovery may be completed.
   c. Scheduling order must be issued within 120 days of service of complaint upon defendant.
   d. Court enters pretrial order (FRCP 16(d)).
   e. Sanctions available on motion or *sua sponte*:
      i. failure to obey scheduling order;
      ii. failure to make an appearance;
      iii. substantial lack of preparedness; or
      iv. failure to participate in good faith.

SUMMARY JUDGMENT

FRCP 56

1. Absence of a genuine issue of material fact. *Anderson v. Liberty Lobby, Inc.*, 477 U.S. 242 (1986).
2. Moving party entitled to judgment as matter of law and establishes:
   a. Nonexistence of a critical fact.
   b. That nonmoving party lacks sufficient evidence to prove critial fact. *Celotex Corp. v. Catrett*, 477 U.S. 317 (1986).
   c. Burden then shifts to nonmoving party to show that there is a genuine issue of material fact. *Bias v. Advantage International Inc.*, 905 F.2d 1558 (1990).
3. Procedure:
   a. Plaintiff may move any time after 20 days from commencement of action. (FRCP 56(a))
   b. Defendant may move immediately. (FRCP 56(b))
   c. Motion must be served at least 10 days before hearing date. (FRCP 56(c))
4. Required evidence (*Adickes v. S. H. Kress & Co.*, 378 U.S. 144 (1970)):
   a. Affidavits:
      i. based on personal knowledge;
      ii. containing facts admissible in evidence;
      iii. demonstrating witness competency.
   b. All products of discovery.
5. Partial summary judgment also available. (FRCP 56 (d))

DEFAULT JUDGMENT

FRCP 55. *Peralta v. Heights Medical Center*, 485 U.S. 80 (1980).

1. Entry of party's default:
   a. Answering party fails to plead or defend.
   b. Default secured by filing affidavit with clerk.
2. Clerk of court enters judgment.

TRIAL/RIGHT TO TRIAL

STAGES OF TRIAL PROCESS

1. Pre-trial conference.
2. Motions in limine.
3. Voir dire.
4. Opening statement.
5. Plaintiff's case-in-chief.
6. Motion (JMOL).
7. Defendant's case-in-chief.
8. Rebuttal evidence.
9. Motions (JMOL).
10. Closing arguments.
11. Jury instructions.
12. Jury deliberations.

RIGHT TO TRIAL

1. Constitution-based (Seventh Amendment). *Teamsters Local No. 391 v. Terry*, 494 U.S. 558 (1990).
2. Applies to cases that mix law and equity. *Ross v. Bernhard*, 396 U.S. 531 (1970).
3. Exceptions:
   a. Bankruptcy cases. *Katchen v. Landy*, 383 U.S. 323 (1966).
   b. Section 1981 cases.

JURY INSTRUCTIONS

Three types:

1. General verdict: finding in favor of one party without explanation.
2. Special verdict: specific written findings on some/all factual issues.
3. Mixture of general/special: See FRCP 49(b).

TRIAL/POST-TRIAL MOTIONS

JUDGMENT AS A MATTER OF LAW (JMOL) (DIRECTED VERDICT)

Pennsylvania R.R. v. Chamberlain, 288 U.S. 333 (1933).

Judge may grant a JMOL or directed verdict if opposing party fails to produce evidence sufficient to support a finding in its favor. (FRCP 50)

1. Timing: generally at close of opposing party's evidence, but may be made at end of opening statements.
2. If renewed at conclusion of all evidence in case, party retains right to move later for post-verdict JMOL.

POST-VERDICT MOTIONS

1. Post-verdict or renewed JMOL (JNOV) requires:
   a. Evidence insufficient to make a case for the jury.
   b. Timeliness: motion must be made within 10 days after judgment or jury dismissal.
2. Motion for a new trial (FRCP 59) requires (*Lind v. Schenley Industries*, 278 F.2d 79 (3d Cir. 1960)):
   a. Verdict against great weight of the evidence. *Peterson v. Wilson*, 141 F.3d 573 (5th Cir. 1998).
   b. Timeliness: must be made within 10 days of entry of judgment.
3. Extraordinary Postjudgment Relief (FRCP 60):
   a. "clerical mistakes."
   b. "mistake, inadvertence or excusable neglect."
   c. "fraud, misrepresentation, misconduct."

APPEAL

REQUIREMENT OF FINALITY

1. Final judgment rule: No appeal may be taken until a final judgment has been issued. *Cohen v. Beneficial Industrial Loan Corp.*, 337 U.S. 541 (1949); *Liberty Mutual Insurance Co. v. Wetzel*, 424 U.S. 737 (1976).
2. Exception – the collateral order doctrine for orders that:
   a. conclusively determine the disputed question;
   b. resolve important issue not related to merits;
   c. are unreviewable by appeal.
3. Partial exception – right to appeal certain interlocutory orders. (28 U.S.C. §1292(a)). *Gulfstream Aerospace Corp. v. Mayacamas Corp.*, 485 U.S. 271 (1988).
4. Partial exception – extraordinary writs (Mandamus). *Kerr v. United States District Court*, 426 U.S. 394 (1976).

STANDARDS OF REVIEW

1. Errors of law ("abuse of discretion"). *Salve Regina College v. Russell*, 499 U.S. 225 (1999).
2. Errors of fact ("clearly erroneous"). *Anderson v. City of Bessemer*, 479 U.S. 564 (1985).
3. Harmless error. *Harnden v. Jayco, Inc.*, 496 F.3d 579 (6th Cir. 2007).

CIVIL PROCEDURE

TERRITORIAL JURISDICTION

Territorial jurisdiction is the authority of the court to exercise jurisdiction over a defendant or property.

TYPES OF JURISDICTION

1. *In personam:* Whether the court has the power to adjudicate claims against a particular person depends on whether the person over whom jurisdiction is sought has a sufficient territorial connection to the forum state.
   - **a.** Defendant is present in state and process is physically served.
   - **b.** Domicile.
   - **c.** Consent. *Carnival Cruise Lines v. Shute*, 499 U.S. 585 (1991); *Hess v. Pawloski*, 274 U.S. 352 (1927).
   - **d.** State long-arm statute grants personal jurisdiction over defendant or property. *Gray v. American Radiator & Standard Sanitary Corp.*, 22 Ill.2d 432 (1961).
2. *In rem:* Jurisdiction over a particular item of property. *Shaffer v. Heitner*, 433 U.S. 186 (1977).
   - **a.** Determines who owns certain property in territorial control of the forum.
   - **b.** Adjudicates ownership interests of world at large to the property.
3. *Quasi in rem:* Rights of particular person to certain property. *McGee v. International Life Insurance Co.*, 355 U.S. 220 (1957).
   - **a.** Suit in which dispute arises out of parties' interests in the property.
   - **b.** Attachment jurisdiction.
     - **i.** Suit in which dispute between the parties has nothing to do with the presence of the property within the forum state.
     - **ii.** Property can be attached by court as "hostage" to a suit against the owner of the property.

DUE PROCESS REQUIREMENTS

Pennoyer v. Neff, 95 U.S. 714 (1877).

1. Fair and adequate notice. *Mullane v. Central Hanover Bank & Trust Co.*, 339 U.S. 306 (1950).
2. Minimum contacts with forum state. *International Shoe Co. v. Washington*, 326 U.S. 310 (1945).

MINIMUM CONTACTS ANALYSIS

International Shoe Co., v. Washington, 326 U.S. 310 (1945).

Defined – The minimal connection with the forum state necessary to justify general jurisdiction.

1. Does the defendant have any contacts within the forum state?
2. Are the contacts purposeful? *Burger King Corp. v. Rudzewicz*, 471 U.S. 462 (1985).
   - **a.** Forseeability of litigation? *World-Wide Volkswagen Corp. v. Woodson*, 444 U.S. 286 (1980).
   - **b.** "Stream of commerce." *Asahi Metal Industry Co. v. Superior Ct.*, 480 U.S. 102 (1987).
   - **c.** "Purposeful availment." *Hanson v. Deckla*, 357 U.S. 235 (1958).
3. Are the contacts continuous, systematic and substantial enough to justify general jurisdiction?
4. If there is no general jurisdiction, are the defendant's purposeful contacts with the forum sufficiently related to the litigation or do they constitute minimum contacts conferring the power to exercise specific jurisdiction?
5. Is the exercise of jurisdiction reasonable? *Burger King Corp. v. Rudzewicz*, 471 U.S. 462 (1985).

FEDERAL SUBJECT MATTER JURISDICTION

DIVERSITY JURISDICTION

28 U.S.C. §1332

1. Complete diversity of citizenship: No plaintiff may be a citizen of the same state as any defendant.
   - **a.** Refers to suits between:
     - **i.** Citizens of different states.
     - **ii.** Citizens of a state and citizens of a foreign state. *Redner v. Sanders*, 2000 WL 1161080 (S.D.N.Y. 2000).
     - **iii.** Citizens of different states and in which citizens of a foreign state are additional parties.
     - **iv.** Plaintiff in a foreign state and citizens of a state or different states.
   - **b.** An individual is a citizen of the state in which he is domiciled (place of fixed residence). *Saadeh v. Farouki*, 107 F.3d 52 (D.C. Cir. 1997).
   - **c.** A corporation is a citizen of any state in which it is incorporated or in which it has its principal place of business. (28 U.S.C. §1332(c)(1))
2. Jurisdictional amount requirement.
   - **a.** In excess of $75,000.
   - **b.** Good-faith allegations of the amount.
   - **c.** Exclusive of interest and costs.

THE ERIE DOCTRINE

Erie R.R. v. Tompkins, 304 U.S. 64 (1938).

In a diversity case, a federal court must apply state substantive law; however, even in diversity cases the federal courts may follow their own express procedural rules & statutes. *Hanna v. Plummer*, 380 U.S. 460 (1965).

1. Is the issue clearly substantive and not even arguably procedural?
2. If not, is federal law specified by federal legislation or an express federal rule?
3. If not, has the state conditioned the enjoyment of a state-created right in issue on enforcement of it according to state law?
4. If not, is the foreseeable impact on outcome of conforming to state law substantially likely to encourage forum shopping and the inequitable administration of the laws? *Byrd v. Blue Ridge Electrical Coop*, 356 U.S. 525 (1958).
5. If yes, are there countervailing considerations of federal policy that outweigh application of state law in diversity cases?

Note: In general *Guaranty Trust Co. v. York*, 326 U.S. 99 (1945), requires state law to apply if a different outcome would result under federal law. *Byrd* & *Hanna* are exceptions.

FEDERAL VENUE 28 U.S.C. §1391

1. District in which any defendant resides, if all reside in same state.
2. District in which substantial part of the events / omissions occurred or in which property is located.
3. "Fallback venue" applies only if otherwise there is no district in which venue is proper.
   - **a.** In diversity cases, where defendants are subject to personal jurisdiction when action commenced.
   - **b.** If no diversity, where any defendant is found. *"Forum non conveniens:"* State or federal court may refuse to exercise jurisdiction because forum has no interest, and controversy may be litigated more conveniently elsewhere. Transfer permitted between federal district courts. (28 U.S.C. §§1404 and 1406). *Piper Aircraft Co. v. Gaynell Reyno, et al.*, 454 U.S. 235 (1981).

SUPPLEMENTAL JURISDICTION

28 U.S.C. §1367. *In re Ameriquest Mortgage Co. Mortgage Lending Practices Litigation*, 2007 U.S. Dist. LEXIS 70805 (N.D. Ill. 2007); *Szendrey-Ramos v. First Bancorp*, 2007 U.S. Dist. LEXIS 74896 (D.P.R. 2007).

In any action in which the federal court has original jurisdiction, it also has supplemental jurisdiction over any other claims in the action that may form part of the same case or controversy. This includes claims involving the joinder or intervention of additional parties. Supplemental jurisdiction is limited in diversity cases. Courts may decline to exercise supplemental jurisdiction if:

1. novel or complex state-law issue;
2. the supplemental claim substantially predominates over the main claim(s);
3. the district court has dismissed all claims; or
4. there are other compelling reasons for declining.

FEDERAL QUESTION JURISDICTION

28 U.S.C. §1331. *Louisville & Nashville R.R. v. Mottley*, 211 U.S. 149 (1908).

1. Confers subject-matter jurisdiction over all suits to enforce federally created rights to relief.
2. In rare instances may also confer federal jurisdiction over suits to enforce state-created rights to relief that necessarily turn on substantial and disputed issues of federal law.

Federal Subject-Matter Judiction continues on page 2

REMOVAL JURISDICTION

28 U.S.C. §1441. *Caterpillar Inc. v. Lewis*, 519 U.S. 61 (1996).

Any civil action that was filed in state court may be removed to federal court for the district in which the case was pending, if the case is within the original jurisdiction of the federal court.

1. Original jurisdiction in federal court.
2. Only defendants may remove, all must agree.
3. Judicial district in which action was pending.

PLEADING

GENERAL TYPES OF PLEADINGS

1. Code-pleading – complaint requires a statement of fact that constitutes a cause of action. *Gillespie v. Goodyear Service Stores*, 258 N.C. 487 (1963).
2. Notice pleading – (FRCP 8) merges law and equity. Complaint merely requires (a) jurisdictional statement, (b) "short and plain" statement of the claim showing pleader is entitled to relief, and (c) demand for judgment. *Bell Atlantic v. Twombly*, 127 S. Ct. 1955 (2007).

ATTACKING THE PLEADINGS (OBJECTIONS)

1. Preliminary Objections. *Haddle v. Garrison*, no. 96-00029-CV-1 (S.D. 1996); *Haddle v. Garrison*, 525 U.S. 121 (1998).
   - **a.** May be raised by motion or in responsive pleading.
   - **b.** Objections to the manner in which action was initiated:
     - **i.** lack of subject-matter jurisdiction;
     - **ii.** lack of personal jurisdiction;
     - **iii.** improper venue;
     - **iv.** insufficient process;
     - **v.** insufficient service of process; and
     - **vi.** failure to join an indispensable party.
2. Formal pleading objections.
   - **a.** Procedural errors.
   - **b.** Motions to strike or motions for more definitive statement.
3. Substantive pleading objections.
   - **a.** Attack legal theory of claim.
4. Federal pleading objections: Pleadings may be attached by responsive pleadings or by motion.
5. Code pleading objections, e.g., demurrer.
6. Motions to dismiss.

THE ANSWER

1. Admissions and denials of allegations in complaint. (FRCP 8(b)). *Zielinski v. Philadelphia Piers, Inc.*, 139 F. Supp. 408 (E.D. Pa. 1956).
2. Affirmative defenses available.
3. Other defenses of a preliminary nature. (FRCP 12(b)). *Huddle v. Garrison*, 525 U.S. 121 (1958).
4. Counterclaim or cross-claim making allegations of liability owed the answering party (federal practice only).

SPECIAL PLEADING REQUIREMENTS

FRCP 9

1. Allegations of fraud or mistake.
2. Special damages.
3. Complex proceedings.
4. Alternative/inconsistent allegations are permitted.

TRUTHFULNESS IN PLEADING

Requires that all parties be candid and proceed in good faith.

1. Verification. Party who files pleading must:
   - **a.** do so under oath; and
   - **b.** sign her name attesting that matters therein are true to best information and belief.
2. Lawyers' certification. (FRCP 11)
3. Courts retain power to sanction bad-faith conduct. *Christian v. Mattel*, 286 F.3d 1118 (2003).

AMENDMENTS TO PLEADINGS

FRCP 15

1. Before trial. *Beeck v. The Aquaslide 'n' Dive Corp.*, 562 F.2d 537 (1977).
   - **a.** After any responsive pleading is served.
   - **b.** Within 20 days after served, if pleading itself does not permit responsive pleading, and action not yet on trial calendar. (FRCP 15)
2. Any time during/after trial with consent of all adverse parties.
3. Relatng back. *Bonerb v. Richard J. Caron Foundation*, 159 F.R.D. 16 (W.D.N.Y. 1994).
   - **a.** Amendments relate back automatically if permitted by applicable statute of limitations.
   - **b.** Amendments relate back to original pleading if claim or defense arose out of the same conduct, transactions, or occurrence.
4. Changing a party. *Moore v. Baker*, 989 F.2d 1129 (1993).
   - **a.** Relates back if:
     - **i.** Same conduct, transaction or occurrence.
     - **ii.** Party received sufficient notice.
     - **iii.** Party knew or should have known, but for a mistake, that the action would have been brought against him.
     - **iv.** Notice for (ii) and (iii) must be provided within 120 days after filing complaint.

VALIDITY AND ENFORCEMENT OF THE JUDGMENT

THE THREE ELEMENTS OF VALIDITY

1. Valid subject-matter jurisdiction. *See above*
2. Valid territorial jurisdiction. *See above*
3. Proper notice. *See* ***Due Process Requirements***.

THE SIX STEP APPROACH [DETERMINING VALIDITY]

1. Local law of trial court subject-matter jurisdiction.
2. Federal constitutional limits on subject-matter jurisdiction. *Kalb v. Feurstein*, 308 U.S. 433 (1940).
3. Local law of trial court territorial jurisdiction.
   - **a.** State courts:
     - **i.** *In personam* jurisdiction: against persons personally served within state.
     - **ii.** *In rem* jurisdiction: against property subject to attachment within state.
     - **iii.** State long-arm statutes authorize service on absent defendant. *Gibbons v. Brown*, 716 So. 2d 868 (Fla. Dist. Ct. App. 1998).
   - **b.** Federal courts:
     - **i.** Have jurisdiction over any served party (FRCP 4) while that person present in the state.
     - **ii.** *In rem* jurisdction: may exercise only in accordance with local law.
     - **iii.** *In personam* jurisdiction: may generally exercise against person served outside state, as authorized by local state law.
     - **iv.** Nationwide service is specifically authorized by FRCP 4(k)(1)(C)–(D) under Federal Interpleader Act and other federal statutes.
4. Federal constitutional limits on territorial jurisdiction. *Baldwin v. Iowa State Traveling Men's Assoc.*, 283 U.S. 522 (1931).
5. Local law of proper notice.
   - **a.** State court service of process:
     - **i.** Careful compliance with technical details.
     - **ii.** Process includes summons and complaint.
     - **iii.** Service requirements.

       Personal:
       - ***a.*** Delivery in hand to named defendant.
       - ***b.*** To entity: delivery to person appointed to accept.

       Substituted:
       - ***a.*** Delivery to person of suitable age and discretion, who lives with defendant.
       - ***b.*** Service by mail may require acknowledgment.

       Constructive:
       - ***a.*** Newspaper publication.
       - ***b.*** Posting at designated location.
     - **iv.** federal court service of process (FRCP 4).
6. Federal constitutional standards for proper notice. *Mullane v. Central Hanover Bank & Trust Co.*, 339 U.S. 306 (1950).

ENFORCEMENT OF JUDGMENTS (PROVISIONAL REMEDIES)

1. Attachment – holding asset when defendant not available. *Connecticut v. Doehr*, 501 U.S. 1 (1991).
2. Garnishment – attachment of wages or other income.
3. Preliminary injunctions / Temporary Restraining Orders (TROs) (FRCP 65) – available ex parte when defendant acting in way that would render the judgment ineffectual. *William Inglis & Sons Baking Co. v. ITT Continental Baking Co.*, 526 F.2d 86 (9th Cir. 1976).
4. Receivership – appointment of overseer to manage assets pendente lite, generally in cases of insolvency. (FRCP 66)
5. Civil arrest – functional equivalent of imprisonment for debt and severely restricted.
6. Notice of Pendency – not strictly a remedy, but notice to third parties concerning property in dispute, etc.

JOINDER

HOW, HOW MANY, AND WHEN CLAIMS AND PARTIES MAY BE AGGREGATED INTO A SINGLE LAWSUIT.

JOINDER OF CLAIMS

1. Joinder of claims is generally permissive.
2. Party asserting original claim, counterclaim, cross-claim, or third-party claim may join as many extant claims. (FRCP 18(a)). *M.K. v. Tenet*, 216 F.R.D. 133 (D.Cl. 2002).
   - **a.** Counterclaims. *Plant v. Blazer Financial Services*, 598 F.2d 1357 (5th Cir. 1979).
     - **i.** Compulsory. (FRCP 13(a))
       - ***a.*** Must arise from same transaction/occurrence.
       - ***b.*** If omitted, waived.
     - **ii.** Permissive. (FRCP 13(b))
       - ***a.*** Does not arise from same transaction/occurrence.
       - ***b.*** Asserted at party's option.
   - **b.** Cross-claims. (FRCP 13(g)). *Lasa per l'industria del Marmo Societa per Azioni v. Alexander*, 414 F. 2d 153 (1969).
     - **i.** Asserted by co-parties.
     - **ii.** Must arise from same transaction/occurrence as:
       - ***a.*** Original claim;
       - ***b.*** Counterclaim; or
       - ***c.*** Property in issue.

JOINDER OF PARTIES – INTERPLEADER

Owner of property subject to multiple claims may invoke to require parties to litigate in single proceeding; *Cohen v. The Republic of the Philippines*, 146 F.R.D. 90 (S.D.N.Y. 1993).

1. Statutory interpleader. *State Farm Fire & Casualty Co. v. Tashire*, 386 U.S. 532 (1967).
   - **a.** Minimal diversity.
   - **b.** Jurisdictional amount minimum: $500.
2. Rule interpleader.
   - **a.** Complete diversity or federal question.
   - **b.** If diversity, jurisdictional amount: $75,000.

JOINDER OF PARTIES – INTERVENTION

Third party initiates joinder to action already in progress.

1. As of right (FRCP 24(a)(2)), requires:
   - **a.** Risk of impairment of interest.
   - **b.** Timely application.
   - **c.** Lack of adequate representation. *Natural Resources Defense Council v. United States Nuclear Regulatory Commission*, 578 F.2d 1341 (10th Cir. 1978).
2. Permissive (FRCP 24(b)(1)-(2)) requires:
   - **a.** Conditional right under federal statute.
   - **b.** Claim or defense and main action have common question of law or fact.

JOINDER OF PARTIES – COMPULSORY

FRCP 19

Applies to a party needed for just adjudication. *Temple v. Synthes Corp.*, 498 U.S. 5 (1990); *Helzberg's Diamond Shops v. Valley West Des Moines Shopping Center*, 564 F.2d 816 (8th Cir. 1977).

1. Complete relief not available in its absence.
2. Absence of party would impair ability to protect interests. *Provident Tradesmens Bank & Trust Co. v. Patterson*, 390 U.S. 102 (1968).
3. Absence of party would expose other parties to substantial risk of inconsistent or multiple obligations.

JOINDER OF PARTIES – CLASS ACTION

Hansberry v. Lee, 311 U.S. 32 (1940); *Communities for Equity v. Michigan High School Athletic Assn.*, 1999 U.S. Dist. LEXIS 5780 (W.D. Mich. 1999).

1. Numerosity: too many class members to join individually.
2. Commonality: common question of law or fact.
3. Typicality: claims of named representatives must match those of the class.
4. Adequacy: named representatives must provide adequate representation.

JOINDER OF PARTIES – IMPLEADER

FRCP 18(a)

1. Joinder of additional party who may be liable to indemnify existing party.
2. Once joined, joinder of additional claims is also allowed.

JOINDER OF PARTIES – PERMISSIVE

Amchem Products v. Windsor, 521 U.S. 591 (1997).

1. Same transaction or occurrence.
2. Common question of law or fact.
3. Complete diversity and jurisdictional amount requirements apply.

PRECLUSION DOCTRINES

MUTUALITY DOCTRINE

Common law doctrine requiring the parties to the second action to be the same or in privity to the parties to the first action.

1. Preclusion cannot be used against person not a party to first action.
2. Exception: Collateral estoppel generally available by party not bound by first litigation. *Parklane Hosiery Co., Inc. v. Shore*, 439 U.S. 322 (1979).

COLLATERAL ESTOPPEL (ISSUE PRECLUSION)

1. Relitigating an issue of law or fact prohibited if issue was
   - **a.** actually litigated and necessarily determined; and
   - **b.** essential to a valid and final judgment.
2. Entered previously in litigation to which that person was a party, provided estopped party had incentive and opportunity to litigate issue conclusively. *Parklane Hosiery Co., Inc. v. Shore*, 439 U.S. 322 (1979).
3. Subject to additional fairness constraints when asserting party not party to prior litigation.
4. Subject to additional fairness constraints when issue was litigated in companion cases that reached inconsistent outcomes. *State Farm Fire & Casualty Co. v. Century Home Components*, 275 Or. 97 (1976).

RES JUDICATA (CLAIM PRECLUSION)

A valid, final judgment rendered on the merits constitutes an absolute bar to a subsequent action between the same parties or those in privity, upon same claim or demand. Requires:

1. Same parties to first and second suits. *Searle Brothers v. Searle*, 588 P.2d 689 (Utah 1978).
2. Final judgment on all parties' claims.
3. Final judgment on the merits.

INTERSYSTEM PRECLUSION

1. State court judgments in state court: the Full Faith and Credit Clause (Art. IV, §1) requires states to give preclusive effect to valid judgments in other states. *Durfee v. Duke*, 375 U.S. 106 (1963).
2. State court judgments in federal court: the Full Faith and Credit Act (28 U.S.C.§1738) requires federal courts to give preclusive effect to valid judgments rendered by state courts. *Gargallo v. Merrill Lynch, Pierce, Fenner & Smith*, 918 F.2d 658 (6th Cir. 1990).

DISCOVERY

BASIC DEVICES

1. Oral and written depositions. (FRCP 30 & 31)
2. Interrogatories. (FRCP 33). *In re Convergent Technologies Securities Litigation*, 108 F.R.D. 328 (1985).
3. Request for production of documents and orders for inspection. (FRCP 34). *Kozlowski v. Sears, Roebuck & Co.*, 73 F.R.D. 73 (1976).
4. Physical and mental examinations. (FRCP 35)
5. Requests for admission (FRCP 36):
   - **a.** admission of truthfulness of facts; or
   - **b.** admission of genuineness of documents.

SCOPE OF DISCOVERY

1. Inclusive – discovery is available for any matter: *Davis v. Precoat Metals*, 2002 WL 1759828 (N.D. Ill. 2002).
   - **a.** Relevant to subject matter of action (FRCP 26(b)(1)),
   - **b.** which appears reasonably calculated to lead to admissible evidence.
2. Exceptions:
   - **a.** Privileged matter (attorney-client, self-incrimination, spousal, physician-patient). *Upjohn Co. v. United States*, 449 U.S. 383 (1981); *Butler v. Rigsby*, 1998 U.S. Dist. LEXIS 4618 (E.D. La. 1998).
   - **b.** Attorney work-product. (FRCP 26(b)(3))
3. Experts. (FRCP 26(b)(4)). *Thompson v. The Haskell Co.*, 65 F. Empl. Prac. Cas. (BNA) 1088 (M.D. Fla. 1994); *Chiquita International Ltd. v. M/V Bolero Reefer*, 1994 U.S. Dist. LEXIS 5820 (S.D.N.Y. 1994).
4. Abuse and sanctions. (FRCP 26 & 27) *Zubulake v. UBS Warburg LLP*, 220 F.R.D. 212 (S.D.N.Y. 2003).
   - **a.** Unreasonable/excessive use of discovery.
   - **b.** Unreasonable compliance or refusal.
5. Duty to supplement responses (FRCP 26(e)):
   - **a.** General rule: no duty to supplement to include later-acquired information or for correction.
   - **b.** Exceptions:
     - **i.** Disclosure materially incomplete or incorrect, if not made known to other parties. (FRCP 26 (e)(1))
     - **ii.** If obtaining information that response was incorrect or failure to correct would constitute concealment.
     - **iii.** If required by agreement among court and parties.

About Aspen Publishing

Aspen Publishing is a leading provider of educational content and digital learning solutions to law schools in the U.S. and around the world. Aspen provides best-in-class solutions for legal education through authoritative textbooks, written by renowned authors, and breakthrough products such as Connected eBooks, Connected Quizzing, and PracticePerfect.

The Aspen Casebook Series (famously known among law faculty and students as the "red and black" casebooks) encompasses hundreds of highly regarded textbooks in more than eighty disciplines, from large enrollment courses such as Torts and Contracts to emerging electives such as Sustainability and the Law of Policing. Study aids such as the *Examples & Explanations* and the *Emanuel Law Outlines* series, both highly popular collections, help law students master complex subject matter.

Major products, programs, and initiatives include:

- **Connected eBooks** are enhanced digital textbooks and study aids that come with a suite of online content and learning tools designed to maximize student success. Designed in collaboration with hundreds of faculty and students, the Connected eBook is a significant leap forward in the legal education learning tools available to students.
- **Connected Quizzing** is an easy-to-use formative assessment tool that tests law students' understanding and provides timely feedback to improve learning outcomes. Delivered through CasebookConnect.com, the learning platform already used by students to access their Aspen casebooks, Connected Quizzing is simple to implement and integrates seamlessly with law school course curricula.
- **PracticePerfect** is a visually engaging, interactive study aid to explain commonly encountered legal doctrines through easy-to-understand animated videos, illustrative examples, and numerous practice questions. Developed by a team of experts, PracticePerfect is the ideal study companion for today's law students.
- The **Aspen Learning Library** enables law schools to provide their students with access to the most popular study aids on the market across all of their courses. Available through an annual subscription, the online library consists of study aids in e-book, audio, and video formats with full text search, note-taking, and highlighting capabilities.
- Aspen's **Digital Bookshelf** is an institutional-level online education bookshelf, consolidating everything students and professors need to ensure success. This program ensures that every student has access to affordable course materials from day one.
- **Leading Edge** is a community centered on thinking differently about legal education and putting those thoughts into actionable strategies. At the core of the program is the Leading Edge Conference, an annual gathering of legal education thought leaders looking to pool ideas and identify promising directions of exploration.

Format for the Casenote® Legal Brief

Nature of Case: This section identifies the form of action (e.g., breach of contract, negligence, battery), the type of proceeding (e.g., demurrer, appeal from trial court's jury instructions) or the relief sought (e.g., damages, injunction, criminal sanctions).

Party ID: Quick identification of the relationship between the parties.

Fact Summary: This is included to refresh your memory and can be used as a quick reminder of the facts.

Rule of Law: Summarizes the general principle of law that the case illustrates. It may be used for instant recall of the court's holding and for classroom discussion or home review.

Facts: This section contains all relevant facts of the case, including the contentions of the parties and the lower court holdings. It is written in a logical order to give you a clear understanding of the case. The plaintiff and defendant are identified by their proper names throughout and are always labeled with a (P) or (D).

Issue: The issue is a concise question that brings out the essence of the opinion as it relates to the section of the casebook in which the case appears. Both substantive and procedural issues are included if relevant to the decision.

Concurrence/Dissent: All concurrences and dissents are briefed whenever they are included by the casebook author.

Analysis: This last paragraph gives you a broad understanding of where the case "fits in" with other cases in the section of the book and with the entire course. It is a hornbook-style discussion indicating whether the case is a majority or minority opinion and comparing the principal case with other cases in the casebook. It may also provide analysis from restatements, uniform codes, and law review articles.

Holding and Decision: This section offers a clear and in-depth discussion of the rule of the case and the court's rationale. It is written in easy-to-understand language and answers the issue presented by applying the law to the facts of the case. When relevant, it includes a thorough discussion of the exceptions to the case as listed by the court, any major cites to the other cases on point, and the names of the judges who wrote the decisions.

Quicknotes: Conveniently defines legal terms found in the case.

Palsgraf v. Long Island R.R. Co.

Injured bystander (P) v. Railroad company (D)

N.Y. Ct. App., 248 N.Y. 339, 162 N.E. 99 (1928).

NATURE OF CASE: Appeal from judgment affirming verdict for plaintiff seeking damages for personal injury.

FACT SUMMARY: Helen Palsgraf (P) was injured on R.R.'s (D) train platform when R.R.'s (D) guard helped a passenger aboard a moving train, causing his package to fall on the tracks. The package contained fireworks which exploded, creating a shock that tipped a scale onto Palsgraf (P).

RULE OF LAW

The risk reasonably to be perceived defines the duty to be obeyed.

FACTS: Helen Palsgraf (P) purchased a ticket to Rockaway Beach from R.R. (D) and was waiting on the train platform. As she waited, two men ran to catch a train that was pulling out from the platform. The first man jumped aboard, but the second man, who appeared as if he might fall, was helped aboard by the guard on the train who had kept the door open so they could jump aboard. A guard on the platform also helped by pushing him onto the train. The man was carrying a package wrapped in newspaper. In the process, the man dropped his package, which fell on the tracks. The package contained fireworks and exploded. The shock of the explosion was apparently of great enough strength to tip over some scales at the other end of the platform, which fell on Palsgraf (P) and injured her. A jury awarded her damages, and R.R. (D) appealed.

ISSUE: Does the risk reasonably to be perceived define the duty to be obeyed?

HOLDING AND DECISION: (Cardozo, C.J.) Yes. The risk reasonably to be perceived defines the duty to be obeyed. If there is no foreseeable hazard to the injured party as the result of a seemingly innocent act, the act does not become a tort because it happened to be a wrong as to another. If the wrong was not willful, the plaintiff must show that the act as to her had such great and apparent possibilities of danger as to entitle her to protection. Negligence in the abstract is not enough upon which to base liability. Negligence is a relative concept, evolving out of the common law doctrine of trespass on the case. To establish liability, the defendant must owe a legal duty of reasonable care to the injured party. A cause of action in tort will lie where harm, though unintended, could have been averted or avoided by observance of such a duty. The scope of the duty is limited by the range of danger that a reasonable person could foresee. In this case, there was nothing to suggest from the appearance of the parcel or otherwise that the parcel contained fireworks. The guard could not reasonably have had any warning of a threat to Palsgraf (P), and R.R. (D) therefore cannot be held liable. Judgment is reversed in favor of R.R. (D).

DISSENT: (Andrews, J.) The concept that there is no negligence unless R.R. (D) owes a legal duty to take care as to Palsgraf (P) herself is too narrow. Everyone owes to the world at large the duty of refraining from those acts that may unreasonably threaten the safety of others. If the guard's action was negligent as to those nearby, it was also negligent as to those outside what might be termed the "danger zone." For Palsgraf (P) to recover, R.R.'s (D) negligence must have been the proximate cause of her injury, a question of fact for the jury.

ANALYSIS

The majority defined the limit of the defendant's liability in terms of the danger that a reasonable person in defendant's situation would have perceived. The dissent argued that the limitation should not be placed on liability, but rather on damages. Judge Andrews suggested that only injuries that would not have happened but for R.R.'s (D) negligence should be compensable. Both the majority and dissent recognized the policy-driven need to limit liability for negligent acts, seeking, in the words of Judge Andrews, to define a framework "that will be practical and in keeping with the general understanding of mankind." The Restatement (Second) of Torts has accepted Judge Cardozo's view.

Quicknotes

FORESEEABILITY A reasonable expectation that change is the probable result of certain acts or omissions.

NEGLIGENCE Conduct falling below the standard of care that a reasonable person would demonstrate under similar conditions.

PROXIMATE CAUSE The natural sequence of events without which an injury would not have been sustained.

Note to Students

Aspen Publishing is proud to offer *Casenote® Legal Briefs*—continuing thirty years of publishing America's best-selling legal briefs.

Casenote® Legal Briefs are designed to help you save time when briefing assigned cases. Organized under convenient headings, they show you how to abstract the basic facts and holdings from the text of the actual opinions handed down by the courts. Used as part of a rigorous study regimen, they can help you spend more time analyzing and critiquing points of law than on copying bits and pieces of judicial opinions into your notebook or outline.

Casenote® Legal Briefs should never be used as a substitute for assigned casebook readings. They work best when read as a follow-up to reviewing the underlying opinions themselves. Students who try to avoid reading and digesting the judicial opinions in their casebooks or online sources will end up shortchanging themselves in the long run. The ability to absorb, critique, and restate the dynamic and complex elements of case law decisions is crucial to your success in law school and beyond. It cannot be developed vicariously.

In addition to *Casenote® Legal Briefs*, Aspen Publishing offers the following study aids:

- *Emanuel® Law Outlines*
- Emanuel® *CrunchTime® Series*

Each of these series is designed to provide you with easy-to-understand explanations of complex points of law. Each volume offers guidance on the principles of legal analysis and, consulted regularly, will hone your ability to spot relevant issues. We have titles that will help you prepare for class, prepare for your exams, and enhance your general comprehension of the law along the way.

To find out more about our law school tools for success, visit us at *www.AspenPublishing.com* or e-mail us at *customer.service@aspenpublishing.com*. We'll be happy to assist you.

How to Brief a Case

A. Decide on a Format and Stick to It

Structure is essential to a good brief. It enables you to arrange systematically the related parts that are scattered throughout most cases, thus making manageable and understandable what might otherwise seem to be an endless and unfathomable sea of information. There are, of course, an unlimited number of formats that can be utilized. However, it is best to find one that suits your needs and stick to it. Consistency breeds both efficiency and the security that when called upon you will know where to look in your brief for the information you are asked to give.

Any format, as long as it presents the essential elements of a case in an organized fashion, can be used. Experience, however, has led *Casenote® Legal Briefs* to develop and utilize the following format because of its logical flow and universal applicability.

NATURE OF CASE: This is a brief statement of the legal character and procedural status of the case (e.g., "Appeal of a burglary conviction").

There are many different alternatives open to a litigant dissatisfied with a court ruling. The key to determining which one has been used is to discover *who is asking this court for what.*

This first entry in the brief should be kept as *short as possible.* Use the court's terminology if you understand it. But since jurisdictions vary as to the titles of pleadings, the best entry is the one that addresses who wants what in this proceeding, not the one that sounds most like the court's language.

RULE OF LAW: A statement of the general principle of law that the case illustrates (e.g., "An acceptance that varies any term of the offer is considered a rejection and counteroffer").

Determining the rule of law of a case is a procedure similar to determining the issue of the case. Avoid being fooled by red herrings; there may be a few rules of law mentioned in the case excerpt, but usually only one is *the* rule with which the casebook editor is concerned. The techniques used to locate the issue, described below, may also be utilized to find the rule of law. Generally, your best guide is simply the chapter heading. It is a clue to the point the casebook editor seeks to make and should be kept in mind when reading every case in the respective section.

FACTS: A synopsis of only the essential facts of the case, i.e., those bearing upon or leading up to the issue.

The facts entry should be a short statement of the events and transactions that led one party to initiate legal proceedings against another in the first place. While some cases conveniently state the salient facts at the beginning of the decision, in other instances they will have to be culled from hiding places throughout the text, even from concurring and dissenting opinions. Some of the "facts" will often be in dispute and should be so noted. Conflicting evidence may be briefly pointed up. "Hard" facts must be included. Both must be *relevant* in order to be listed in the facts entry. It is impossible to tell what is relevant until the entire case is read, as the ultimate determination of the rights and liabilities of the parties may turn on something buried deep in the opinion.

Generally, the facts entry should not be longer than three to five *short* sentences.

It is often helpful to identify the role played by a party in a given context. For example, in a construction contract case the identification of a party as the "contractor" or "builder" alleviates the need to tell that that party was the one who was supposed to have built the house.

It is always helpful, and a good general practice, to identify the "plaintiff" and the "defendant." This may seem elementary and uncomplicated, but, especially in view of the creative editing practiced by some casebook editors, it is sometimes a difficult or even impossible task. Bear in mind that the *party presently* seeking something from this court may not be the plaintiff, and that sometimes only the cross-claim of a defendant is treated in the excerpt. Confusing or misaligning the parties can ruin your analysis and understanding of the case.

ISSUE: A statement of the general legal question answered by or illustrated in the case. For clarity, the issue is best put in the form of a question capable of a "yes" or "no" answer. In reality, the issue is simply the Rule of Law put in the form of a question (e.g., "May an offer be accepted by performance?").

The major problem presented in discerning what is *the* issue in the case is that an opinion usually purports to raise and answer several questions. However, except for rare cases, only one such question is really the issue in the case. Collateral issues not necessary to the resolution of the matter in controversy are handled by the court by language known as *"obiter dictum"* or merely *"dictum."* While dicta may be included later in the brief, they have no place under the issue heading.

To find the issue, ask *who wants what* and then go on to ask *why did that party succeed or fail in getting it.* Once this is determined, the "why" should be turned into a question.

The complexity of the issues in the cases will vary, but in all cases a single-sentence question should sum up the issue. *In a few cases,* there will be two, or even more rarely, three issues of equal importance to the resolution of the case. Each should be expressed in a single-sentence question.

Since many issues are resolved by a court in coming to a final disposition of a case, the casebook editor will reproduce the portion of the opinion containing the issue or issues most relevant to the area of law under scrutiny. A noted law professor gave this advice: "Close the book; look at the title on the cover." Chances are, if it is Property, you need not concern yourself with whether, for example, the federal government's treatment of the plaintiff's land really raises a federal question sufficient to support jurisdiction on this ground in federal court.

The same rule applies to chapter headings designating sub-areas within the subjects. They tip you off as to what the text is designed to teach. The cases are arranged in a casebook to show a progression or development of the law, so that the preceding cases may also help.

It is also most important to remember to *read the notes and questions* at the end of a case to determine what the editors wanted you to have gleaned from it.

HOLDING AND DECISION: This section should succinctly explain the rationale of the court in arriving at its decision. In capsulizing the "reasoning" of the court, it should always include an application of the general rule or rules of law to the specific facts of the case. Hidden justifications come to light in this entry: the reasons for the state of the law, the public policies, the biases and prejudices, those considerations that influence the justices' thinking and, ultimately, the outcome of the case. At the end, there should be a short indication of thedisposition or procedural resolution of the case (e.g., "Decision of the trial court for Mr. Smith (P) reversed").

The foregoing format is designed to help you "digest" the reams of case material with which you will be faced in your law school career. Once mastered by practice, it will place at your fingertips the information the authors of your casebooks have sought to impart to you in case-by-case illustration and analysis.

B. Be as Economical as Possible in Briefing Cases

Once armed with a format that encourages succinctness, it is as important to be economical with regard to the time spent on the actual reading of the case as it is to be economical in the writing of the brief itself. This does not mean "skimming" a case. Rather, it means reading the case with an "eye" trained to recognize into which "section" of your brief a particular passage or line fits and having a system for quickly and precisely marking the case so that the passages fitting any one particular part of the brief can be easily identified and brought together in a concise and accurate manner when the brief is actually written.

It is of no use to simply repeat everything in the opinion of the court; record only enough information to trigger your recollection of what the court said. Nevertheless, an accurate statement of the "law of the case," i.e., the legal principle applied to the facts, is absolutely essential to class preparation and to learning the law under the case method.

To that end, it is important to develop a "shorthand" that you can use to make marginal notations. These notations will tell you at a glance in which section of the brief you will be placing that particular passage or portion of the opinion.

Some students prefer to underline all the salient portions of the opinion (with a pencil or colored underliner marker), making marginal notations as they go along. Others prefer the color-coded method of underlining, utilizing different colors of markers to underline the salient portions of the case, each separate color being used to represent a different section of the brief. For example, blue underlining could be used for passages relating to the rule of law, yellow for those relating to the issue, and green for those relating to the holding and decision, etc. While it has its advocates, thecolor-coded method can be confusing and time-consuming (all that time spent on changing colored markers). Furthermore, it can interfere with the continuity and concentration many students deem essential to the reading of a case for maximum comprehension. In the end, however, it is a matter of personal preference and style. Just remember, whatever method you use, underlining must be used sparingly or its value is lost.

If you take the marginal notation route, an efficient and easy method is to go along underlining the key portions of the case and placing in the margin alongside them the following "markers" to indicate where a particular passage or line "belongs" in the brief you will write:

N (NATURE OF CASE)
RL (RULE OF LAW)
I (ISSUE)
HL (HOLDING AND DECISION, relates to the RULE OF LAW behind the decision)
HR (HOLDING AND DECISION, gives the RATIONALE or reasoning behind the decision)
HA (HOLDING AND DECISION, applies the general principle(s) of law to the facts of the case to arrive at the decision)

Remember that a particular passage may well contain information necessary to more than one part of your brief, in which case you simply note that in the margin. If you are using the color-coded underlining method instead of marginal notation, simply make asterisks or checks in the margin next to the passage in question in the colors that indicate the additional sections of the brief where it might be utilized.

The economy of utilizing "shorthand" in marking cases for briefing can be maintained in the actual brief writing process itself by utilizing "law student shorthand" within the brief. There are many commonly used words and phrases for which abbreviations can be substituted in your briefs (and in your class notes also). You can develop abbreviations that are personal to you and which will save you a lot of time. A reference list of briefing abbreviations can be found on page x of this book.

C. Use Both the Briefing Process and the Brief as a Learning Tool

Now that you have a format and the tools for briefing cases efficiently, the most important thing is to make the time spent in briefing profitable to you and to make the most advantageous use of the briefs you create. Of course, the briefs are invaluable for classroom reference when you are called upon to explain or analyze a particular case. However, they are also useful in reviewing for exams. A quick glance at the fact summary should bring the case to mind, and a rereading of the rule of law should enable you to go over the underlying legal concept in your mind, how it was applied in that particular case, and how it might apply in other factual settings.

As to the value to be derived from engaging in the briefing process itself, there is an immediate benefit that arises from being forced to sift through the essential facts and reasoning from the court's opinion and to succinctly express them in your own words in your brief. The process ensures that you understand the case and the point that it illustrates, and that means you will be ready to absorb further analysis and information brought forth in class. It also ensures you will have something to say when called upon in class. The briefing process helps develop a mental agility for getting to the *gist* of a case and for identifying, expounding on, and applying the legal concepts and issues found there. The briefing process is the mental process on which you must rely in taking law school examinations; it is also the mental process upon which lawyers rely in serving their clients and in making a living.

Abbreviations for Briefs

acceptance	acp
affirmed	aff
answer	ans
assumption of risk	a/r
attorney	atty
beyond a reasonable doubt	b/r/d
bona fide purchaser	BFP
breach of contract	br/k
cause of action	c/a
common law	c/l
Constitution	Con
constitutional	con
contract	K
contributory negligence	c/n
cross	x
cross-complaint	x/c
cross-examination	x/ex
cruel and unusual punishment	c/u/p
defendant	D
dismissed	dis
double jeopardy	d/j
due process	d/p
equal protection	e/p
equity	eq
evidence	ev
exclude	exc
exclusionary rule	exc/r
felony	f/n
freedom of speech	f/s
good faith	g/f
habeas corpus	h/c
hearsay	hr
husband	H
injunction	inj
in loco parentis	ILP
inter vivos	I/v
joint tenancy	j/t
judgment	judgt
jurisdiction	jur
last clear chance	LCC
long-arm statute	LAS
majority view	maj
meeting of minds	MOM
minority view	min
Miranda rule	Mir/r
Miranda warnings	Mir/w
negligence	neg
notice	ntc
nuisance	nus
obligation	ob
obscene	obs
offer	O
offeree	OE
offeror	OR
ordinance	ord
pain and suffering	p/s
parol evidence	p/e
plaintiff	P
prima facie	p/f
probable cause	p/c
proximate cause	px/c
real property	r/p
reasonable doubt	r/d
reasonable man	r/m
rebuttable presumption	rb/p
remanded	rem
res ipsa loquitur	RIL
respondeat superior	r/s
Restatement	RS
reversed	rev
Rule Against Perpetuities	RAP
search and seizure	s/s
search warrant	s/w
self-defense	s/d
specific performance	s/p
statute	S
statute of frauds	S/F
statute of limitations	S/L
summary judgment	s/j
tenancy at will	t/w
tenancy in common	t/c
tenant	t
third party	TP
third party beneficiary	TPB
transferred intent	TI
unconscionable	uncon
unconstitutional	unconst
undue influence	u/e
Uniform Commercial Code	UCC
unilateral	uni
vendee	VE
vendor	VR
versus	v
void for vagueness	VFV
weight of authority	w/a
weight of the evidence	w/e
wife	W
with	w/
within	w/i
without	w/o
without prejudice	w/o/p
wrongful death	wr/d

Table of Cases

CHAPTER 1

An Introduction to Civil Procedure

Quick Reference Rules of Law

United States v. Hall

United States (P) v. Criminal defendant (D)

472 F.2d 261 (5th Cir. 1972)

NATURE OF CASE: Appeal from guilty verdict of contempt charge following nonjury trial.

FACT SUMMARY: As part of a desegregation plan, a federal district court issued a restraining order that was violated by Hall (D), who was not a party to the original segregation suit.

RULE OF LAW

A federal district court has power to punish for contempt a person who violates its order even though the person punished is not a party to the litigation out of which the case arose.

FACTS: As part of a desegregation plan, a federal district court issued an interim ex parte order restraining unauthorized persons from entering certain school grounds. The court served notice on Hall (D) who, nevertheless, went upon the grounds, stating his purpose was to violate the desegregation order. Hall (D) was not a party to the segregation suit.

ISSUE: Does a federal district court have power to punish for contempt a person who violates the court's order even though the person punished is not a party to the litigation out of which the order arose?

HOLDING AND DECISION: (Wisdom, J.) Yes. A federal district court has power to punish for contempt a person who violates its order even though the person punished is not a party to the litigation out of which the case arose. The activities of Hall (D) threatened the rights of the parties as adjudicated in the underlying desegregation suit, which had established that the original plaintiffs had a constitutional right to attend a desegregated school. The activities of persons contributing to racial disorder, which was the goal of Hall (D) in entering the school premises, imperiled the court's fundamental power to make a binding adjudication between the parties properly before it. Because school desegregation orders often strongly excite community passions, such orders, like in rem orders, are particularly vulnerable to disruption by an indefinable class of persons who, like Hall (D), are neither parties nor acting at the instigation of parties. Affirmed.

ANALYSIS

Although a literal reading of Rule 65(d) of the Federal Rules of Civil Procedure forbids federal courts to issue in rem type injunctions against persons not parties nor acting in concert with parties to a suit, the instant court noted that federal courts continue to issue such injunctions because they possess the power to do so at common law and because Rule 65(d) was intended to embody rather than to limit their common-law powers.

Quicknotes

EX PARTE A proceeding commenced by one party without providing any opposing parties with notice or that is uncontested by an adverse party.

INJUNCTION A court order requiring a person to do or prohibiting that person from doing a specific act.

IN REM An action against property.

Goldberg v. Kelly

Recipients of financial aid (P) v. State of New York (D)

397 U.S. 254 (1970)

NATURE OF CASE: Appeal from judgment invalidating welfare termination procedure.

FACT SUMMARY: New York welfare recipients of Aid to Families with Dependent Children (P) sued the state of New York (D) for refusal to adopt a pretermination hearing procedure prior to termination of benefits.

RULE OF LAW

The Due Process Clause of the Fourteenth Amendment to the United States Constitution requires that an Aid to Families with Dependent Children recipient be afforded an evidentiary hearing prior to termination of benefits.

FACTS: New York welfare recipients of Aid to Families with Dependent Children (P) sued the state of New York (D), alleging that New York officials were about to terminate such aid without prior notice and hearing, thereby denying them due process of law. At the time the suits were filed, however, there was no requirement of prior notice or hearing of any kind before termination of financial aid.

ISSUE: Does the Due Process Clause of the Fourteenth Amendment to the United States Constitution require that an Aid to Families with Dependent Children recipient be afforded an evidentiary hearing before termination of benefits?

HOLDING AND DECISION: (Brennan, J.) Yes. The Due Process Clause of the Fourteenth Amendment to the United States Constitution requires that an Aid to Families with Dependent Children recipient be afforded an evidentiary hearing prior to termination of benefits. When welfare is discontinued, only a pretermination evidentiary hearing provides the recipient with procedural due process, because for qualified recipients, welfare provides the means to obtain essential food, clothing, housing, and medical care. Thus, the crucial factor in this context is that termination of aid pending resolution of a controversy over eligibility may deprive an eligible recipient of the very means by which to live while he or she waits. Because such persons lack independent resources, their situation becomes immediately desperate and, in turn, adversely affects their ability to seek redress from the welfare bureaucracy. Affirmed.

DISSENT: (Black, J.) As a matter of constitutional law, a pretermination evidentiary hearing for recipients of state-funded welfare payments finds no precedent in the American legal system. The Fourteenth Amendment should not be given such an unnecessarily broad construction. New experiments in carrying out a welfare program should not be frozen into our constitutional structure. They should be left to the legislative branch to determine.

ANALYSIS

The Court noted that an Aid to Families with Dependent Children pretermination hearing need not take the form of a judicial or quasi-judicial trial and that a "fair hearing" will provide the recipient with a full administrative review. Hence, a complete record and a comprehensive opinion need not be provided at the pretermination stage and "minimum procedural safeguards" are justified. At the very least, however, the affected individual must have an opportunity to state his or her case orally to an impartial decision maker.

Quicknotes

EVIDENTIARY HEARING Hearing pertaining to the evidence of the case.

FOURTEENTH AMENDMENT No person shall be deprived of life, liberty, or property without the due process of law.

FOURTEENTH AMENDMENT DUE PROCESS CLAUSE Provides that protections mandated by the Constitution and observed by the federal government are equally applicable, and therefore must be observed by the states.

PRETERMINATION HEARING A hearing held prior to the termination of a property interest.

PROCEDURAL DUE PROCESS The constitutional mandate that if the state or federal government acts so as to deny a citizen of a life, liberty, or property interest the individual is first entitled to notice and the right to be heard.

QUASI-JUDICIAL Function of administrative officers to hear and determine matters.

Mathews, Secretary of Health, Education, and Welfare v. Eldridge

Secretary of Health, Education, and Welfare (D) v. Social Security disability recipient (P)

424 U.S. 319 (1976)

NATURE OF CASE: Appeal from judgment declaring unconstitutional administrative procedures established by the Secretary of Health, Education, and Welfare for discontinuing federally funded disability payments.

FACT SUMMARY: Eldridge (P) challenged the constitutional validity of the administrative procedures established by Health, Education, and Welfare (D) for assessing whether there exists a continuing disability entitling him to Social Security payments.

RULE OF LAW

The Due Process Clause of the Fifth Amendment to the United States Constitution does not require that the recipient be afforded an opportunity for an evidentiary hearing prior to termination of Social Security disability benefit payments.

FACTS: After obtaining medical reports, the state agency charged with monitoring his medical condition notified Eldridge (P) that it had made a tentative decision that his disability had ceased, advising him that he could request additional time to seek reconsideration. Instead of requesting reconsideration, Eldridge (P) commenced suit challenging the constitutional validity of the administrative procedures established by Health, Education, and Welfare (D) for assessing whether there exists a continuing disability, specifically contending that a pretermination hearing was required.

ISSUE: Does the Due Process Clause of the Fifth Amendment to the United States Constitution require that the recipient be afforded an opportunity for an evidentiary hearing prior to termination of Social Security disability benefit payments?

HOLDING AND DECISION: (Powell, J.) No. The Due Process Clause of the Fifth Amendment to the United States Constitution does not require that the recipient be afforded an opportunity for an evidentiary hearing prior to termination of Social Security disability benefit payments. The disabled worker's need for uninterrupted payments is likely to be less than that of a welfare recipient. In addition to the possibility of access to private resources, other forms of government assistance will become available if the termination of disability benefits places a worker or his or her family below the subsistence level. In addition, the existing pretermination procedures are fair and comparatively reliable, involving the more sharply focused and easily documented evaluation of a recipient's medical condition, rather than the more vague matter of his or her financial need. Hence, there is less reason here than in some other situations to depart from the ordinary principle that something less than an evidentiary hearing is sufficient prior to adverse administrative action. Experience with the constitutionalizing of governmental procedures suggests that the ultimate additional cost in terms of money and administrative burden would be substantial. Reversed.

DISSENT: (Brennan, J.) The Court's consideration that a discontinuance of disability benefits causes a recipient only limited deprivation is not argument but speculation.

ANALYSIS

The Court points out that the specific dictates of due process require consideration of three factors: (1) private interests affected; (2) risk of erroneous deprivation of such interests through the procedures used and the probative value of additional or substitute procedural safeguards; and (3) the government's interest, including the function involved and the fiscal and administrative burdens that the additional or substitute procedural requirement would entail.

Quicknotes

DUE PROCESS CLAUSE Clauses, found in the Fifth and Fourteenth Amendments to the United States Constitution, providing that no person shall be deprived of "life, liberty, or property, without due process of law."

EVIDENTIARY HEARING Hearing pertaining to the evidence of the case.

FIFTH AMENDMENT Provides no person shall be compelled to serve as a witness against oneself, be subject to trial for the same offense twice, or be deprived of life, liberty, or property without due process of law.

PRETERMINATION HEARING A hearing held prior to the termination of a property interest.

Jones v. Flowers

Property owner (P) v. Purchaser (D)

547 U.S. 220 (2006)

NATURE OF CASE: Appeal from grant of summary judgment to defendant.

FACT SUMMARY: After Jones (P) failed to pay his property taxes, the state of Arkansas (D) moved to sell his property for unpaid taxes. After two certified mailings to the home were returned, the state sold the property to Flowers (D).

RULE OF LAW

When a government has learned that its attempt at notice has failed, due process requires the government to do something more before the property may be sold at a tax sale.

FACTS: Jones (P) failed to pay property taxes on a house he owned but no longer occupied. The State of Arkansas (the State) (D) mailed two separate certified letters to the house, stating that the house would be put up for sale if the taxes were not paid. The certified letters, requiring a signature, were returned to the State (D) as undelivered. The State (D) was aware of that fact. The State (D) also published a notice of the tax sale just before the house was put up for sale. Flowers (D) purchased the house. Jones (P) then brought suit, alleging that he was not given proper notice of the tax sale. The State (D) and Flowers (D) argued that due process does not require actual notice and moved for summary judgment on those grounds. The trial court agreed and granted both parties summary judgment. The Arkansas Supreme Court affirmed. Jones (P) appealed.

ISSUE: When a government has learned that its attempt at notice has failed, does due process require the government to do something more before the property may be sold at a tax sale?

HOLDING AND DECISION: (Roberts, C.J.) Yes. When a government has learned that its attempt at notice has failed, due process requires the government to do something more before the property may be sold at a tax sale. Typically, due process does not require actual notice. Instead, this Court has stated that due process requires a government to provide notice reasonably calculated, under the circumstances, to make parties aware of a tax foreclosure sale and afford them an opportunity to be heard. Normally, service by mail or certified mail will suffice. However, the distinction here is that the State (D) was aware that its attempts to notify Jones (P) of the possible sale of his house had failed. In these situations, due process requires the State (D) to take additional steps where practicable. Here, the State (D) could have mailed the letters by regular mail, thus avoiding the signature requirement. It could have also posted a notice on the door of the home. The State (D) is not required to do a comprehensive search for the current whereabouts of the property owner. Lastly, the notice of the sale by publication in a newspaper was not constitutionally adequate because it was possible to give Jones (P) notice via service by regular mail or notice on his door. Reversed and remanded.

DISSENT: (Thomas, J.) The State's (D) two attempts to notify Jones (P) of the sale by certified mail, along with the publication in a newspaper, satisfied due process. The time for determination of whether notice is reasonably calculated to reach a party is the time the notice is sent, not subsequently. The Court's new policy is also burdensome on state and local governments.

ANALYSIS

In this six to three decision the majority's reasoning stands upon more solid footing. Chief Justice Roberts used the following example to undercut the dissent's argument that valid notice is determined at the time the notice is sent. If a tax collector gave a stack of notices to a mail carrier and then watched the mail carrier place them down a sewer drain, due process would dictate that the tax collector would have the obligation to create new notices.

Quicknotes

DUE PROCESS Clauses, found in the Fifth and Fourteenth Amendments to the United States Constitution, providing that no person shall be deprived of "life, liberty, or property, without due process of law."

NOTICE Communication of information to a person by one authorized or by an otherwise proper source.

Hamdi v. Rumsfeld

Alleged enemy combatant (P) v. Federal government/U.S. Secretary of Defense (D)

542 U.S. 507 (2004)

NATURE OF CASE: Habeas petition from designation and detention as an enemy combatant.

FACT SUMMARY: Hamdi (P) was charged as an enemy combatant and detained by the U.S. military. He challenged his status and the constitutionality of holding him without formal charges or proceedings.

RULE OF LAW

A United States citizen designated and detained as an enemy combatant has a due process right to challenge the underlying factual support for that designation before a neutral arbitrator.

FACTS: On September 11, 2001, al Qaeda terrorists attacked the United States and caused the deaths of 3,000 American citizens. In response, the President, authorized by Congress, sent military troops to Afghanistan to locate and subdue the terrorists and the Taliban regime supporting them. Yaser Esam Hamdi (P) was born in America but had lived most of his life in Saudi Arabia. He was captured by allied troops while fighting with the Taliban and turned over to the U.S. military. The Government (D) classified Hamdi (P) as an "enemy combatant" and decided to hold him indefinitely without formal charges or proceedings. Hamdi (P) challenged this designation as unconstitutional. The Fourth Circuit Court of Appeals held no further hearing was required and the United States Supreme Court granted certiorari.

ISSUE: Does a United States citizen designated and detained as an enemy combatant have a due process right to challenge the underlying factual support for that designation before a neutral arbitrator?

HOLDING AND DECISION: (O'Connor, J.) Yes. A United States citizen designated and detained as an enemy combatant has a due process right to challenge the underlying factual support for that designation before a neutral arbitrator. This Court finds that Congress did in fact authorize the detention of persons such as Hamdi (P) because Hamdi (P) was detained pursuant to an Act of Congress. Contrary to the Fourth Circuit's holding, it is not undisputed that Hamdi (P) was captured in a combat zone because all that is certain is that Hamdi (P) resided in that area. Hamdi (P) has thus not made any concessions abdicating his rights, if any, to further hearing. The Government (D) next argues that the Court should only consider whether broader authorization existed for the detention and not whether an individual detainee is entitled to further proceedings. A citizen, however, has a right to be free from unlawful detention without due process of law. The Court must weigh the governmental interest in confining enemy combatants against the individual liberty rights of the detainee. After due consideration, it is not necessary to provide initial due process hearings for captures, but those who must be detained further are entitled to further proceedings. The detainee must have an opportunity to demonstrate that the Government's (D) factual assertions are untrue. Vacated and remanded.

DISSENT: (Scalia, J.) How the law is applied to the facts of this case must take into consideration the special nature of the offending activity. Hamdi (P) was detained by the Government (D) because the Government (D) suspected that he participated in waging war against the United States (D). The relevant question is whether there is a different, special procedure for imprisonment of a citizen accused of wrongdoing by aiding the enemy in wartime. Justice O'Connor argued that captured enemy combatants (other than those suspected of war crimes) have traditionally been detained until the cessation of hostilities and then released. That may be an accurate description of wartime practice with respect to enemy aliens, but the tradition with respect to American citizens has been different. Citizens aiding the enemy have been treated as traitors subject to the criminal process. The Government (D) must prosecute for treason or another crime in federal court unless wartime allows for the enactment of the Suspension Clause. As no one contends this is a Suspension Clause situation, nothing allows for the detention of this man without due process proceedings. This is especially true given that this man is a U.S. citizen and not a foreign-born captive.

DISSENT: (Thomas, J.) We have held in prior cases that legislative authority to detain enemy combatants is unnecessary. Due process requires only a good faith determination by the executive branch whether to detain an individual during wartime. The executive branch, acting pursuant to both statutory and constitutional authority, may unilaterally decide to detain an individual if the executive makes determination that the detention will protect the public. Judicial second guessing of such a determination should not be allowed. Moreover, allowing hearings on Hamdi's (P) detention may harm the intelligence gathering process and may even force the government to divulge classified material.

Continued on next page.

ANALYSIS

While the Court did not directly address presidential authority to designate and detain enemy combatants, it did temper the government's attempts to unilaterally control wartime captures as they related to American citizens. Although many supported the President's actions after the terrorist attacks of 2001, many more recognized the danger in vesting too much power in the executive branch even in wartime. Mistakes may be made; and captured U.S. citizens should be entitled to place their case before an objective party.

Quicknotes

CERTIORARI A discretionary writ issued by a superior court to an inferior court in order to review the lower court's decisions; the Supreme Court's writ ordering such review.

DUE PROCESS Clauses, found in the Fifth and Fourteenth Amendments to the United States Constitution, providing that no person shall be deprived of "life, liberty, or property, without due process of law."

HABEAS CORPUS A proceeding in which a defendant brings a writ to compel a judicial determination of whether he is lawfully being held in custody.

Boddie v. Connecticut

Welfare recipient (P) v. State (D)

401 U.S. 371 (1971)

NATURE OF CASE: Appeal from dismissal of complaint challenging constitutionality of fee requirements as applied to indigents for commencement of divorce litigation.

FACT SUMMARY: Indigent welfare recipients (P) sued the State (D), arguing that to require indigents to pay fees for access to courts in marital dissolution proceedings violates due process.

RULE OF LAW

Due process prohibits a state from denying, solely because of inability to pay, access to its courts to individuals who seek judicial dissolution of their marriages.

FACTS: Indigent welfare recipients (P) sued the State (D) in federal district court in a class action challenging certain state procedures for commencement of marital dissolution litigation, including requirements for payment of court fees and costs for service of process, which they could not afford to pay and that, therefore, allegedly restricted their access to the courts in their efforts to bring an action for divorce. The district court ruled against the plaintiffs, and the United States Supreme Court granted certiorari.

ISSUE: Does due process prohibit a state from denying, solely because of inability to pay, access to its courts to individuals who seek judicial dissolution of their marriages?

HOLDING AND DECISION: (Harlan, J.) Yes. Due process prohibits a state from denying, solely because of inability to pay, access to its courts to individuals who seek judicial dissolution of their marriages. Given the basic position of the marriage relationship in American society's hierarchy of values and the concomitant state monopolization of the means for legally dissolving this relationship, it is a violation of due process for a state to deny, solely because of an individual's inability to pay, access to its courts for the purpose of seeking a divorce. Marriage involves interests of basic importance in American society and, in the instant case, meaningful opportunity to be heard, within the limits of practicality, must be protected against denial by particular laws, such as here, that operate to jeopardize it for particular individuals. Reversed.

CONCURRENCE: (Brennan, J.) Here, the State (D) has denied procedural due process to individuals, like the plaintiffs, by denying them access to the State's (D) courts solely on account of their indigency. However, the Court's decision should have gone further than it did and should not have depended solely on the factor that only the State (D) can grant a divorce. That is because as a practical matter a state has a monopoly on all judicial proceedings, not just those relating to marriage and divorce, and the right to be heard in some way at some time extends to all such proceedings. Moreover, in this case, not only is due process implicated, but equal protection is as well since the State (D) denies a hearing only to those individuals who cannot pay certain fees. The validity of such partial denial, or differentiation in treatment, can be scrutinized under equal protection as well as due process principles. Because courts are the central dispute-settling institutions in our society, they are bound to do equal justice under law to rich and poor alike. If money can determine whether a person gets into court at all, the great principle of equal protection becomes a mockery. Accordingly, the State's (D) fee requirement, as applied to indigents, is a denial of equal protection.

DISSENT: (Black, J.) Absent some specific federal constitutional or statutory provision, marriage and divorce in America are completely under state control. In determining applicability of the due process clause, civil lawsuits are not like criminal prosecutions and the government is not usually involved as an actual party; hence, there is no deprivation of life, liberty, or property.

ANALYSIS

In concluding that the due process clause requires an indigent applicant an opportunity to go into court to obtain a divorce even if such person cannot afford to pay the court fees, the Court emphasized that it went no further than necessary to dispose of the case before it and did not decide that access for all individuals to the courts is a right that is, in all circumstances, guaranteed by the Due Process Clause.

Quicknotes

DUE PROCESS CLAUSE Clauses, found in the Fifth and Fourteenth Amendments to the United States Constitution, providing that no person shall be deprived of "life, liberty, or property, without due process of law."

INDIGENT A person who is poor and thus is unable to obtain counsel to defend himself in a criminal proceeding and for whom counsel must be appointed.

MARITAL DISSOLUTION Legal termination of the marital relationship.

Lassiter v. Department of Social Services of Durham County, North Carolina

Parent (D) v. State agency (P)

452 U.S. 18 (1981)

NATURE OF CASE: Appeal from a termination of parental rights.

FACT SUMMARY: Lassiter (D) contended she was entitled to the appointment of counsel in a procedure to terminate her parental rights.

RULE OF LAW

There is no constitutional right to appointed counsel, unless the party, if she loses, may be deprived of her physical liberty.

FACTS: Lassiter (D) lost custody of her infant son, William, after a trial court found she had neglected him and failed to provide him with adequate medical care. Following this, Lassiter (D) was charged with murder and convicted and sentenced to 25 to 40 years of imprisonment. The Department of Social Services (P) brought a proceeding to terminate her parental rights. At the hearing, Lassiter (D) was not represented by counsel, and she did not indicate that she was indigent. Following the taking of testimony, her parental rights were terminated. Lassiter (D) appealed, contending that she was in fact indigent and that she was entitled to appointed counsel prior to the termination of her parental rights. The Supreme Court of North Carolina denied the asserted right to appointed counsel, and the United States Supreme Court granted review.

ISSUE: Is there a constitutional right to appointed counsel, unless the party, if she loses, may be deprived of her physical liberty?

HOLDING AND DECISION: (Stewart, J.) No. There is no right to appointed counsel, unless the party, if she loses, may be deprived of her physical liberty. The basis for Lassiter's (D) assertion of a right to counsel is based upon the Due Process Clause of the Fourteenth Amendment. This clause has been interpreted on many occasions as requiring appointed counsel only where the right to personal liberty is in jeopardy. These situations almost always involve criminal proceedings. The result of the termination of parental rights is not one that encompasses the possibility of a deprivation of personal liberty. As a result, there is no right to appointed counsel, and no abuse of discretion was displayed by the trial court in failing to supply such counsel. As a result, the holding of the North Carolina Supreme Court must be affirmed.

DISSENT: (Blackmun, J.) The case at issue involves the interest of a parent in the companionship, care, custody, and management of his or her children. A more fundamental right cannot be imagined, and the deprivation of such right clearly approaches, if not exceeds, the right to personal liberty. As a result, the right to appointment of counsel must be recognized in this situation in order to uphold the policy behind maintaining the family unit. Without such counsel, Lassiter (D) has been deprived of an opportunity to be meaningfully heard prior to the termination of her fundamental right as a parent.

ANALYSIS

The seminal case in due process discussions of the type illustrated in this case is that found in *Mathews v. Eldridge*, 424 U.S. 319 (1976). In that case, a formula involving three elements was developed, and courts were required to evaluate such elements in deciding the requirements of due process. Those three elements include the private interests at stake, the government's interests, and the risk that the procedures used will lead to erroneous decisions. The use of these factors in this case allows the Court to conclude that while a parent has an extremely high private interest in maintaining the parental rights, the government's interests and the risk of the procedures used leading to an erroneous decision simply outweighed those rights. The procedure by which the rights were terminated was found to be adequate, and the governmental interest in protecting the child was found to be paramount. As a result, it was found that due process was not violated in this case.

Quicknotes

DUE PROCESS CLAUSE Clauses, found in the Fifth and Fourteenth Amendments to the United States Constitution, providing that no person shall be deprived of "life, liberty, or property, without due process of law."

FOURTEENTH AMENDMENT DUE PROCESS CLAUSE Provides that protections mandated by the Constitution and observed by the federal government are equally applicable, and therefore must be observed by the States.

INDIGENT A person who is poor and thus is unable to obtain counsel to defend himself in a criminal proceeding and for whom counsel must be appointed.

CHAPTER 2

Remedies and Stakes

Quick Reference Rules of Law

PAGE

1. *Fuentes v. Shevin.* Before a state may authorize its agents to seize a party's property upon the application of another party, the Fourteenth Amendment requires that the possessor be given the opportunity to have a pre-seizure hearing to challenge the seizure. *12*

2. *Winter v. Natural Resources Defense Council, Inc.* A plaintiff who seeks a preliminary injunction must establish he is likely to succeed on the merits, he is likely to suffer irreparable harm in the absence of preliminary relief, the balance of equities tips in his favor, and an injunction is in the public interest. *14*

3. *Department of Homeland Security et al. v. New York, et al.* An application for stay pending appeal should be granted to stay enforcement of a universal injunction that purports to apply to anyone in the nation, not just to the plaintiffs in an action, or even to a definable group having something to do with the plaintiffs' claimed injury. *17*

4. *Walgreen Co. v. Sara Creek Property Co.* Where damages would be a costly and inadequate remedy, injunctive relief should be granted. *18*

5. *Brown v. Plata.* A remedial order issued by a three-judge district court convened pursuant to the Prison Litigation Reform Act of 1995 (PLRA), which requires a state to significantly reduce its prison population to remedy Eighth Amendment violations resulting from overcrowding, meets the PLRA's requirements and procedures where: the PLRA's requirement of allowing a state a reasonable amount of time to comply with previous court orders is satisfied; evidence supports the court's finding that overcrowding is the primary cause of Eighth Amendment violations; evidence supports the court's finding that no other relief would remedy the Eighth Amendment violations; the court has given substantial weight to public safety; and the evidence supports the court's determination of the appropriate number at which the prison population should be capped. *19*

6. *Carey v. Piphus.* In an action based on denial of procedural due process, only nominal damages may be awarded in the absence of actual injury. *24*

7. *Marek v. Chesny.* Attorney fees incurred by a plaintiff subsequent to an offer of settlement will not be paid when the plaintiff recovers less than the offer. *25*

8. *City of Riverside v. Rivera.* An award of attorneys' fees under 42 U.S.C. § 1988 is not per se "unreasonable" within the meaning of the statute if it exceeds the amount of damages recovered by the plaintiff in the underlying civil rights action. *26*

9. *Walker v. City of Birmingham.* The subject of an injunction that has been issued by a court of competent jurisdiction may be held in contempt for disobeying the injunction where the subject has not challenged the validity of the injunction or any underlying law through the judicial system, notwithstanding that both the process involved in the injunction's issuance and the law underpinning the injunction may have been unconstitutional. *27*

Fuentes v. Shevin

Owner of chattels (P) v. Court (D)

407 U.S. 67 (1972)

NATURE OF CASE: Appeals in consolidated cases from judgments upholding states' prejudgment replevin procedures against due process attack.

FACT SUMMARY: Fuentes (P), who had a stove and stereo seized by the sheriff prior to the adjudication of a suit filed by Firestone Tire and Rubber Co. for nonpayment of the installment sales contract pursuant to which Fuentes (P) had purchased the items, argued the state's (Florida's) prejudgment replevin procedure, which permitted a writ of replevin to issue and chattels to be seized without notice to their possessor and without offering the possessor an opportunity to be heard prior to the seizure, was unconstitutional insofar as it deprived her of her property without due process. A similar statute in Pennsylvania was similarly attacked, and the cases were consolidated on appeal.

RULE OF LAW

Before a state may authorize its agents to seize a party's property upon the application of another party, the Fourteenth Amendment requires that the possessor be given the opportunity to have a pre-seizure hearing to challenge the seizure.

FACTS: Fuentes (P) purchased a gas stove and service policy, and later a stereo, from Firestone Tire and Rubber Co. (Firestone) pursuant to a conditional sales contract, a type of installment contract. After a year, a dispute arose between Fuentes (P) and Firestone over the servicing of the stove. Firestone filed an action for replevin of both the stove and the stereo, claiming Fuentes (P) had defaulted on her installment payments. Before she was served with the complaint, Firestone obtained a writ of replevin and the sheriff seized the stove and stereo pursuant to that writ. The state's (Florida's) prejudgment replevin statute did not require a convincing showing that the goods were wrongfully detained by the possessor before seizure, and a private party could merely file a complaint, post a bond, and make an ex parte request to the court's clerk for a writ of replevin on the bare assertion that it was entitled to the property. The possessor was provided neither with notice the writ was being issued nor an opportunity to challenge the issuance of the writ prior to seizure of the property, though they were guaranteed a hearing after the seizure. Fuentes (P) attacked the prejudgment replevin statute as unconstitutional under the Fourteenth Amendment, contending it deprived her of her property without due process. A similar prejudgment replevin statute in Pennsylvania was challenged on the same grounds. Under the Pennsylvania scheme, a possessor who wanted to challenge the seizure had to initiate a suit post-seizure to do so. The federal district courts in both cases upheld the legislation as constitutional, and the United States Supreme Court granted certiorari in both cases and consolidated them.

ISSUE: Before a state may authorize its agents to seize a party's property upon the application of another party, does the Fourteenth Amendment require that the possessor be given the opportunity to have a pre-seizure hearing to challenge the seizure?

HOLDING AND DECISION: (Stewart, J.) Yes. Before a state may authorize its agents to seize a party's property upon the application of another party, the Fourteenth Amendment requires that the possessor be given the opportunity to have a pre-seizure hearing to challenge the seizure. Procedural due process requires that a party whose rights are being affected be given a meaningful opportunity to be heard; and in order that they may enjoy that right, they must be notified. The constitutional right to be heard is a basic aspect of the duty of government to follow a fair process of decision-making when it acts to deprive a person of his possessions. This right to be heard minimizes substantively unfair or mistaken deprivations of property, a danger that is especially great when the state seizes goods simply upon the application of and for the benefit of a private party. Without due process of law, there would be no safeguards to protect a person's property from governmental interference. The right to speak out in one's own defense before an impartial arbitrator is a fundamental right that must be protected. If the right to notice and a hearing is to serve its full purpose, then it is clear it must be granted at a time when the deprivation can still be prevented. While return of possession and damages can be granted at a later hearing, nothing can undo the fact that a person's property was arbitrarily taken from him without procedural due process of law. That the hearing required by due process is subject to waiver, and is not fixed in form, does not affect its root requirement that an individual be given an opportunity for a hearing before he is deprived of any significant property interest, except for extraordinary situations where some valid governmental interest is at stake that justifies postponing the hearing until after the event. The statute's requirements of requesting a writ, posting bond, and stating in a conclusory fashion the property is wrongfully held merely test the applicant's own belief in his rights. Since his private gain is at stake,

Continued on next page.

the danger is all too great that his confidence in his cause will be misplaced. While possession may be reinstated by the posting of a counter-bond, it is well settled that a temporary, non-final deprivation of property is nonetheless violative of the Due Process Clause of the Fourteenth Amendment. Moreover, the Due Process Clause encompasses both the possessory rights to property and situations where the title is in dispute. Further, the district courts erred in rejecting the possessors' constitutional claim on the ground the household goods seized were not items of "necessity" and therefore did not require due process protection, as the Fourteenth Amendment imposes no such limitation. Situations requiring a postponement of notice and hearing are truly unusual. They require an important governmental purpose, a special need for prompt action, and are initiated by and for the benefit of the government as opposed to a private individual (e.g., war effort, economic disaster, etc.). The statutes at bar did not serve such governmental interests. The contention that the parties waived their constitutional rights is also without merit, since waiver requires clear and explicit language indicating exactly the rights to be waived. For the above-mentioned reasons, both Florida's and Pennsylvania's prejudgment replevin statutes violate the Due Process Clause of the Fourteenth Amendment. Vacated and remanded.

ANALYSIS

In California, Michigan, and numerous other states, the writ of replevin is now referred to as claim and delivery. In California, this action is defined in § 511.010, et seq. of the Code of Civil Procedure. A hearing is required for the granting of a writ of possession (comparable to the prior writ of replevin) under the guidelines set out in § 512.010. Exceptions to this hearing requirement are made for property that has been feloniously taken, for property in the form of a credit card, and for property acquired in the normal course of trade or business for commercial use. It must be alleged that the property is not necessary for the support of the defendant or his family; that there is a danger that the property will become unavailable to levy or that its value will be substantially impaired; and that the ex parte issuance of a writ is necessary to protect the property (§ 512.020). At the hearing, the court will make its determination based on affidavits, pleadings, and other evidence on record. Upon showing of good cause, the court may admit additional evidence or continue the hearing until the new evidence can be obtained (§ 512.050). Finally, with regard to waiver of a hearing requirement, it appears it is permissible if the parties are acting at arm's length and have equal bargaining power, *D.H. Overmeyer Co. v. Frick Co.*, 405 U.S. 174 (1972); however, if the consumer has no option but to buy on credit, the parties are not equal in bargaining power and the clause is unconscionable, *Kosches v. Nichols*, 327 N.Y.S. 2d 968 (1971). This is but another example of consumer protection. The businessman can waive his constitutional rights, but the consumer cannot.

Quicknotes

GARNISHMENT Satisfaction of a debt by deducting payments directly from the debtor's wages before they are paid to him by his employer; due process requires that the debtor be first given notice and an opportunity to be heard.

PROCEDURAL DUE PROCESS The constitutional mandate that if the state or federal government acts so as to deny a citizen of a life, liberty, or property interest the individual is first entitled to notice and the right to be heard.

REPLEVIN An action to recover personal property wrongfully taken.

Winter v. Natural Resources Defense Council, Inc.

U.S. Navy (D) v. Environmental defense organization (P)

555 U.S. 7 (2008)

NATURE OF CASE: Appeal from affirmance of grant of a preliminary injunction in action asserting violations of the National Environmental Policy Act of 1969, the Endangered Species Act, and the Coastal Zone Management Act.

FACT SUMMARY: The Natural Resources Defense Council (P) filed suit against the U.S. Navy (the Navy) (D) to stop the Navy (D) from using sonar in its training programs due to the adverse effect sonar might have on marine mammals.

RULE OF LAW

A plaintiff who seeks a preliminary injunction must establish he is likely to succeed on the merits, he is likely to suffer irreparable harm in the absence of preliminary relief, the balance of equities tips in his favor, and an injunction is in the public interest.

FACTS: The U.S. Navy (the Navy) (D) prepares for war through training exercises at sea. The exercises include training in the use of modern sonar to detect and track enemy submarines, and sonar has been part of the training for 40 years. Active sonar, which involves emitting pulses of sound underwater and then receiving the acoustic waves that echo off the target, is the most effective technology for identifying submerged submarines in torpedo range. In one instance, the Navy (D) used "mid-frequency active" (MFA) sonar during integrated training exercises in the waters off southern California (SOCAL). The Navy (D) had conducted similar exercises for 40 years and claimed its exercises throughout this period did not significantly harm the 37 or so species of marine mammals contained in the SOCAL waters. The Natural Resources Defense Council (the Council) (P) and other parties believed that MFA harmed marine mammals that shared the waters with the Navy (D). They believed these harms included permanent hearing loss, decompression sickness, and major behavioral disruptions. A federal law—the Marine Mammal Protection Act of 1972—prohibits harassing marine mammals, but the Secretary of Defense may exempt any action or category of actions from the law if such actions are necessary for national defense. The Navy (D) had been granted a two-year exemption for the SOCAL training but was required to take certain precautions to mitigate potential harms to marine mammals. Another federal law—the National Environmental Policy Act of 1969 (NEPA)—requires federal agencies "to the fullest extent possible" to prepare an environmental impact statement (EIS) for every major federal action significantly affecting the quality of the human environment, unless the agency determines the proposed action will not have a significant impact on the environment and bases that conclusion on a shorter environmental assessment (EA). The Navy (D) had concluded the training exercises would not have a significant impact on the environment and issued an EA to that effect in 2007. The Council (P) and others then filed suit seeking to enjoin the Navy (D) from using MFA in its training programs on the grounds such use violated NEPA, the Endangered Species Act (ESA), and the Coastal Zone Management Act. In particular, the Council (P) contended the Navy (D) should have prepared an EIS before conducting the latest round of SOCAL exercises. The district court entered a preliminary injunction prohibiting the Navy (D) from using MFA sonar during its training exercises. The court of appeals held this injunction was overbroad and remanded to the district court for a narrower remedy. The district court then entered another preliminary injunction, imposing six restrictions on the Navy's (D) use of sonar during its SOCAL training exercises. The Navy (D) objected to two of these restrictions: that the Navy (D) shut down MFA sonar when a marine mammal was spotted within 2,200 yards of a vessel, and that it power down sonar by 6 decibels during conditions known as "surface ducting." The Navy (D) then sought relief from these restrictions from the Executive Branch. The Council on Environmental Quality (CEQ) authorized the Navy to implement "alternative arrangements" to NEPA compliance in light of "emergency circumstances." The CEQ allowed the Navy (D) to continue its training exercises under voluntary mitigation procedures the Navy (D) had previously adopted. The Navy (D) moved to vacate the district court's preliminary injunction in light of the CEQ's actions. The district court refused to do so, and the court of appeals affirmed. The United States Supreme Court granted certiorari.

ISSUE: Must a plaintiff who seeks a preliminary injunction establish he is likely to succeed on the merits, he is likely to suffer irreparable harm in the absence of preliminary relief, the balance of equities tips in his favor, and an injunction is in the public interest?

HOLDING AND DECISION: (Roberts, C.J.) Yes. A plaintiff who seeks a preliminary injunction must establish he is likely to succeed on the merits, he is likely to suffer irreparable harm in the absence of preliminary relief, the balance of equities tips in his favor, and an injunction

Continued on next page.

is in the public interest. First, the district court and the Ninth Circuit held that when a plaintiff demonstrates a strong likelihood of prevailing on the merits, a preliminary injunction may be entered based only on a "possibility" of irreparable harm. This "possibility" standard is too lenient. Irreparable injury must be likely, not merely possible, for an injunction to be justified. It is an extraordinary remedy that can only be awarded on a clear showing the plaintiff is entitled to such relief. But even though the courts both stated the incorrect standard, it appears from the record they found the National Resources Defense Council (the Council) (P) had in fact established a "near certainty" of irreparable harm, so the statement of the incorrect standard did not cause harm. Second, even if the Council (P) had shown irreparable injury from the Navy's (D) training exercises, any injury is outweighed by the public interest and the Navy's (D) interest in effective, realistic training of its sailors. Consideration of these factors requires denial of the preliminary injunction. The threat posed by enemy submarines and the need for extensive sonar training to counter the threat is absolutely necessary. The seriousness of the possible harm to the ecological, scientific, and recreational interests advanced by the Council (P) is substantial, but the balance of equities and consideration of the overall public interest tip strongly in favor of the Navy (D). This balancing is also supported by the fact that this is not a case in which the defendant is conducting a new type of activity with completely unknown effects on the environment. Part of the harm the National Environmental Policy Act of 1969 (NEPA) attempts to prevent in requiring an environmental impact statement (EIS) is that without one there may be little if any information about prospective environmental harms and potential mitigating measures. Here, in contrast, the Council (P) was seeking to enjoin—or substantially restrict—training exercises that had been taking place in the waters off southern California (SOCAL) for the last 40 years, about the impacts of which there was a great deal of information. The most serious possible injury caused by the sonar would be to harm an unknown number of the marine mammals the Council (P) studies and observes; but forcing the Navy (D) to deploy an inadequately trained antisubmarine force jeopardizes the safety of the fleet. For these and other reasons, the district court abused its discretion by imposing a 2,200–yard shutdown zone and by requiring the Navy to power down its mid-frequency active (MFA) sonar during significant surface ducting conditions. This is not a judgment on the underlying merits of the claims, but this judgment does make clear that it would be an abuse of discretion to enter a permanent injunction after final decision on the merits, along the same lines as the preliminary injunction. Judgment reversed and preliminary injunction vacated.

DISSENT: (Ginsburg, J.) In imposing manageable measures to mitigate harm until completion of the EIS, the district court conscientiously balanced the equities and did not abuse its discretion. Here, the Navy's (D) conduct was designed to undermine NEPA and took an extraordinary course. The EIS requirement of NEPA is designed to ensure important effects will not be overlooked or underestimated only to be discovered after resources have been committed or the die otherwise cast, and it also serves the purpose of informing the public and other agencies so these interested stakeholders may act appropriately in response to proposed agency action. Thus, in light of these purposes, the timing of the EIS is critical. The Navy's (D) publication of its EIS in this case, scheduled to occur after the 14 exercises were completed, defeated NEPA's informational and participatory purposes. This inverted timing was the very reason why the district court had to confront the question of mitigation measures at all. Had the Navy (D) prepared a legally sufficient EIS before beginning the SOCAL exercises, NEPA would have functioned as its drafters intended. Instead of seeking assistance from Congress, the Navy (D) resorted to the Executive, through the Council on Environmental Quality (CEQ). CEQ's hasty decision on a one-sided record was no substitute for the district court's considered judgment based on a two-sided record. More fundamentally, even an exemplary CEQ review could not have affected the short circuit the Navy (D) sought, since CEQ lacks authority to absolve an agency of its statutory duty to prepare an EIS. Equity jurisdiction allows for flexibility and courts must evaluate claims for equitable relief on a sliding scale, awarding relief based on a lower likelihood of harm when the likelihood of success is very high. Thus, although the majority is correct that relief is not warranted simply to prevent the possibility of some remote future injury, the injury need not have been inflicted when application is made or be certain to occur; a strong threat of irreparable injury before trial is an adequate basis. Accordingly, the district court was correct in concluding the Council (P) made the required showing here, and, in fact, the Navy's (P) own environmental assessment (EA) predicted substantial and irreparable harm to marine mammals. The likely harms enumerated in the EA were not insubstantial and justifiably could be balanced against the critical interests served by the training exercises, especially since military interests do not always trump other considerations. Therefore, in light of the likely, substantial harm to the environment, the Council's (P) almost inevitable success on the merits of its claim that NEPA required the Navy (D) to prepare an EIS, the history of the litigation at bar, and the public interest the mitigation measures the district court imposed were within its discretion.

Continued on next page.

ANALYSIS

It is unusual for the United States Supreme Court to hear a challenge to a preliminary injunction. Typically, it hears the merits of a petitioner's claims. But the court made very clear that its belief in the overriding national security interest associated with the Navy's training program should lead the lower court to reject a permanent injunction after a decision on the merits as well, thus influencing a final judgment by the district court even if the district court finds that the Navy violated an environmental statute. This case also illustrates the Court's rejection of the Ninth Circuit's "mere possibility" test, which the United States government had been seeking for some time.

Quicknotes

IRREPARABLE HARM Such harm that because it is too great, too small, or of a continuing character it cannot be properly compensated in damages, and the remedy for which is typically injunctive relief.

PRELIMINARY INJUNCTION A judicial mandate issued to require or restrain a party from certain conduct; used to preserve a trial's subject matter or to prevent threatened injury.

Department of Homeland Security et al. v. New York, et al.

Federal agency (D) v. State (P)

140 S. Ct. 599 (2020)

NATURE OF CASE: Application for stay from order enjoining enforcement of federal agency rule as it applied universally to anyone in the entire country.

FACT SUMMARY: After the Department of Homeland Security (the Government) (D) promulgated a new rule, numerous parties all over the country challenged the rule on many grounds, and many courts enjoined the rule's enforcement. When a federal district court in New York issued a universal injunction against the rule, barring its enforcement against anyone in the entire country, the Government (D) sought a nationwide stay of the injunction pending appeal.

RULE OF LAW

An application for stay pending appeal should be granted to stay enforcement of a universal injunction that purports to apply to anyone in the nation, not just to the plaintiffs in an action, or even to a definable group having something to do with the plaintiffs' claimed injury.

FACTS: The Department of Homeland Security (the Government) (D) promulgated a new rule defining the term "public charge" as that term is used in the immigration laws. Numerous states, organizations, and individuals brought suits all over the nation asserting that the rule violated the Constitution, the Administrative Procedure Act, and the immigration laws themselves. Some courts enjoined enforcement of the rule within certain jurisdictions. However, when a federal district court in New York issued a universal injunction against the rule, the Government (D) sought a nationwide stay of the injunction pending appeal. The United States Supreme Court considered the government's (D) application for stay.

ISSUE: Should an application for stay pending appeal be granted to stay enforcement of a universal injunction that purports to apply to anyone in the nation, not just to the plaintiffs in an action, or even to a definable group having something to do with the plaintiffs' claimed injury?

HOLDING AND DECISION: (Gorsuch, J.) Yes. An application for stay pending appeal should be granted to stay enforcement of a universal injunction that purports to apply to anyone in the nation, not just to the plaintiffs in an action, or even to a definable group having something to do with the plaintiffs' claimed injury. The requested stay is granted. However, issuing such a stay does not solve the real problem, which is an increasingly common practice of trial courts ordering relief that transcends the cases before them. Whether framed as injunctions of "nationwide," "universal," or "cosmic" scope, these orders share the same basic flaw—they direct how the defendant must act toward persons who are not parties to the case. In part, this problem arises because equitable remedies, such as injunctions, like legal remedies are meant to redress the injuries sustained by a particular plaintiff in a particular lawsuit. If a court goes beyond the parties in a case, it exceeds its judicial role of resolving cases and controversies. Moreover, the routine issuance of universal injunctions is patently unworkable, sowing chaos for litigants, the government, courts, and all those affected by potentially conflicting decisions, and such injunctions have little basis in traditional equitable practice, because they force judges to make rushed, high-stakes, low-information decisions. The use of such injunctions also greatly encourages forum-shopping, since plaintiffs generally are not bound by adverse decisions in cases to which they were not a party, and greatly increases the chance that orders will conflict.

ANALYSIS

On appeal, in *New York v. United States Department of Homeland Security*, 969 F.3d 42 (2020), the Second Circuit Court of Appeals upheld the preliminary injunction issued by the Southern District of New York, but modified the injunction to cover only New York, Connecticut, and Vermont. In doing so, the Second Circuit noted that although the law permits district courts to enter nationwide injunctions, and that such injunctions may be an appropriate remedy in certain circumstances, the issuance of unqualified nationwide injunctions is a less desirable practice where numerous challenges to the same agency action are being litigated simultaneously in district and circuit courts across the country.

Quicknotes

NATIONAL INJUNCTION *See* "Universal injunction."

NATIONWIDE INJUNCTION *See* "Universal injunction."

UNIVERSAL INJUNCTION (Also known as "national injunction" or "nationwide injunction") is an equitable remedy issued by a court that binds the federal government even as to parties not before the court.

Walgreen Co. v. Sara Creek Property Co.

Retail tenant (D) v. Owner of shopping center (P)

966 F.2d 273 (7th Cir. 1992)

NATURE OF CASE: Appeal from grant of permanent injunction against owner of shopping center.

FACT SUMMARY: Walgreen Co. (D) brought suit for permanent injunction against Sara Creek Property Co. (Sara Creek) (P), the owner of shopping center, to prevent Sara Creek from breaching its lease by renting space to a competing pharmacy. Injunction was granted to Walgreen (D), and Sara Creek (D) appealed.

RULE OF LAW

Where damages would be a costly and inadequate remedy, injunctive relief should be granted.

FACTS: Walgreen Co. (P) leased retail space from Sara Creek Property Co. (Sara Creek) (D) in a shopping mall and ran a pharmacy in the leased space. Walgreen (P) brought a diversity suit for breach of contract against Sara Creek (D) when it learned that, in violation of a lease provision, Sara Creek (D) was about to rent space to a second pharmacy within a few hundred feet of Walgreen's pharmacy (P). Walgreen (P) also requested an injunction against Sara Creek (D) to prevent it from leasing space to the competing drugstore.

ISSUE: Should injunctive relief be granted where damages would be a costly and inadequate remedy?

HOLDING AND DECISION: (Posner, J.) Yes. Injunctive relief should be granted where damages would be a costly and inadequate remedy. The choice between remedies requires a balancing of the costs and benefits of the alternatives. Here, the effect of upholding the injunction would be to substitute for the costly processes of forensic fact determination the less costly processes of private negotiation. In other words, it would cost society less to grant the injunction and allow the parties to work out in private negotiations just how much compensation the plaintiff drugstore, Walgreen (P), would be willing to take to dissolve the injunction, than it would cost to bring the apparatus of the state to bear in a trial to determine the amount in money damages that would compensate Walgreen (P) for its losses if Sara Creek (D) breaks the lease and allows a competing pharmacy to open in the same shopping center. Here, there were 10 years left on Walgreen's (P) lease, and determining its revenues that far into the future, discounted by the effects of the competing pharmacy on its business and adjusting for present value, would be fraught with uncertainty. The Court was satisfied that the analytical approach of the trial judge did not exceed the bounds of reasonable judgment in concluding that the costs (including forgone benefits) of the damages remedy would exceed the costs (including forgone benefits) of an injunction. Affirmed.

ANALYSIS

The court noted that a plaintiff who seeks an injunction has the burden of persuasion. Because damages are the norm, the plaintiff must show why his or her case is "abnormal."

Quicknotes

BREACH OF CONTRACT Unlawful failure by a party to perform its obligations pursuant to contract.

INJUNCTION A court order requiring a person to do, or prohibiting that person from doing, a specific act.

INJUNCTIVE RELIEF A court order issued as a remedy, requiring a person to do, or prohibiting that person from doing, a specific act.

Brown v. Plata

State governor (D) v. Mentally or physically ill state prisoner (P)

563 U.S. 493 (2011)

NATURE OF CASE: Appeal from decision of three-judge district court convened under the Prison Litigation Reform Act of 1995 ordering the release of prisoners to remedy the unconstitutional consequences of overcrowding in the California (D) prison system.

FACT SUMMARY: California (D) contended that a remedial order issued by a three-judge district court pursuant to the Prison Litigation Reform Act of 1995 (PLRA), which required California (D) to significantly reduce its prison population within two years, was erroneous because it did not comply with the PLRA's requirements and procedures.

RULE OF LAW

A remedial order issued by a three-judge district court convened pursuant to the Prison Litigation Reform Act of 1995 (PLRA), which requires a state to significantly reduce its prison population to remedy Eighth Amendment violations resulting from overcrowding, meets the PLRA's requirements and procedures where: the PLRA's requirement of allowing a state a reasonable amount of time to comply with previous court orders is satisfied; evidence supports the court's finding that overcrowding is the primary cause of Eighth Amendment violations; evidence supports the court's finding that no other relief would remedy the Eighth Amendment violations; the court has given substantial weight to public safety; and the evidence supports the court's determination of the appropriate number at which the prison population should be capped.

FACTS: California's (D) prisons were designed to house a population just under 80,000, but its prison population had grown to almost double that. In other words, the prison population was at about 200% of design capacity. This resulted, on average, in an inmate in one of California's (D) prisons needlessly dying every six to seven days due to constitutional deficiencies in the California (D) prisons' medical delivery system. The consequences of overcrowding also included needless suffering and pain, the increased, substantial risk for transmission of infectious illness, and a suicide rate approaching an average of one per week. The resulting conditions were the subject of two federal class actions. In *Coleman v. Brown,* filed in 1990, the district court [E.D. Cal.] found that prisoners (P) with serious mental illness did not receive minimal, adequate care. A Special Master appointed to oversee remedial efforts reported 12 years later that the state of mental health care in California's (D) prisons was deteriorating due to increased overcrowding. In *Plata v. Brown,* filed in 2001 [N.D. Cal.], California (D) conceded that deficiencies in prison medical care violated prisoners' (P) Eighth Amendment rights and stipulated to a remedial injunction. However, when California (D) had not complied with the injunction by 2005, the court appointed a Receiver to oversee remedial efforts. Three years later, the Receiver described continuing deficiencies caused by overcrowding. Believing that a remedy for unconstitutional medical and mental health care could not be achieved without reducing overcrowding, the Coleman and Plata plaintiffs (P) moved their respective district courts to convene a three-judge district court empowered by the Prison Litigation Reform Act of 1995 (PLRA), 18 U.S.C. § 3626, to order reductions in the prison population. The judges in both actions granted the request, and the cases were consolidated before a single three-judge court. Under the PLRA, only a three-judge court may limit a prison population. Before convening such a court, a district court must have entered an order for less intrusive relief that failed to remedy the constitutional violation and must have given the defendant state a reasonable time to comply with its prior orders. Once convened, the three-judge court must find by clear and convincing evidence that crowding is the primary cause of the violation and that no other relief will remedy the violation. The court must also ensure that the relief is narrowly drawn, extends no further than necessary, and is the least intrusive means necessary to correct the violation. Additionally, the court must give substantial weight to any adverse impact on public safety or the operation of a criminal justice system caused by the ordered relief. After hearing testimony and making extensive findings of fact, the court ordered California (D) to reduce its prison population to 137.5% of design capacity within two years. Assuming California (D) would not be able to increase capacity through new construction, the order required a prison population reduction of 38,000 to 46,000 persons. Because it appeared all but certain that California (D) could not complete sufficient construction to comply fully with the order, the prison population would have to be reduced to at least some extent. The court did not order California (D) to achieve this reduction in any particular manner. Instead, the court ordered California (D) to formulate a plan for compliance and to submit its plan for approval by the court. California (D), contending that the remedial order did not satisfy the PLRA's requirements and procedures, appealed directly to the United States

Continued on next page.

Supreme Court (the Court), as authorized by federal law, and the Court granted review.

ISSUE: Does a remedial order issued by a three-judge district court convened pursuant to the Prison Litigation Reform Act of 1995 (PLRA), which requires a state to significantly reduce its prison population to remedy Eighth Amendment violations resulting from overcrowding, meet the PLRA's requirements and procedures where: the PLRA's requirement of allowing a state a reasonable amount of time to comply with previous court orders is satisfied; evidence supports the court's finding that overcrowding is the primary cause of Eighth Amendment violations; evidence supports the court's finding that no other relief would remedy the Eighth Amendment violations; the court has given substantial weight to public safety; and the evidence supports the court's determination of the appropriate number at which the prison population should be capped?

HOLDING AND DECISION: (Kennedy, J.) Yes. A remedial order issued by a three-judge district court convened pursuant to the Prison Litigation Reform Act of 1995 (PLRA), which requires a state to significantly reduce its prison population to remedy Eighth Amendment violations resulting from overcrowding, meets the PLRA's requirements and procedures where: the PLRA's requirement of allowing a state a reasonable amount of time to comply with previous court orders is satisfied; evidence supports the court's finding that overcrowding is the primary cause of Eighth Amendment violations; evidence supports the court's finding that no other relief would remedy the Eighth Amendment violations; the court has given substantial weight to public safety; and the evidence supports the court's determination of the appropriate number at which the prison population should be capped.

California (D) contended that it was error to convene the three-judge court without affording it more time to comply with the prior orders in Coleman and Plata. This contention is without merit. The district court orders in those cases were intended to remedy constitutional violations and were given ample time to succeed—12 years in Coleman and 5 years in Plata. Contrary to California's (D) claim, the district courts were not required to wait to see whether their more recent efforts would yield equal disappointment and thus were not required to give more time for subsequent remedial efforts to succeed. The district courts had a solid basis to doubt that additional efforts to build new facilities and hire new staff would achieve a remedy, given the ongoing deficiencies recently reported by both the Special Master and the Receiver. Therefore, the district courts acted reasonably in convening the three-judge district court.

Also contrary to California's (D) assertion, the three-judge court did not err in finding that crowding was the primary cause of Eighth Amendment violations in the California (D) prison system. The trial record documented the severe impact of burgeoning demand on the provision of care. The evidence showed that there were high vacancy rates for medical and mental health staff, e.g., 20% for surgeons and 54.1% for psychiatrists; that these numbers understated the severity of the crisis because California (D) had not budgeted sufficient staff to meet demand; and that even if vacant positions could be filled, there would be insufficient space for the additional staff. Such a shortfall contributed to significant delays in treating mentally ill prisoners, who were housed in administrative segregation for extended periods while awaiting transfer to scarce mental health treatment beds. There were also backlogs of up to 700 prisoners waiting to see a doctor for physical care. Crowding created unsafe and unsanitary conditions that hampered the effective delivery of medical and mental health care. It also promoted unrest and violence. Increased violence requires increased reliance on lockdowns to keep order, and lockdowns further impede the effective delivery of care. Overcrowding's effects were particularly acute in prison reception centers, which processed 140,000 new or returning prisoners annually and which housed some prisoners for their entire incarceration period. Numerous experts testified that crowding was the primary cause of the constitutional violations. Further, California's (D) complaint that the three-judge court excluded evidence of current conditions in the prisons lacked a factual basis, as California (D) failed to point to any significant evidence that it was unable to present and that would have changed the outcome of the proceedings.

The three-judge court acknowledged that the violations were caused by factors in addition to overcrowding and that reducing crowding in the prisons would not entirely cure the violations. The three-judge court nevertheless did not err in finding that overcrowding was the primary cause in the sense of being the foremost cause of the violation. This understanding of the primary cause requirement is consistent with the text of the PLRA. Overcrowding need only be the foremost, chief, or principal cause of the violation. If Congress had intended to require that crowding be the only cause, it would have said so. A reading of the PLRA that would render population limits unavailable in practice would raise serious constitutional concerns. A finding that overcrowding is the "primary cause" of a violation is therefore permissible, despite the need for additional steps to remedy the violation.

The evidence supported the three-judge court's finding that "no other relief [would] remedy the violation." California (D) argues that the violation could have been remedied through a combination of new construction,

Continued on next page.

transfers of prisoners out of state, hiring of medical personnel, and continued efforts by the Plata Receiver and Coleman Special Master. The order in fact permits California (D) to comply with the population limit by transferring prisoners to county facilities or facilities in other states or by constructing new facilities to raise the prisons' design capacity. If California (D) does find an adequate remedy other than a population limit, it may seek modification or termination of the three-judge court's order on that basis. The evidence at trial, however, supports the three-judge court's conclusion that an order limited to other remedies would not provide effective relief—especially given that the California (D) legislature has not been willing or able to allocate the resources necessary to meet the prison crisis absent a reduction in overcrowding, and that there is no reason to believe it will begin to do so in the face of unprecedented budgetary shortfalls.

Furthermore, the prospective relief ordered here was narrowly drawn, extended no further than necessary to correct the violation, and was the least intrusive means necessary to correct the violation. The population limit does not fail narrow tailoring simply because prisoners beyond the plaintiff class will have to be released through parole or sentencing reform to meet the required reduction or because reducing overcrowding will have positive effects beyond facilitating timely and adequate access to medical care, such as reducing violence and ameliorating unsafe living conditions. A narrow and otherwise proper remedy for a constitutional violation is not invalid simply because it will have collateral effects. Nor does the PLRA require that result. The PLRA states that a remedy shall extend no further than necessary to remedy the violation of the rights of a "particular plaintiff or plaintiffs." This means only that the scope of the order must be determined with reference to the constitutional violations established by the specific plaintiffs (P) before the court. Even prisoners with no present physical or mental illness might become afflicted, and all prisoners in California (D) are at risk so long as they are provided inadequate care. Prisoners in the general population will become sick and will become members of the plaintiff classes with routine frequency. Relief targeted only at present members of the plaintiff classes might therefore fail to adequately protect future class members who will develop serious physical or mental illness.

The three-judge court also gave "substantial weight" to any potential adverse impact on public safety from its order. The PLRA's "substantial weight" requirement does not require the court to certify that its order has no possible adverse impact on the public. Here, statistical evidence showed that prison populations had been lowered without adversely affecting public safety in some California counties, several states, and Canada. The court found that various available methods of reducing overcrowding—good time credits and diverting low-risk offenders to community programs—would have little or no impact on public safety, and its order took account of such concerns.

To comply with the PLRA, a court must set a population limit at the highest level consistent with an efficacious remedy, and it must order the population reduction to be achieved in the shortest period of time reasonably consistent with public safety. Here, the three-judge court's conclusion that the prison population should be capped at 137.5% of design capacity was not clearly erroneous. The court concluded that the evidence supported a limit between a 130% limit and a 145% limit. The court made the most precise determination it could in light of the record before it. The PLRA's narrow tailoring requirement is satisfied so long as such equitable, remedial judgments are made with the objective of releasing the fewest possible prisoners consistent with an efficacious remedy. In light of substantial evidence supporting an even more drastic remedy, the three-judge court complied with the requirement of the PLRA in this case.

Finally, the three-judge court did not err in providing a two-year deadline for relief. The court has the authority, and responsibility, to amend its order as warranted by the exercise of sound discretion, and the court must remain open to a showing by either California (D) or the plaintiffs (P) that its injunction should be altered to ensure that the rights and interests of the parties are given all due and necessary protection. For example, the court may grant a motion to extend the deadline if California (D) meets appropriate preconditions designed to ensure that the plan will be implemented without undue delay. Such observations reflect the fact that the existing order, like all ongoing equitable relief, must remain open to appropriate modification. They are not intended to cast doubt on the validity of the order's basic premise. Affirmed.

DISSENT: (Scalia, J.) The institutional reform the three-judge court has undertaken violates the PLRA's terms, ignores bedrock limitations on the power of Article III judges, and takes federal courts beyond their institutional capacity. This case alleges a prison system with inadequate medical facilities, but it is inconceivable that anything more than a small proportion of prisoners (P) in the plaintiff classes have personally received sufficiently atrocious treatment that their Eighth Amendment right was violated. No tenable procedural principles justify certifying a class of plaintiffs so they may assert a claim of systemic unconstitutionality. One possible justification is that although some or most plaintiffs in the class do not individually have viable Eighth Amendment claims, the class as a whole collectively suffered an Eighth Amendment violation. That theory, however, is contrary to the bedrock rule that the sole purpose of classwide

Continued on next page.

adjudication is to aggregate claims that are individually viable. A second possibility is that every member of the plaintiff class has suffered an Eighth Amendment violation merely by virtue of being a patient in a poorly run prison system, and that the purpose of the class is merely to aggregate all those individually viable claims. Under this theory, every prisoner who happens to be a patient in a system that has systemic weaknesses has suffered cruel or unusual punishment, even if that person cannot make an individualized showing of mistreatment. Such a theory, however, is contrary to established Eighth Amendment jurisprudence. Nevertheless, even assuming, arguendo, that the plaintiffs (P) have established a systemic Eighth Amendment violation, the three-judge court's decrowding order, which is in the form of a structural injunction, is unsupportable. Structural injunctions depart from the historical practice of courts' issuing injunctions that require a single act, turning judges into long-term administrators of complex social institutions such as schools, prisons, and police departments. Indeed, they require judges to play a role essentially indistinguishable from the role ordinarily played by executive officials. The majority's decision not only affirms the structural injunction but vastly expands its use by holding that an entire system is unconstitutional because it may produce constitutional violations. One of the most pernicious aspects of structural injunctions is that they force judges to engage in a form of factfinding-as-policymaking that is outside the traditional judicial role. The factfinding judges traditionally engage in primarily involves the determination of past or present facts based exclusively upon a closed trial record. In a very limited category of cases, judges have also traditionally been called upon to make some predictive judgments. However, a judge who manages a structural injunction will inevitably be required to make very broad empirical predictions necessarily based in large part upon policy views—the sort of predictions regularly made by legislators and executive officials but inappropriate for the judiciary. Here, for example, the three-judge court cast its predictions of the effect on public safety of its decrowding order as findings based on expert testimony. The notion that the judges relied solely on this testimony is fanciful: it is impossible for judges to make "factual finding" without inserting their own policy judgments when the factual findings are, in fact, policy judgments. When, as in this case, a court issues an injunction, it must make a factual assessment of the anticipated consequences of the injunction. When the injunction undertakes to restructure a social institution, assessing the factual consequences of the injunction is necessarily the sort of predictive judgment that our system of government allocates to other government officials. The court's reliance on the un-cross-examined findings in the reports of the Receiver and Special Master likewise bears no resemblance to ordinary judicial decision making. Further, a court may not order a prisoner's release unless it determines that the prisoner's constitutional rights are being violated and that such release, and no other relief, will remedy the violation. A court may not, however, order the release of prisoners who have suffered no violations of their constitutional rights merely to make it less likely that that will happen to them in the future. The PLRA states that it shall not be construed to repeal or detract from otherwise applicable limitations on the remedial powers of the courts; the PLRA, therefore, is best understood as an attempt to constrain the discretion of courts issuing structural injunctions—not as a mandate for their use.

DISSENT: (Alito, J.) Undesirable prison conditions that do not violate the Constitution are beyond the federal courts' reach. Both the PLRA and general principles concerning injunctive relief dictate that a prisoner release order cannot properly be issued unless the relief is necessary to remedy an ongoing violation. Thus, the propriety of the relief ordered here cannot be assessed without ascertaining the nature and scope of any ongoing constitutional violations. The three-judge court, however, erroneously relied heavily on outdated information and findings and refused to permit California (D) to introduce new evidence. Additionally, the power of the federal courts to restructure the operation of state and local entities is not plenary, and once a constitutional violation is found, a federal court is required to tailor the scope of the remedy to fit the nature and extent of the violation. Here, however, the majority's conclusion that no remedy short of a massive release of prisoners can remedy California's (D) failure to provide constitutionally adequate health care is implausible on its face and is not supported by the requisite clear and convincing evidence. Although general overcrowding contributes to many of California's (D) prison system's healthcare problems, it by no means follows that reducing overcrowding is the only or the best or even a particularly good way to alleviate those problems. Although some class members will presumably be among those who are discharged, the decrease in the number of prisoners needing mental health treatment or other forms of extensive medical care will be much smaller than the total number of prisoners released, and thus the release will produce at best only a modest improvement in the burden on the medical care system. The three-judge court, seemingly intent on attacking the broader problem of general overcrowding, rejected all of California's (D) proposals that did not involve prisoner release. In doing so, the court made three critical errors. First, the court did not assess those proposals and other remedies in light of conditions proved to exist at the time the release order was framed. Second, the court failed to distinguish between conditions that fall below the level that may be desirable

Continued on next page.

as a matter of public policy and conditions that do not meet the minimum level mandated by the Constitution. Third, the court rejected alternatives that would not have provided immediate relief, notwithstanding that nothing in the PLRA suggests that public safety may be sacrificed to implement an immediate remedy rather than a less dangerous one that requires a more extended but reasonable period of time. Absent these errors, it is possible that a less drastic, yet adequate, remedial plan could have been crafted. For example, sanitary procedures could be improved, or sufficient medical supplies and equipment could be purchased. Perhaps the number of medical and other staff positions could be increased by increasing salaries, improving working conditions, and providing better training and performance monitoring. Measures such as these—all of which will require expenditures—could be combined with targeted reductions in critical components of the prison population. Finally, the three-judge court erred in concluding that loosing 46,000 criminals would not have an adverse impact on public safety. When a trial court selects between the competing views of experts on broad empirical questions such as the efficacy of preventing crime through the incapacitation of convicted criminals, the trial court's choice is very different from a classic finding of fact and is not entitled to the same degree of deference on appeal.

ANALYSIS

In contradistinction to structural injunctions, such as the one issued by the three-judge court in this case, mandatory injunctions that are issued upon termination of litigation usually require a single simple act. In fact, courts of equity historically avoided rendering decrees that called for more than a single affirmative act. For example, where specific performance of contracts was sought, it was the categorical rule that no decree would issue that required ongoing supervision. Thus, by avoiding ongoing involvement with litigants, courts can simplify their workloads by avoiding prolonged entanglement with litigants. Once the ordered act is achieved, the litigant's obligation to the court and the court's coercive power over the litigant cease, and the court does not need to engage in any ongoing supervision of the litigant's conduct, which presumably results in greater efficiency of the court system.

Quicknotes

CRUEL AND UNUSUAL PUNISHMENT Punishment that is excessive or disproportionate to the offense committed and that is prohibited by the Eighth Amendment to the United States Constitution.

EIGHTH AMENDMENT The Eighth Amendment to the United States Constitution prohibits the imposition of excessive bail, fines, and cruel and unusual punishment.

Carey v. Piphus

School officials (D) v. Suspended student (P)

435 U.S. 247 (1978)

NATURE OF CASE: Appeal of award of damages for civil violations.

FACT SUMMARY: Damages in excess of a nominal amount were awarded in absence of proof of injury.

RULE OF LAW

In an action based on denial of procedural due process, only nominal damages may be awarded in the absence of actual injury.

FACTS: Piphus (P) was suspended from school for several days. He was reinstated but brought an action under 28 U.S.C. § 1983, contending he was denied procedural due process. The district court found no actual injury and dismissed. The court of appeals reversed, holding that Piphus (P) was entitled to injunctive relief and that denial of procedural due process was compensable even in the absence of actual injury. The United States Supreme Court accepted renewal of the latter portion of the appellate court's holding.

ISSUE: In an action based on denial of procedural due process, may damages in excess of a nominal amount be awarded in the absence of proof of injury?

HOLDING AND DECISION: (Powell, J.) No. In an action based on denial of procedural due process, only nominal damages may be awarded in the absence of actual injury. The basic purpose of § 1983 is to compensate individuals for injuries caused by the deprivation of constitutional rights. The structure under which this is done borrows from tort law. Just as tort law requires injury for compensation to be merited, so does § 1983. It cannot be assumed that denial of procedural due process, in itself, is an injury. Many will suffer no distress when such denial leads to no injury, and in such cases compensation would be inappropriate. It is injury caused by deprivation, not the deprivation itself, which is compensable. Here, no evidence on the issue of injury was put forth, so actual damages would be inappropriate. Reversed and remanded.

ANALYSIS

The decision was apparently rather purposefully limited in scope. The Court always limited its terms to procedural due process. Substantive due process was not mentioned. Also, the Court said in a footnote that punitive damages might be awarded in the absence of actual injury.

Quicknotes

INJUNCTIVE RELIEF A court order issued as a remedy, requiring a person to do, or prohibiting that person from doing, a specific act.

NOMINAL DAMAGES A small sum awarded to a plaintiff in order to recognize that he sustained an injury that is either slight or incapable of being established.

PROCEDURAL DUE PROCESS The constitutional mandate that if the state or federal government acts so as to deny a citizen of a life, liberty, or property interest the individual is first entitled to notice and the right to be heard.

PUNITIVE DAMAGES Damages exceeding the actual injury suffered for the purposes of punishment, deterrence, and comfort to plaintiff.

Marek v. Chesny

Offeror (D) v. Settlement offeree (P)

473 U.S. 1 (1985)

NATURE OF CASE: Appeal of denial of award of attorney fees.

FACT SUMMARY: Chesny (P) refused a settlement offer in a § 1983 action and was awarded less in trial.

RULE OF LAW

Attorney fees incurred by a plaintiff subsequent to an offer of settlement will not be paid when the plaintiff recovers less than the offer.

FACTS: Chesny (P) sued Marek (D) under 42 U.S.C. § 1983. Prior to trial, Marek (D) and the other defendants offered $100,000 to settle. Chesny (P) refused and was awarded $60,000 at trial. The court awarded Chesny (P) $32,000 in costs and fees incurred before the offer but refused to award costs and fees subsequent to the offer, per Fed. R. Civ. P. 68, which shifts to the plaintiff all costs incurred subsequent to an offer of judgment not exceeded by the ultimate recovery. The district court held that fees recoverable by a plaintiff in a § 1983 action were considered costs for purposes of Fed. R. Civ. P. 68. The Seventh Circuit Court of Appeals disagreed and reversed. The United States Supreme Court granted certiorari.

ISSUE: Will attorney fees incurred by a plaintiff subsequent to an offer of settlement be paid when the plaintiff recovers less than the offer?

HOLDING AND DECISION: (Burger, C.J.) No. Attorney fees incurred by a plaintiff subsequent to an offer of settlement will not be paid when the plaintiff recovers less than the offer. Legislative history shows when Fed. R. Civ. P. 68 was drafted attorney fees were considered part of costs. When 42 U.S.C. § 1988 was enacted, enabling successful plaintiffs to recover costs and fees, Congress was aware that Fed. R. Civ. P. 68 included fees in its operation, and it could have exempted plaintiffs in § 1983 actions from the force of Fed. R. Civ. P. 68, but it did not do so. In the absence of this, the salutary effect of Fed. R. Civ. P. 68, the encouragement of settlements, should not be hindered. Reversed.

DISSENT: (Brennan, J.) The Court's reasoning is wholly inconsistent with the history and structure of the Federal Rules of Civil Procedure. Its application to the over 100 attorney fees statutes enacted by Congress will produce absurd variations in the operation of Fed. R. Civ P. 68 among the statutes. This is contrary to the purpose of the Federal Rules of Civil Procedure, which is a uniform procedure in federal courts.

ANALYSIS

42 U.S.C. § 1988 was enacted in 1976. As the Court states, it provides that prevailing plaintiffs in § 1983 actions will be awarded costs and fees. The purpose of the section was to ensure that civil rights plaintiffs obtained effective access to the judicial process.

Quicknotes

42 U.S.C. § 1983 Provides that every person who under color of state law subjects or causes to be subjected any citizen of the United States or person within its jurisdiction to be deprived of rights, privileges, and immunities guaranteed by the federal constitution and laws is liable to the injured party at law or in equity.

42 U.S.C. § 1988 Allows for attorney fees to be awarded the prevailing party in an action pursuant to § 1983.

CERTIORARI A discretionary writ issued by a superior court to an inferior court in order to review the lower court's decisions; the United States Supreme Court's writ ordering such review.

SETTLEMENT OFFER An offer made by one party to a lawsuit to the other agreeing upon the determination of rights and issues between them, thus disposing of the need for judicial determination.

City of Riverside v. Rivera

City (D) v. Individuals (P)

477 U.S. 561 (1986)

NATURE OF CASE: Appeal from judgment affirming award of attorneys' fees in federal civil rights suit.

FACT SUMMARY: Individuals (P) sued City of Riverside (D) for civil rights violations under 42 U.S.C. § 1983 for using "unnecessary physical force" in breaking up a party.

RULE OF LAW

An award of attorneys' fees under 42 U.S.C. § 1988 is not per se "unreasonable" within the meaning of the statute if it exceeds the amount of damages recovered by the plaintiff in the underlying civil rights action.

FACTS: Individuals (P) sued City of Riverside (D) for civil rights violations under 42 U.S.C. § 1983 for using "unnecessary physical force" in breaking up a party. Upon trial, the individuals (P) were awarded $33,350 for their claims. The individuals (P) also sought attorneys' fees under 42 U.S.C. § 1988 for 1,946.75 hours expended by their two attorneys and were awarded $245,456.25 as attorneys' fees.

ISSUE: Is an award of attorneys' fees under 42 U.S.C. § 1988 per se "unreasonable" within the meaning of the statute if it exceeds the amount of damages recovered by the plaintiff in the underlying civil rights action?

HOLDING AND DECISION: (Brennan, J.) No. An award of attorneys' fees under 42 U.S.C. §1988 is not per se "unreasonable" within the meaning of the statute if it exceeds the amount of damages recovered by the plaintiff in the underlying civil rights action. The district court had carefully considered the results obtained by the attorneys and properly concluded that the attorneys were entitled to recover for all hours expended on the litigation because the amount of time reflected sound legal judgment under the circumstances and counsels' excellent performances entitled them to be compensated at prevailing market rates, even though they were relatively young when the litigation began. It would have been inappropriate to adjust the fee downward to account for the fact that the attorneys had prevailed only on some on their claims and against only some of the defendants. The relatively small size of the actual damages award did not imply that the attorneys' success was limited. Furthermore, the district court paid particular attention to the fact that the case presented complex and interrelated issues of fact and law and that a fee award in this civil rights action would advance the public interest. Affirmed.

DISSENT: (Burger, C.J.) The fee award is unreasonable and constitutes a grave abuse of discretion. The attorneys' level of experience did not justify the fee.

DISSENT: (Rehnquist, J.) It was patently unreasonable for the attorneys to have spent 1,946.75 hours in light of the facts that they ultimately prevailed against only the City (D) and five police officers, no restraining orders or injunctions were ever issued, and the City (D) was never compelled to change a single practice or policy as a result of the suit.

ANALYSIS

Although the amount of damages a plaintiff recovers is relevant to the amount of the attorneys' fees to be awarded under 42 U.S.C. § 1988, the Court made clear that it is only one of many factors that a court should consider. Furthermore, the Court emphasized that unlike most private tort litigants, a civil rights plaintiff seeks to vindicate important civil and constitutional rights that cannot be valued solely in monetary terms.

Quicknotes

42 U.S.C. § 1983 Provides that every person who under color of state law subjects or causes to be subjected any citizen of the United States or person within its jurisdiction to be deprived of rights, privileges, and immunities guaranteed by the federal constitution and laws is liable to the injured party at law or in equity.

42 U.S.C. § 1988 Allows for attorney fees to be awarded the prevailing party in an action pursuant to § 1983.

INJUNCTION A court order requiring a person to do, or prohibiting that person from doing, a specific act.

RESTRAINING ORDER An order prohibiting a defendant from certain activities until a hearing regarding an injunction on such activities may be conducted.

Walker v. City of Birmingham

Protest organizer (D) v. City (P)

388 U.S. 307 (1967)

NATURE OF CASE: Appeal from state's highest court's affirmance of state trial court's criminal contempt conviction of individuals who deliberately violated an ex parte temporary injunction based on an ordinance alleged to be unconstitutional as a restraint on free speech.

FACT SUMMARY: After a temporary injunction was issued ex parte at the City of Birmingham's (Birmingham's) (P) request to prevent mass demonstrations without a permit, as required by a city ordinance, Walker (D), Dr. Martin Luther King (D), and other protest organizers (D) went ahead with a demonstration without attempting to challenge or vacate the injunction or the underlying ordinance; subsequently they were held in criminal contempt for violating the injunction, jailed, and fined. In their defense, the protesters (D) contended that the injunction and the underlying ordinance were unconstitutional and that the ordinance's administration had been discriminatory and arbitrary, but the state trial court refused to consider these contentions.

RULE OF LAW

The subject of an injunction that has been issued by a court of competent jurisdiction may be held in contempt for disobeying the injunction where the subject has not challenged the validity of the injunction or any underlying law through the judicial system, notwithstanding that both the process involved in the injunction's issuance and the law underpinning the injunction may have been unconstitutional.

FACTS: Walker (D), Dr. Martin Luther King, Jr. (Dr. King) (D), and others organized a demonstration in the City of Birmingham (Birmingham) (P) to protest racial discrimination and segregation. A Birmingham (P) city commissioner refused twice to issue a permit for the demonstration pursuant to the city's parade ordinance, allegedly making it patently clear that under no circumstances would a permit issue to these particular protesters. However, no formal application to the full three-person commission was made as stipulated by the permit ordinance, although such permits had previously uniformly been issued to all other groups even though those groups had not been required to apply to the full commission. Birmingham (P) then applied to a circuit (trial) court judge for a temporary injunction to enjoin the protestors from engaging in the protest demonstrations for which they had sought a permit. The application was ex parte, with no notice to the protest organizers (D). Birmingham (P) alleged that the anticipated demonstration would pose a threat to safety and peace and would be in violation of numerous municipal ordinances. Based on these allegations, the court issued a writ for temporary injunction, copies of which were provided to the organizers (D) the next day. Walker (D), Dr. King (D), and the other organizers held a press conference and made it known that they would disobey the injunction because, they asserted, it was "raw tyranny under the guise of maintaining law and order." They distributed a statement written by Dr. King (D) indicating that the protesters (D) respected the Constitution, federal law, and federal injunctions but that "recalcitrant forces in the Deep South . . . will use the courts to perpetuate the unjust and illegal system of racial separation." The statement further asserted that public officials, law enforcement agencies, and legislatures in the Deep South had openly defied the United States Supreme Court's mandates of desegregation and that, therefore, the protesters (D) could not "in all good conscience obey such an injunction which is an unjust, undemocratic and unconstitutional misuse of the legal process." The statement added that "[j]ust as in all good conscience we cannot obey unjust laws, neither can we respect the unjust use of the courts." (The full statement was included in the Court's decision as an appendix). The next day, which was Good Friday, a demonstration was held in the City of Birmingham (P). Two days later, on Easter Sunday, more demonstrations were held. The next day, the city officials who had requested the injunction applied to the circuit court for an order to show cause why the protest organizers (D) should not be held in contempt for violating it. At the ensuing hearing, they sought to attack the constitutionality of the injunction on the ground that it was vague and overbroad and that it restrained free speech. They also sought to attack the Birmingham (P) parade ordinance upon similar grounds and upon the additional ground that the ordinance had previously been administered in an arbitrary and discriminatory manner. The circuit judge refused to consider any of these contentions, pointing out that there had been neither a motion to dissolve the injunction nor an effort to comply with it by applying for a permit from the city commission before engaging in the Good Friday and Easter Sunday demonstrations. Consequently, the court held that the only issues before it was whether it had jurisdiction to issue the temporary injunction and whether thereafter the protest organizers (D) had knowingly violated it. The court ruled against the protest organizers (D), held them in criminal

Continued on next page.

contempt, and had them fined and jailed. The state's highest court affirmed. The United States Supreme Court granted certiorari to consider the constitutionality of the protest organizers' (D) criminal contempt convictions.

ISSUE: May the subject of an injunction that has been issued by a court of competent jurisdiction be held in contempt for disobeying the injunction where the subject has not challenged the validity of the injunction or any underlying law through the judicial system, notwithstanding that both the process involved in the injunction's issuance and the law underpinning the injunction may have been unconstitutional?

HOLDING AND DECISION: (Stewart, J.) Yes. The subject of an injunction that has been issued by a court of competent jurisdiction may be held in contempt for disobeying the injunction where the subject has not challenged the validity of the injunction or any underlying law through the judicial system, notwithstanding that both the process involved in the injunction's issuance and the law underpinning the injunction may have been unconstitutional. The state court had sufficient jurisdiction to issue the injunction in upholding the permit ordinance, and the injunction was not patently invalid upon its face since government has a strong interest in regulating public streets and places. Where expression is made through use of such public places, as in mass demonstrations, First Amendment interests are weaker than if the expression is made purely by speech. The protest organizers (D) did not attempt to apply to the state courts for an authoritative construction of the ordinance, even though its breadth and generality could have raised serious constitutional concerns, nor did they attempt to modify or dissolve the injunction after it was granted, even though the breadth and vagueness of the injunction itself would also unquestionably be subject to substantial constitutional question. However, the way to have raised those constitutional questions was to apply to the Alabama courts to have the injunction modified or dissolved. It cannot be presumed that the state courts would have ignored constitutional claims, nor can it be said that the parade ordinance was void on its face. Moreover, the protest organizers (D) could have applied for a parade permit after they had received the injunction. Had they done so and had the permit been refused, it is clear their claim of arbitrary or discriminatory administration of the ordinance would have been considered by the state circuit court upon a motion to dissolve the injunction. The rule of law that Alabama (P) followed reflects a belief that in the fair administration of justice no person can be judge in their own case, however exalted their station, however righteous their motives, and irrespective of their race, color, politics, or religion. Accordingly, it cannot be held that the protest organizers (D) were constitutionally free to ignore all the procedures of the law and carry their battle to the streets. Because they took the law into their own hands, they properly were held in contempt. Affirmed.

DISSENT: (Warren, C.J.) The facts do not lend support to the conclusion that Walker (D), Dr. King (D), and the other protest organizers (D) disregarded the judicial process. Instead, the facts show that the parade ordinance was unconstitutional on its face and was unconstitutionally applied, and that the injunction was likewise unconstitutional, as it contained no time limit and was issued pursuant to faulty (ex parte) process. Thus, contrary to the majority's conclusion, the protest organizers (D) were not presuming to act as judges in their own case, nor did they have a disregard for the judicial process. They did not flee, but instead appeared in the Alabama (P) courts after they violated the injunction to challenge its constitutionality and that of the ordinance it parroted. Thus, they were in a position similar to persons who challenge the constitutionality of a statute by violating it and then defending the ensuing criminal prosecution on constitutional grounds. It shows no disrespect for law to violate a statute on the ground that it is unconstitutional and then to challenge that law's constitutionality. The ordinance violated was patently unconstitutional on its face since it permitted local officials to act as censors over the views presented to the public, and this unconstitutionality was compounded by convincing evidence that local officials indeed used their power to stifle views they disliked. The Court should not have given its seal of approval to such a gross misuse of the judicial process.

DISSENT: (Douglas, J.) The record shows that the protest organizers (D) attempted to obtain a permit pursuant to Birmingham's (P) ordinance and were rebuffed in a manner that made clear that any further attempt to obtain a permit would be futile. A statute that is clearly a prior restraint on speech and patently unconstitutional on its face need not be honored. However, through the use of the ex parte injunction process, the state insulates such unconstitutional legislation from challenge by mere incorporation of the identical stifling, overbroad, and vague restraints on the exercise of the First Amendment freedoms into an even more vague and pervasive injunction obtained without challenge or scrutiny. What is at stake, therefore, is neither violence nor the state's right to control its streets but the insulation from attack of ex parte orders and legislation upon which they are based, even when that legislation is patently unconstitutional. Thus, the state courts are armed with the power to punish as "contempt" what they otherwise could not punish at all. Constitutional restrictions against abridgments of First Amendment freedoms limit judicial equally with legislative and executive power. Thus, convictions for contempt of court orders that invalidly abridge First Amendment

Continued on next page.

freedoms must be condemned equally with convictions for violation of statutes that do the same thing.

ANALYSIS

The ordinance that the protest organizers were prohibited by the injunction from violating was later overturned as unconstitutional. However, the rationale of this case—that the proper procedure to subvert an injunction is to subject it to review and not to disobey it—remains legally strong, regardless of its shortcomings in the face of the particular facts of the case at bar.

Quicknotes

CERTIORARI A discretionary writ issued by a superior court to an inferior court in order to review the lower court's decisions; the Supreme Court's writ ordering such review.

CRIMINAL CONTEMPT CITATION Conduct by a party to a proceeding intended to obstruct the court's effective administration of justice or to otherwise disrespect its authority.

EX PARTE A proceeding commenced by one party without providing any opposing parties with notice or that is uncontested by an adverse party.

FIRST AMENDMENT Prohibits Congress from enacting any law respecting an establishment of religion or prohibiting the free exercise of religion; abridging freedom of speech or of the press; the right of peaceful assembly; and the right to petition for a redress of grievances.

INJUNCTION A court order requiring a person to do, or prohibiting that person from doing, a specific act.

ORDINANCE Law or statute usually enacted by a municipal government.

RESTRAINING ORDER An order prohibiting a defendant from certain activities until a hearing regarding an injunction on such activities may be conducted.

CHAPTER 3

Thinking Like a Trial Lawyer, Pleadings, and Joinder

Quick Reference Rules of Law

Conley v. Gibson

Union members (P) v. Labor union (D)

355 U.S. 41 (1957)

NATURE OF CASE: Appeal from dismissal of complaint alleging that labor union failed fairly to represent Black union members.

FACT SUMMARY: Black union members (P) brought class action against their labor union (D) alleging that, because they were Black, the union (D) failed to represent them fairly in negotiations between them and their employer in seniority and other job protection matters.

RULE OF LAW

The Federal Rules of Civil Procedure do not require a complaint to set out in detail the facts upon which the claim is based.

FACTS: A labor contract existed between a railroad and a union that gave the employees certain protections from discharge and loss of seniority rights. Black union members (P), arguing violation of these rights, brought a class action against their labor union (D) alleging that, because they were Black, the union (D) failed to represent them fairly in negotiations between them and the railroad as to these seniority and other job protection matters.

ISSUE: Do the Federal Rules of Civil Procedure require a complaint to set out in detail the facts upon which the claim is based?

HOLDING AND DECISION: (Black, J.) No. The Federal Rules of Civil Procedure do not require a complaint to set out in detail the facts upon which the claim is based. All the Rules require is "a short and plain statement of the claim" that will give the defendant fair notice of what the plaintiff's claim is and the grounds upon which it rests. Here, the complaint sufficiently alleged that the Black union members (P) were discharged wrongfully by their railroad employer and that their union (D), acting according to plan, refused to protect their jobs as it did those of White employees or to help them with their grievances, all because they were Black. Reversed and remanded.

ANALYSIS

The Court noted that simplified "notice pleading," as in this case, is made possible by the liberal opportunity for discovery and other pretrial procedures established by the Federal Rules of Civil Procedure to disclose more precisely the basis of both claim and defense and to define more narrowly the disputed facts and issues.

Quicknotes

CLAIM The demand for a right to payment or equitable relief; the fact or facts giving rise to such demand.

PLEADING A statement setting forth the plaintiff's cause of action or the defendant's defenses to the plaintiff's claims.

Bell Atlantic Corp. v. Twombly

Telephone companies (D) v. Telephone subscribers (P)

550 U.S. 544 (2007)

NATURE OF CASE: Appeal of judgment on the pleadings.

FACT SUMMARY: Telephone and Internet subscribers (P) alleged in a complaint that local telephone companies (D) were violating antitrust laws. The district court dismissed the complaint for failure to state a claim, and the Second Circuit Court of Appeals reversed.

RULE OF LAW

In order for a complaint to survive dismissal on the pleadings, the complaint must include enough facts to state a claim to relief that is plausible on its face.

FACTS: Telephone and Internet subscribers (P) alleged in a complaint that local telephone companies (D) were violating antitrust laws by agreeing not to compete with each other and by agreeing to exclude other potential competitors, which allowed monopoly power in the market. The district court dismissed the complaint for failure to state a claim, and the Second Circuit Court of Appeals reversed.

ISSUE: In order for a complaint to survive dismissal on the pleadings, must the complaint include enough facts to state a claim to relief that is plausible on its face?

HOLDING AND DECISION: (Souter, J.) Yes. In order for a complaint to survive dismissal on the pleadings, the complaint must include enough facts to state a claim to relief that is plausible on its face. In this case, in order to state an antitrust claim under the Sherman Act, the complaint must state enough factual matter to suggest that an agreement between the alleged conspirators was made. The complaint fails to show a plausible claim. The holding in *Conley v. Gibson*, 355 U.S. 41 (1957), which stated that a "complaint should not be dismissed for failure to state a claim unless it appears beyond doubt that the plaintiff can prove no set of facts in support of his claim which would entitle him to relief," must have been read by the court of appeals to say that any statement showing the theory of a claim will suffice unless its factual impossibility may be shown from the face of the pleadings. But the standard interpreted by the *Conley* case should now be set aside, insofar as it has been held up as a minimum standard of adequate pleading for a complaint to survive dismissal. Because antitrust conspiracy was not suggested by the facts in the complaint, the complaint failed to state a claim and must be dismissed. Enough facts to state a claim to relief that is plausible on its face are required for a complaint to survive. That the claim is conceivable is not enough. It must be plausible. Reversed and remanded.

DISSENT: (Stevens, J.) This case alleges that the telephone companies (D) acted in concert to cheat customers (P). Plaintiffs alleged the conspiracy, and because the complaint was dismissed in advance of the answer, the allegation has not even been denied. The case should therefore proceed. The departure from settled procedural law seems to stem from the enormous expense of private antitrust litigation, and the risk that jurors may mistakenly conclude that evidence of parallel conduct proves that the parties acted in accordance with agreement when they in fact merely made similar independent decisions. These concerns do not justify the dismissal of an adequately pleaded complaint. The Court seems to have appraised the plausibility of the ultimate factual allegation, rather than its legal sufficiency.

ANALYSIS

The Court was careful to say, in the text of the opinion and in footnotes, that it did not apply a heightened pleading standard or broaden the scope of Fed. R. Civ. P. 9. The risk of abusive litigation in certain subjects, like antitrust, requires the plaintiff to state factual allegations with greater particularity than Fed. R. Civ. P. 8 requires, and the Court's concern in this case was not that the allegations in the complaint were insufficiently particularized, but that the complaint failed to show a plausible claim to relief. It is the totality of the claim in the complaint that the Court says must indicate a plausible claim, which is beyond merely conceivable.

Quicknotes

PLEADING A statement setting forth the plaintiff's cause of action or the defendant's defense to the plaintiff's claims.

SHERMAN ACT Prohibits unreasonable restraint of trade.

Ashcroft v. Iqbal

Former U.S. Attorney General (D) v. Pakistani citizen (P)

556 U.S. 662 (2009)

NATURE OF CASE: Certiorari to determine complaint sufficiency in constitutional claim.

FACT SUMMARY: Javaid Iqbal (P), a Pakistani citizen, was arrested in the United States on criminal charges and detained by federal officials soon after the 9/11 terrorist attacks. He claimed his confinement conditions violated his constitutional rights. The federal official defendants moved to dismiss Iqbal's (P) complaint as facially insufficient.

RULE OF LAW
A well-pleaded complaint requires nonconclusory, plausible, factual pleadings.

FACTS: United States officials arrested Javaid Iqbal (P), a Pakistani citizen and Muslim, on criminal charges and detained him after the 9/11 terrorist attacks. Iqbal (P) filed a federal complaint alleging he was deprived of certain constitutional rights while confined. He alleged the deprivations occurred because of his race, religion, or national origin. He named former U.S. Attorney General John Ashcroft (D) and Federal Bureau of Investigation Director Robert Mueller (D) in addition to several others. Ashcroft (D) and Mueller (D) moved to dismiss the complaint as facially insufficient and raised the defense of qualified immunity based on their official status at the time of the confinement. The district court denied the motion and Ashcroft (D) and Mueller (D) took an interlocutory appeal to the Second Circuit Court of Appeals. The Second Circuit affirmed, and the United States Supreme Court granted certiorari.

ISSUE: Does a well-pleaded complaint require nonconclusory, plausible, factual pleadings?

HOLDING AND DECISION: (Kennedy, J.) Yes. A well-pleaded complaint requires nonconclusory, plausible, factual pleadings. Iqbal's (P) complaint alleges the federal government had a policy of detaining Arab Muslims after the 9/11 attacks until the individuals were "cleared" by the Federal Bureau of Investigation. Iqbal (P) claimed U.S. Attorney General John Ashcroft (D) was the "architect" of this policy and Federal Bureau of Investigation Director Mueller (D) was instrumental in its "adoption, promulgation, and implementation." This Court held in *Bell Atlantic Corp. v. Twombly*, 550 U.S. 544 (2007), that pleadings require factual content that allows the court to draw the reasonable inference that the defendant is liable for the alleged misconduct. The plausibility standard did not rise to a probability but requires more than conclusions of misconduct. *Twombly* supported the principles that a court accepts factual allegations as true but need not accept conclusory allegations as true. Fed. R. Civ. P. 8 may now permit more flexibility, but it does not permit mere conclusions. Further, only a complaint that states a plausible claim survives a motion to dismiss. The courts may begin their analysis with determining which pleadings include factual allegations that will be entitled to a presumption of truth. Here, Iqbal (P) states only conclusory allegations that Ashcroft (D) was the principal architect and Mueller (D) was the principal implementer of the policies. These conclusory allegations are not entitled to a presumption of truth. Iqbal (P) fails to include factual allegations supporting his conclusions that Ashcroft (D) and Mueller (D) knew of the federal officials' behavior regarding his confinement. The consideration then becomes whether the complaint suggests an entitlement to relief. It does not. Iqbal (P) was plausibly held for reasons other than race, religion, or national origin. Detaining such suspects until cleared does not violate constitutional protections. Iqbal (P) argues *Twombly* should be limited to antitrust pleadings, but nothing supports this theory. *Twomby* is the pleading standard for all civil actions. Iqbal (P) finally argues Fed. R. Civ. P. 9(b) permits him "general" rather than "specific" pleading for an alleged constitutional violation. Rule 9(b) does not override the factual pleading requirements of Rule 8 but merely requires even greater specificity for the enumerated claims. Reversed and remanded.

DISSENT: (Souter, J.) Consistent with *Twombly*, nonconclusory allegations should be taken as true unless they are "sufficiently fantastic to defy reality." The key allegations here are not conclusory and the complaint was facially sufficient.

DISSENT: (Breyer, J.) The lower court expressly rejected minimally intrusive discovery in favor of dismissal. That would have been appropriate because the discovery could have been in anticipation of a summary judgment motion.

ANALYSIS

Pleading requirements have become stricter so general notice is no longer sufficient. The defendant is not merely put on notice of the plaintiff's claim but is entitled to factual allegations informing it of the support for the claim. Some analysts were concerned about the future of litigation because of a fear that pleadings

Continued on next page.

would have to be so specific that most plaintiffs would not be able to proceed. Most courts, however, have required factual pleading for a long time and did not become more stringent after *Iqbal.* The rule stated in *Iqbal* is "plausibility" not "probability" so the allegations do not have to be proven on the face of the complaint, but the facts alleged must be plausible and permit a reasonable inference of defendant's misconduct.

Quicknotes

INTERLOCUTORY APPEAL The appeal of an issue that does not resolve the disposition of the case but is essential to a determination of the parties' legal rights.

Bower v. Weisman

Former partner (P) v. Former partner (D)

639 F. Supp. 532 (S.D.N.Y. 1986)

NATURE OF CASE: Motions for a more definite statement, to dismiss for failure to state claim with particularity, and to dismiss for failure to state a claim upon which relief can be granted.

FACT SUMMARY: After her 15-year relationship with Weisman (D) ended, Bower (P) sought to enforce an agreement under which Weisman (D) agreed to continue to provide her and her daughter with financial security. Weisman (D) allegedly breached the agreement, and she filed a seven-count claim against him. He filed three motions with respect to each count of the claim.

RULE OF LAW

A complaint is deficient if it (1) fails to clearly identify which defendant it refers to, where there are multiple defendants; (2) only generally states that three defendants intentionally misrepresented and defrauded by making promises and representations, without stating specifics; or (3) fails to set forth facts to support a claim.

FACTS: After her 15-year relationship with Weisman (D) ended, Bower (P) sought to enforce an agreement under which Weisman (D) agreed to continue to provide her and her daughter with financial security and a home, provided she didn't remarry or move from the country. Weisman (D) allegedly breached the agreement, and Bower (P) filed a seven-count claim against him. Count one asserted a tort and contract claim for money damages for breach of the agreement; count two asserted claims of fraud, misrepresentation, and deceit in connection with the agreement; count three alleged breach of contract and conversion concerning Weisman's (D) attempt to remove Bower (P) from a townhouse he owned, and his alleged conversion of art and furniture; counts four and five charged Weisman (D) and his two companies (D) with trespass and false imprisonment in connection with his dispatch of armed guards at the house, allowing access to only Bower (P), her daughter, and medical personnel; and counts six and seven claimed intentional infliction of emotional distress and private nuisance, also in connection with Weisman's (D) action to recover the townhouse. Weisman (D) filed three motions with respect to several counts of the complaint. He moved for a more definite statement under Fed. R. Civ. P. 12(e) with respect to which of the three defendants is charged with each act; to dismiss for failure to state fraud with particularity under Fed. R. Civ. P. 9(b); and to dismiss for failure to state a claim upon which relief can be granted under Fed. R. Civ. P. 12(b)(6).

ISSUE: Is a complaint deficient if it (1) fails to clearly identify which defendant it refers to, where there are multiple defendants; (2) only generally states that three defendants intentionally misrepresented and defrauded by making promises and representations, without stating specifics; or (3) fails to set forth facts to support a claim?

HOLDING AND DECISION: (Sweet, J.) Yes. A complaint is deficient if it (1) fails to clearly identify which defendant it refers to, where there are multiple defendants; (2) only generally states that three defendants intentionally misrepresented and defrauded by making promises and representations, without stating specifics; or (3) fails to set forth facts to support a claim. First, Bower's (P) claim fails to distinguish between Weisman (D) and his two co-defendants, both of which are companies he owns. The essence of a complaint is to inform the defendant as to the general nature of the action to allow him to effectively respond. Bower (P) had to identify which defendant is referred to in each charge, or Weisman (D) would not be able to effectively respond to Bower's (P) complaint. In addition, Bower's (P) pleadings are vague and fail to provide the specificity required by Fed. R. Civ. P. 9(b) with respect to her second claim for misrepresentation, fraud, and deceit. The second claim is therefore dismissed. Finally, Bower's (P) fifth claim for false imprisonment is dismissed because she failed to set forth any facts that would support her claim that she was confined at the townhouse. Bower's (P) seventh claim for private nuisance is also dismissed, because she failed to show that there was a substantial and unreasonable interference with her property rights, which are required for the claim of nuisance.

ANALYSIS

Though this case has a very fact-specific holding, it illustrates the slight tension between Fed. R. Civ. P. 8(a)(2), which requires only a short and plain statement of the claim showing that the pleader is entitled to relief, and other Federal Rules of Civil Procedure requiring some level of specificity. The Rules, as so stated by the court, must be read in conjunction with each other, which in practice can sometimes lead to confusion.

Continued on next page.

Quicknotes

COMPLAINT The initial pleading commencing litigation that sets forth a claim for relief.

NUISANCE An unlawful use of property that interferes with the lawful use of another's property.

PLEADING A statement setting forth the plaintiff's cause of action or the defendant's defenses to the plaintiff's claims.

Freedom from Religion Foundation, Inc. v. Emanuel County School System

Parents of public-school children (P) v. Public school system (D)

109 F. Supp. 3d 1353 (S.D. Ga. 2015)

NATURE OF CASE: Plaintiffs' motion to use pseudonyms for themselves and their children in action brought under 42 U.S.C. § 1983 alleging violation of the Establishment Clause of the First Amendment by endorsement of teacher-led prayer in a public school.

FACT SUMMARY: Parents (P) and children (P) who brought a suit against the Emanuel County School System (D) under 42 U.S.C. § 1983, alleging violation of the Establishment Clause of the First Amendment by endorsement of teacher-led prayer in a public school, moved for leave of court to proceed using pseudonyms rather than their actual names in the litigation to avoid reprisals from the community for bringing the action.

RULE OF LAW

A court may grant leave for plaintiffs to use pseudonyms rather than their actual names in litigation initiated by the plaintiffs where the plaintiffs are parents and young children challenging teacher-led prayer in a public school; the teachers have bullied and proselytized the non-praying children; reprisals against plaintiffs litigating church-state issues are commonplace; the case concerns primarily a legal issue rather one involving the plaintiffs' credibility; and the defendants know the identities of the plaintiffs.

FACTS: Freedom from Religion Foundation, Inc. (P) and some of its members (P) brought a suit against the Emanuel County School System (ECS) (D) under 42 U.S.C. § 1983, alleging violation of the Establishment Clause of the First Amendment by endorsement of teacher-led prayer in a public school. The individual members (P) claimed that some of the teachers in their children's kindergarten and first grade classes in a public elementary school in the ECS were leading prayer in the classroom. They also claimed that although they had informed the ECS Superintendent that these prayer and proselytizing practices violated the Constitution, the practices did not cease. Instead, the teachers not only continued to lead prayer in the classroom, but they also began to punish the non-participating children (P) by making them sit in the hallway while the rest of the class prayed, trying to persuade them to ignore their parents (P) and join in the class prayers, and assuring one child (P) that her mother (P) was "a bad person for not believing in God." Given these circumstances, the individual plaintiffs—the parents (P) and children (P)—moved the court for leave to proceed using pseudonyms rather than their actual names in the litigation to avoid reprisals from the broader community for bringing the action. Some of the defendants opposed the motion.

ISSUE: May a court grant leave for plaintiffs to use pseudonyms rather than their actual names in litigation initiated by the plaintiffs where the plaintiffs are parents and young children challenging teacher-led prayer in a public school; the teachers have bullied and proselytized the non-praying children; reprisals against plaintiffs litigating church-state issues are commonplace; the case concerns primarily a legal issue rather one involving the plaintiffs' credibility; and the defendants know the identities of the plaintiffs?

HOLDING AND DECISION: (Smith, Mag. J.) Yes. A court may grant leave for plaintiffs to use pseudonyms rather than their actual names in litigation initiated by the plaintiffs where the plaintiffs are parents and young children challenging teacher-led prayer in a public school; the teachers have bullied and proselytized the non-praying children; reprisals against plaintiffs litigating church-state issues are commonplace; the case concerns primarily a legal issue rather one involving the plaintiffs' credibility; and the defendants know the identities of the plaintiffs. As a rule, the public has a presumptive right to know the identity of the litigants who use the courts to resolve their disputes. However, litigants may proceed pseudonymously in exceptional cases where their privacy rights outweigh the constitutionally imbedded presumption of openness in judicial proceedings. This Eleventh Circuit Court of Appeals uses a multi-factor balancing test for weighing these competing interests, and the determination of the various factors must be made on a case-by-case basis. Initially, a court must ask (1) whether the plaintiffs who seek anonymity are challenging governmental activity; (2) whether the prosecution of their suit compels them to disclose information of the "utmost intimacy"; and (3) whether plaintiffs will be compelled to admit their intention to engage in illegal conduct, thus risking criminal prosecution. Additional factors are whether the plaintiffs are minors; whether the plaintiffs are threatened with violence or physical harm by proceeding in their own names; and whether their anonymity poses a unique threat of fundamental unfairness to the defendants. These factors must

Continued on next page.

be considered and weighed in their totality. Here, the plaintiffs clearly are challenging governmental activity, i.e., the defendants' alleged policy of allowing teacher-led prayer in a public-school classroom. It is not that suing the government weighs in favor of granting a request for anonymity; rather, the operative principle is that a suit against a private party weighs against a plaintiff's request for anonymity. Here, the plaintiffs are suing not only a governmental entity but also the individual administrators and teachers who allegedly punished their children for refusing to participate in classroom prayer. So, the fact that the plaintiffs have named a governmental entity as a defendant does not establish their right to anonymity. Indeed, because the plaintiffs are also suing the school officials in their individual capacities, this factor weighs against their request for anonymity. The second factor also comes into play, since the plaintiffs will be compelled to disclose information of the "utmost intimacy," given that their suit touches upon their beliefs about religion, a topic deemed by this circuit to be "the quintessentially private matter." This factor alone, however, does not automatically entitle the plaintiffs to Doe status, and, in Establishment Clause cases, something more is required than just an intrusion into a plaintiff's religious privacy before a court will allow the plaintiff to proceed using a pseudonym. Here, that additional showing is that the children involved are very young. Even where the evidence of retaliatory violence is not particularly strong, the balance can tip in favor of anonymity in a case involving child litigants seeking to prevent the state from intruding into a matter of the "utmost intimacy." Although it is difficult, if not impossible, to quantify the risk of harm a plaintiff faces when litigating such a socially-charged issue as the constitutionality of teacher-led prayer in a public school setting, in this case there need not be any speculation as to whether the plaintiffs will suffer any harm, for they have stated in an unrebutted declaration that such harm has already occurred: the children were pressured to ignore their parents and adopt a theistic belief system, and made to suffer when they failed to do so. That the evidence of retaliatory harm relates to defendants' own actions rather than the post-filing behavior of other members of the community does not diminish its significance. If these defendants—who are educated professionals charged with the welfare and protection of very young children—are willing to pressure those children to ignore their parents and join in classroom prayer, and then ostracize them when they refuse to do so, it is permissible to infer that other, less responsible members of the local community (or the broader Internet community) might engage in even more extreme conduct if they learn the identities of the plaintiffs in this litigation. Therefore, the defendants' argument, that the plaintiffs' concern about their welfare is "unsubstantiated," is unconvincing. Further, many reported cases have described the most vicious, and sometimes criminal, acts committed against those who have commenced litigation under the Establishment Clause. Although it is not certain that such acts will be committed in response to the litigation at bar, reprisals against plaintiffs litigating church-state issues are still commonplace. Finally, contrary to the defendants' argument that it would be inherently unfair to allow the plaintiffs to proceed anonymously in a suit that not only attacks the defendants' reputation and integrity but that seeks compensatory and punitive damages against them in their individual capacities, the potential harm to defendants is not so great as to override the plaintiffs' privacy interest or need to shield their children from any further harm. The case primarily concerns the resolution of a legal question rather than a determination of the plaintiffs' credibility regarding hotly disputed factual allegations. Thus, there does not appear to be a compelling need for the defendants to publicize the plaintiffs' names in order to "shake out" information bearing on their credibility. Moreover, the defendants know the plaintiffs' identities. Where the defendants already know the plaintiffs' names, their interest in fairness is diminished because the defendants may depose the plaintiffs, request ordinary discovery, and otherwise litigate the case normally. For these reasons, the balance of the competing interests at issue weighs in favor of allowing the plaintiffs to proceed anonymously. Moreover, the plaintiffs' use of fictitious names will not unduly prejudice the public interest, since all of the pleadings and other filings in the case will remain unsealed, so that the public will be well aware of the nature of the suit, the positions of the parties, and the issues at play, and the public and the press will have full access to all court proceedings, including the trial itself. The plaintiffs' motion is granted.

ANALYSIS

As this case illustrates, no one factor is dispositive as to whether the public interest in knowing the identity of all the parties must yield to protecting a party's privacy in a very private matter. Instead, it is the court's task to review all the circumstances of a given case and then decide whether the customary practice of disclosing the plaintiff's identity should yield to the plaintiff's privacy concerns. Nevertheless, courts have recognized that some private matters involve such a high degree of intimacy that prejudice can be presumed if a plaintiff's identity is disclosed. For instance, courts have recognized that abortion is a paradigmatic example of the type of highly sensitive and personal matter that warrants a grant of anonymity. Similarly, the public interest in open judicial proceedings typically gives way in cases

Continued on next page.

involving sexual assaults upon minors or the existence of a stigmatizing disease.

Quicknotes

ESTABLISHMENT CLAUSE The constitutional provision prohibiting the government from favoring any one religion over others or engaging in religious activities or advocacy.

Singletary v. Pennsylvania Department of Corrections

Mother of inmate (P) v. Prison and prison employees (D)

266 F.3d 186 (3d Cir. 2001)

NATURE OF CASE: Appeal from denial of a motion to amend a complaint to add a defendant.

FACT SUMMARY: Subsequent to filing suit and after the running of the limitations period, Dorothy Singletary (P) sought to add a newly named defendant under the "relation back" doctrine.

RULE OF LAW

After the statute of limitations has run, a new party may not be added to a suit under the "relation back" doctrine unless such party received notice of the institution of the action within 120 days of the filing of the original complaint.

FACTS: On October 6, 1996, Edward Singletary committed suicide while incarcerated at SCI-Rockview. On October 6, 1998, Dorothy Singletary (P), Edward's mother, filed a civil rights lawsuit under 42 U.S.C. § 1983, naming as defendants Pennsylvania Department of Corrections (PADOC) (D), SCI-Rockview (D), Joseph Mazurkiewicz (former Superintendent of SCI-Rockview) (D), and "Unknown Corrections Officers" (D). On July 28, 2000, nearly two years after the statute of limitations had run, Dorothy Singletary (P) moved for leave to amend her original complaint to substitute Robert Regan, a psychologist at SCI-Rockview (D), for "Unknown Corrections Officers." She also moved to have the amended complaint relate back to her original complaint under Fed. R. Civ. P. 15(c)(3). The district court denied Dorothy Singletary's (P) motion to amend her complaint to add Regan as a defendant on the grounds that that claim would be barred by the statute of limitations because it did not meet the conditions for "relation back" under Fed. R. Civ. P. 15(c)(3). The district court also granted summary judgment in favor of PADOC (D), SCI-Rockview (D), and Joseph Mazurkiewicz (D).

ISSUE: After the statute of limitations has run, may a new party be added to a suit under the "relation back" doctrine where such party did not receive notice of the institution of the action within 120 days of the filing of the original complaint?

HOLDING AND DECISION: (Becker, C.J.) No. After the statute of limitations has run, a new party may not be added to a suit under the "relation back" doctrine unless such party received notice of the institution of the action within 120 days of the filing of the original complaint. In order for an amended complaint that substitutes newly named defendants to successfully relate back under Fed. R. Civ. P. 15(c)(3), three conditions must be met. Fed. R. Civ. P. 15(c)(3)(A) states that one of the three conditions is that the newly named party must have received notice of the institution of the action (a) within 120 days after the filing of the original complaint, and (b) the notice is sufficient that the defendant is not prejudiced in maintaining his defense. In the context of Fed. R. Civ. P. 15(c), "notice" does not require actual service of process on the party sought to be added to the complaint. Notice concerning the institution of an action may be actual, constructive, or imputed. Constructive or implied notice can be by two methods: (a) the shared attorney method or (b) the identity of interest method. Notice can be implied under the shared attorney method where the attorney's later relationship with the newly named defendant gives rise to the inference that the attorney, within the 120-day period, had some communication or relationship with, and thus gave notice of the action to, the newly named defendant. Notice can be implied under the identity of interest method where the parties are so closely related in their business operations or other activities that the institution of an action against one serves to provide notice of the litigation to the other. Dorothy Singletary (P) argues Regan received timely notice under the shared attorney method because he shared his attorney with SCI-Rockview (D), an originally named party. Dorothy Singletary (P) also argues that Regan received timely notice under the identity of interest method because he had an identity of interest with SCI-Rockview (D). The facts do not support Dorothy Singletary's (P) contention that Regan shared an attorney with the other defendants. The attorney who represented the defendants through the 120-day period following the filing of the original complaint never represented Regan. That attorney was replaced by another. The attorney who took over after the 120-day period, and who had connection with Regan and the defendants, did not become attorney for the defendants until well after the relevant 120-day period. The facts also do not support Dorothy Singletary's (P) contention that Regan received constructive or implied notice by way of the identity of interest method. Regan was a staff-level employee at SCI-Rockview (D) with no administrative or supervisory duties. His position alone cannot serve as a basis for finding an identity of interest with his employer because he was not highly enough placed in the prison hierarchy to support a conclusion that his interests as an employee were identical to the prison's interests. Absent other circumstances that permit the inference that notice was actually received, a non-management employee like

Continued on next page.

Regan does not share a sufficient nexus of interests with his or her employer so that notice given to the employer can be imputed to the employee for Fed. R. Civ. P. 15(c)(3) purposes. Because Regan did not receive actual, constructive, or implied notice of the institution of the action within 120 days of the filing of the original complaint, the district court correctly denied Dorothy Singletary's (P) motion for leave to amend her complaint. Affirmed.

ANALYSIS

Issue whether the facts satisfy the second requirement for relating back an amendment under Fed. R. Civ. P. 15(c)(3)(B) was not resolved by the court because the first condition, dealing with notice, was not met; and the case was disposed of on that issue alone. The court does note that the language of Fed. R. Civ. P. 15(c)(3)(B) is unclear. Specifically, there is a division in authority as to whether not knowing the identity of a potential defendant is the same as mistaking the identity of a defendant. Most courts seem to take the position that not knowing the identity of a defendant is not a mistake concerning the defendant's identity. Therefore, "the bulk of authority from other courts of appeals takes the position that the amendment of a 'John Doe' complaint, i.e., the substituting of real names for 'John Does' or 'Unknown Persons' named in an original complaint, does not meet the 'but for a mistake' requirement in 15(c)(3)(B)." *Singletary v. Pennsylvania Department of Corrections*, 266 F.3d 186, 201 (3d Cir. 2001). While the court notes that it is bound by a case that held that not knowing the identity of a defendant can be a mistake under Fed. R. Civ. P. 15(c)(3)(B), the court expressed concern over the state of the law on Fed. R. Civ. P. 15(c)(3), and, in particular, other Circuits' interpretation of the "mistake" requirement. The court recommended to the Advisory Rules Committee a modification of Fed. R. Civ. P. 15(c)(3) to bring the Rule into accord with the prevailing opinion about it.

Quicknotes

42 U.S.C. § 1983 Provides that every person who under color of state law subjects or causes to be subjected any citizen of the United States or person within its jurisdiction to be deprived of rights, privileges, and immunities guaranteed by the federal Constitution and laws is liable to the injured party at law or in equity.

ACTUAL NOTICE Direct communication of information that would cause an ordinary person of average prudence to inquire as to its truth.

COMPLAINT The initial pleading commencing litigation that sets forth a claim for relief.

CONSTRUCTIVE NOTICE Knowledge of a fact imputed to an individual who was under a duty to inquire and who could have learned of the fact through the exercise of reasonable prudence.

RELATION BACK DOCTRINE Doctrine that holds that a party may not amend its pleading to set forth a new or different claim or defense unless it involves the subject matter of the original pleading; under Fed. R. Civ. P. 15, if a party amends its pleading as a matter of course before a responsive pleading is served, such amendment is said to relate back to the original pleading if it involves the subject matter of the original pleading.

STATUTE OF LIMITATIONS A law prescribing the period in which a legal action may be commenced.

Krupski v. Costa Crociere S.p.A.

Cruise ship passenger (P) v. Cruise owner (D)

560 U.S. 538 (2010)

NATURE OF CASE: Appeal of circuit court judgment.

FACT SUMMARY: Wanda Krupski (P) injured herself while on a cruise. She brought suit against the wrong party and sought to amend a complaint to name the proper defendant after the limitations period lapsed. The Eleventh Circuit Court of Appeals held that the amended complaint did not relate back because she should have known the identity of the proper defendant.

RULE OF LAW

Federal Rule of Civil Procedure 15(c) permits an amended complaint to relate back to a previously filed complaint if the proper defendant knew or should have known within the time of service that but for a mistake in identity, the plaintiff would have asserted the claims against the proper defendant.

FACTS: Wanda Krupski (P) was injured while a passenger on the cruise ship Costa Magica. She sued Costa Cruise S.p.A. (D), the business through which she had booked her cruise and had sent her travel documents. In its answer to the complaint, Costa Cruise (D) stated that it was only the North American sales and booking agent for the ship operator, Costa Crociere (D), which was the proper defendant. Krupski (P) amended her complaint to add Costa Crociere (D) as a party. But Costa Crociere (D), which was represented by the same attorney as Costa Cruise (D), argued that the expiration of the contractual one-year limitations period had expired. The Eleventh Circuit Court of Appeals held that Federal Rule of Civil Procedure 15(c) was not satisfied because Krupski (P) knew or should have known the identity of the proper defendant before the expiration of the limitations period, and that because she chose not to sue Costa Crociere (D), she didn't make the type of mistake about the identity of the defendant that Rule 15(c) contemplated. The court also held that relation back was not appropriate because the plaintiff had unduly delayed in seeking to amend.

ISSUE: Does Federal Rule of Civil Procedure 15(c) permit an amended complaint to relate back to a previously filed complaint if the proper defendant knew or should have known within the time of service that but for a mistake in identity, the plaintiff would have asserted the claims against the proper defendant?

HOLDING AND DECISION: (Sotomayor, J.) Yes. Federal Rule of Civil Procedure 15(c) permits an amended complaint to relate back to a previously filed complaint if the proper defendant knew or should have known within the time of service that but for a mistake in identity, the plaintiff would have asserted the claims against the proper defendant. Whether an amendment relates back under Rule 15(c)(1)(C) depends on what the party to be added knew or should have known, not on the amending party's knowledge or timeliness in seeking to amend the pleading. Rule 15 asks what the prospective defendant "knew or should have known," not what the plaintiff "knew or should have known," as was understood by the Eleventh Circuit. Costa Crociere (D) should have known that Krupski's (P) failure to name it as a defendant was due to a mistake concerning the proper party's identity. Reversed and remanded.

ANALYSIS

This decision illustrates a very basic fact about being human: People can make mistakes even when they know all the facts. The Eleventh Circuit found that because Krupski (P) knew about the existence of Costa Crociere (D), and that the company was the owner of the ship, she could not have made a mistake when she chose to sue Costa Cruise (D). But Fed. R. Civ. P. 15(c) does not require that the mistake of the plaintiff be reasonable. It requires only that a mistake was made.

Quicknotes

FED. R. CIV. P. 15(C) Provides that a claim or defense arising out of the conduct or occurrence set forth in the original pleading will relate back to the date of the original pleading.

Chaplin v. DuPont Advance Fiber Systems

Seven employees (P) v. Employer (D)

303 F. Supp. 2d 766 (E.D. Va. 2004), *aff'd,* 124 Fed. Appx. 771 (4th Cir. 2005)

NATURE OF CASE: Motion for Rule 11 sanctions.

FACT SUMMARY: Seven DuPont employees (P), who are White, Christian, and Confederate Southern Americans, brought an action under Title VII of the 1964 Civil Rights Act, alleging employment discrimination based on national origin, religion, and race. DuPont (D) sought sanctions under Fed. R. Civ. P. 11(b)(1) for filing a complaint for an improper purpose, under Rule 11(b)(2) for stating claims without sufficient basis in law, and under Rule 11(b)(3) for stating claims without sufficient basis in fact.

RULE OF LAW

(1) Sanctions for filing a complaint with improper purpose are not necessarily warranted where the complaint "creatively" pursues a new legal theory.

(2) Sanctions for filing a complaint containing claims that lack legal authority are not necessarily warranted where there is no authoritative precedent precluding the claims.

(3) Sanctions for filing a complaint containing claims that lack factual basis are necessarily warranted where there is no factual basis whatsoever to support the complaint's allegations.

FACTS: DuPont Advance Fiber Systems, DuPont Spruance, and DuPont Textiles & Interiors, Inc. (collectively, DuPont) (D) instituted in 2000 a policy banning the display of offensive symbols on DuPont (D) property. The policy included a ban on the display of the Confederate battle flag, specifically on the wearing or displaying of Confederate symbols on clothing, newspapers, pictures, photographs, and bumper stickers. Seven DuPont employees (P), who are White, Christian, and Confederate Southern Americans, brought an action under Title VII of the 1964 Civil Rights Act, alleging employment discrimination based on national origin, religion, and race. One plaintiff had been ordered to discontinue wearing clothing bearing the Confederate symbols, another plaintiff had been told "it was not a good idea" to wear his Confederate belt buckle, two plaintiffs had been ordered to remove bumper stickers from their vehicles, and another plaintiff had been told to stop wearing a Confederate t-shirt or risk a reprimand and he had been ordered to sit in the back of the room during an off-site, DuPont-sponsored multicultural workshop because he had worn such a shirt. DuPont (D) sought sanctions under Fed. R. Civ. P.11(b)(1) for filing a complaint for an improper purpose, under Fed. R. Civ. P. 11(b)(2) for stating claims without sufficient basis in law, and under Fed. R. Civ. P.11(b)(3) for stating claims without sufficient basis in fact.

ISSUE:

(1) Are sanctions for filing a complaint with improper purpose necessarily warranted where the complaint "creatively" pursues a new legal theory?

(2) Are sanctions for filing a complaint containing claims that lack legal authority necessarily warranted where there is no authoritative precedent precluding the claims?

(3) Are sanctions for filing a complaint containing claims that lack factual basis necessarily warranted where there is no factual basis whatsoever to support the complaint's allegations?

HOLDING AND DECISION: (Hudson, J.)

(1) No. Sanctions for filing a complaint with improper purpose are not necessarily warranted where the complaint "creatively" pursues a new legal theory. The purpose of Rule 11 is not to thwart an attorney's enthusiasm or creativity in pursuing factual or legal theories. Regardless of the merits of the claims, the attorney's purpose in filing the lawsuit was not to harass DuPont Advance Fiber Systems, DuPont Spruance, and DuPont Textiles & Interiors, Inc. (collectively, DuPont) (D) but to broaden the interpretation of "national origin" protection under Title VII. Therefore, the motion for sanctions under Fed. R. Civ. P. 11(b)(1) is denied.

(2) No. Sanctions for filing a complaint containing claims that lack legal authority are not necessarily warranted where there is no authoritative precedent precluding the claims. Where an argument has absolutely no chance of success under existing authoritative precedent, it may be sanctionable. While there is no authoritative case law anywhere in the country to support the claim of national origin discrimination in this case, there also is no binding case to the contrary. Therefore, the motion for sanctions under Fed. R. Civ. P. 11(b)(2) is denied.

(3) Yes. Sanctions for filing a complaint containing claims that lack factual basis are necessarily warranted where there is no factual basis whatsoever to support the complaint's allegations. The complaint lists many facts, both supported and unsupported, backing their

Continued on next page.

national origin discrimination claim, and whether they have merit or not, they satisfy Fed. R. Civ. P. 11(b)(3). However, there is absolutely no evidence that DuPont (D) denied them a religious accommodation that they requested, or that DuPont's (D) policy discriminates against Caucasians. Therefore, with respect to counts alleging religious and race discrimination, the complaint is frivolous and unwarranted, and the motion for sanctions is granted.

ANALYSIS

It would seem easiest to comply with Fed. R. Civ. P. 11(b)(3), as compared with Fed. R. Civ. P. 11(b)(1) and (b)(2); the complaint simply must have a factual basis. Sanctions for Fed. R. Civ. P. 11(b)(3) violations are, therefore, easier to pursue. On the other hand, if a complaint is arguably proper and arguably based on the law, or on some extended legal theory, the Rule is satisfied.

Quicknotes

SANCTIONS A penalty imposed in order to ensure compliance with a statute or regulation.

A.D. v. La Quinta Holdings, Inc.; Choice Hotels Intl., Inc.; Wyndham Hotels & Resorts, Inc.; et al.

Alleged sex-trafficking victim (P) v. Hotel (D)

2022 WL 4357989 (M.D. Fla. 2022)

NATURE OF CASE: Motion to sever in action for violation of the Trafficking Victims Protection Reauthorization Act of 2008, 18 U.S.C. § 1595.

FACT SUMMARY: A.D. (P) brought suit alleging she had been a victim of sex trafficking at a number of hotels (D) in violation of the Trafficking Victims Protection Reauthorization Act of 2008 (TVPRA), 18 U.S.C. § 1595. One of the hotels (D) moved to sever, contending that the defendant hotels (D) had been improperly joined together.

RULE OF LAW

Separate defendants should not be joined in a single action where, although the claims against each defendant may raise similar legal issues, the claims are not logically related because they arose from separate transactions or occurrences rather than from common operative facts or concerted activity.

FACTS: A.D. (P) alleged she was a victim of sex trafficking at various hotels (D) in violation of the Trafficking Victims Protection Reauthorization Act of 2008 (TVPRA), 18 U.S.C. § 1595. The 20 defendants in the case were the alleged hotel (D) franchisors, owners, operators, and/or franchisees of the properties where the trafficking allegedly occurred. One of the defendants, Choice Hotels International, Inc. (Choice) (D), moved to sever, contending that the defendant hotels (D) had been improperly joined together. Specifically, Choice (D) argued that joinder of the 20 defendants would result in an overcomplicated, inefficient trial of the important issues in the case. In response, A.D. (P) argued that Federal Rule of Civil Procedure 20 warranted joining the defendants in one action since a "logical relationship" existed between the defendants sufficient to show that A.D.'s (P) TVPRA claim arose from the same sex trafficking occurrence along with common questions of law and fact. A.D. (P) also asserted it would be logically impossible to sever the claims against all the defendants because her indivisible injuries resulted from repeated victimization and trafficking at the various hotels (D). The federal district court considered the motion.

ISSUE: Should separate defendants be joined in a single action where, although the claims against each defendant may raise similar legal issues, the claims are not logically related because they arose from separate transactions or occurrences rather than from common operative facts or concerted activity?

HOLDING AND DECISION: (Steele, J.) No. Separate defendants should not be joined in a single action where, although the claims against each defendant may raise similar legal issues, the claims are not logically related because they arose from separate transactions or occurrences rather than from common operative facts or concerted activity. Pursuant to Federal Rule of Civil Procedure 20, defendants may be joined in one action if "(A) any right to relief is asserted against them jointly, severally, or in the alternative with respect to or arising out of the same transaction, occurrence, or series of transactions or occurrences; and (B) any question of law or fact common to all defendants will arise in the action." Fed. R. Civ. P. 20(a)(2). Notwithstanding that joinder is strongly encouraged, district courts have wide discretion to sever parties based on misjoinder. Here, joinder was inappropriate, and the requested severance will, therefore, be granted. In determining whether claims arise from the same series of transactions or occurrences, the logical relationship test is applied. Under this test, a logical relationship exists if the claims rest on the same set of facts or the same operative facts serve as the basis of the claims against each defendant. A.D.'s (P) joinder ignores the individualized nature of the claim as well as the practical difficulties that would arise from joinder, given that the claim involves conduct by different alleged sex trafficking ventures, different hotel brands, different owners and employees, different geographic locales, different witnesses, different indicia of sex trafficking, and different time periods. Thus, the sex trafficking that occurred at each defendant hotel's (D) property was a separate "transaction" or "occurrence," and each defendant's knowledge of trafficking, or what they did or failed to do giving rise to a claim for relief does not overlap between defendants. Here, too, the absence of concerted activity is fatal to A.D.'s (P) attempt at joinder, as A.D. (P) has failed to present sufficient factual evidence that the different hotels (D) acted in any concerted activity. Finally, even if joinder were technically appropriate under Rule 20(a), considerations of judicial economy, case management, prejudice to parties, and fundamental fairness require severance. Under the TVPRA, A.D. (P) must show

Continued on next page.

that each defendant knew or should have known that A.D. (P) was being trafficked, and that each defendant participated in a sex trafficking venture and knowingly benefited from such conduct. Therefore, it is inevitable that the factual circumstances giving rise to the claim against each defendant will vary (e.g., the different ventures, hotel owners and employees, locations, witnesses and time periods, and the knowledge of each defendant) and resolution of the claim against each defendant will require an individualized inquiry. Accordingly, severance will make the cases more manageable and reduce the risk of prejudice by separating each claim as to each defendant. Fundamental fairness also weighs in favor of severance, because otherwise the court would have to consider all of the alleged trafficking occurring at every hotel to be the same as to each defendant. Choice's (D) motion as to severance, therefore, is granted.

ANALYSIS

In its motion, Choice Hotels International, Inc. (Choice) (D) also argued that A.D.'s complaint should be dismissed as an impermissible shotgun pleading. Specifically, Choice (D) argued that the complaint (1) alleged conclusory, vague and immaterial facts about sex trafficking and the hospitality industry's failure to stop it, (2) asserted a claim against multiple defendants without specifying which of the defendants was responsible for which acts, and (3) merely reiterated the elements of the claims without alleging specific facts or circumstances that gave rise to Choice's (D) liability. Shotgun pleadings are unacceptable because they fail to give defendants adequate notice of the claims against them and the grounds upon which each claim rests, and because they exact an intolerable toll on the trial court's docket. Here, the court agreed that portions of the complaint constituted an improper shotgun pleading since it contained immaterial allegations, and at times commingles factual allegations against all defendants and failed to specify which of the defendants were responsible for which acts or omissions. Accordingly, the court concluded that dismissal of the complaint without prejudice was appropriate.

Quicknotes

JOINDER OF PARTIES The joining of parties in one lawsuit.

SEVERANCE OF PARTIES The separation of one of more parties from a single lawsuit so that each separated party may be tried in a separate lawsuit.

SHOTGUN PLEADING Impermissible pleading that fails to provide an opposing party with fair and adequate notice of claims or defenses against them, and precludes an effective responsive pleading, usually alleging conclusory, vague and immaterial facts; asserting a claim or claims against multiple defendants without specifying which of the defendants is responsible for which acts; or merely reiterating the elements of claims without alleging specific facts or circumstances that give rise to, or support, the claims.

Podhorn v. Paragon Group, Inc.

Tenant (P) v. Landlord (D)

606 F. Supp. 185 (D. Mo. 1985)

NATURE OF CASE: Motion to dismiss.

FACT SUMMARY: A landlord (D) sued tenants in state court for failure to pay rent. The tenants did not counterclaim but later filed a federal claim against the landlord (D) that was based on the same tenancy that gave rise to the state court claim.

RULE OF LAW

A claim arising out of the transaction that is the subject matter of the opposing party's claim, and that does not require for its adjudication the presence of third parties over whom the court does not have jurisdiction, must be stated as a counterclaim, even where the counterclaim may not have been triable in the court where the original pleading was filed.

FACTS: Paragon Group, Inc. (D), which owned the apartment building in which Paul, Liana, and Renata Podhorn (P) lived, sued them in state court for failure to pay rent. The Podhorns (P) did not file a counterclaim, and default judgment was entered. [The Podhorns (P) then filed suit against Paragon Group (D), alleging constructive eviction, breach of implied warranty of habitability, false swearing, false credit report, breach of implied covenant of quiet enjoyment, negligence, abuse of process, tort, conversion, and malicious prosecution.] Paragon Group (D) moved to dismiss the claim on grounds that it should have been filed as a compulsory counterclaim in the state court action because it arose from the same tenancy that gave rise to the state court claim.

ISSUE: Must a claim arising out of the transaction that is the subject matter of the opposing party's claim, and that does not require for its adjudication the presence of third parties over whom the court does not have jurisdiction, be stated as a counterclaim, even where the counterclaim may not have been triable in the court where the original pleading was filed?

HOLDING AND DECISION: (Hungate, J.) Yes. A claim arising out of the transaction that is the subject matter of the opposing party's claim, and that does not require for its adjudication the presence of third parties over whom the court does not have jurisdiction, must be stated as a counterclaim, even where the counterclaim may not have been triable in the court where the original pleading was filed. The Podhorns' (P) claim arose out of the transaction that gave rise to Paragon Group's (D) rent action in the state court case, and the Podhorns (P) were therefore required to file their federal court claims as compulsory counterclaims. Their failure to do so bars them from having those claims heard. The fact that the state court was without jurisdiction to hear their counterclaim if filed, because the claim exceeded the statutory limit, does not relieve the Podhorns (P) of their obligation to file it. The issue of jurisdiction would have been resolved through assignment to a judge who could hear the claim. Motion to dismiss granted.

ANALYSIS

Though the opinion lists very little in the way of facts, one might imagine a claim that might not have arisen from the same transaction or occurrence as the landlord's nonpayment of rent claim, such as breaking and entering by the landlord, and it becomes clear that the holding may be too broad in scope. The court seems to say that any issue arising during a tenancy that is based on any action by the landlord must be pled as a counterclaim, whether related to the landlord-tenant relationship or not.

Quicknotes

CLAIM The demand for a right to payment or equitable relief; the fact or facts giving rise to such demand.

COUNTERCLAIM An independent cause of action brought by a defendant to a lawsuit in order to oppose or deduct from the plaintiff's claim.

Gross v. Hanover Insurance Co.

Insured (P) v. Insurer (D)

138 F.R.D. 53 (S.D.N.Y. 1991)

NATURE OF CASE: Motion under Federal Rule of Civil Procedure 14(a) to implead third-party defendants.

FACT SUMMARY: Gross (P) brought claim against Hanover Insurance Co. (Hanover) (D), his insurer, for theft of jewelry consigned to a retail jewelry store. Hanover (D) sought to implead Joseph Rizzo and Anthony Rizzo, an employee and owner of the store at the time of the theft.

RULE OF LAW

A third-party defendant may be impleaded under Federal Rule of Civil Procedure 14(a), in the sound discretion of the court, when such third party is purportedly liable to the defendant for all or part of the defendant's liability to the plaintiff.

FACTS: Gross (P) consigned jewelry to a store from which the jewelry was stolen and brought suit against Hanover Insurance Co. (Hanover) (D), his insurer. Hanover (D), under Rule 14(a), sought to implead the owner of the jewelry store and the owner's brother, who worked there, on evidence that the brother had been involved in the theft and, hence, that the owner and brother would be liable to reimburse the insurer (D) for the stolen goods.

ISSUE: May a defendant implead a third party under Federal Rule of Civil Procedure 14(a), in the sound discretion of the court, when such third party is purportedly liable to the defendant for all or part of the defendant's liability to the plaintiff?

HOLDING AND DECISION: (Leisure, J.) Yes. A third-party defendant may be impleaded under Federal Rule of Civil Procedure 14(a), in the sound discretion of the court, when such third party is purportedly liable to the defendant for all or part of the defendant's liability to the plaintiff. The interest in judicial economy is served by permitting Hanover Insurance Co. (D) to implead the store owner and his brother. Any prejudice felt by Gross (P), the insured, due to the need for additional discovery, was sufficiently outweighed by the benefits of more efficient litigation to be gained by permitting impleader. Furthermore, federal and state court decisions both hold that third-party impleader practice encompasses, as here, subrogation claims. Motion to implead granted.

ANALYSIS

The court emphasized that the district court has considerable discretion in deciding whether to permit a third-party complaint.

Quicknotes

DISCOVERY Pretrial procedure during which one party makes certain information available to the other.

IMPLEADER Procedure by which a third party, who may be liable for all or part of liability, is joined to an action so that all issues may be resolved in a single suit.

SUBROGATION The substitution of one party for another in assuming the first party's rights or obligations.

THIRD-PARTY COMPLAINT A complaint filed by the defendant against a party not yet involved in a lawsuit, alleging liability on the part of the third party for all or part of the damages being sought by the plaintiff.

Temple v. Synthes Corporation, Ltd.

Patient (P) v. Medical device manufacturer (D)

498 U.S. 1042 (1991)

NATURE OF CASE: Appeal of dismissal with prejudice of action for damages for products liability, medical malpractice, and negligence.

FACT SUMMARY: Temple's (P) federal suit against Synthes Corporation, Ltd. (D), the manufacturer of a plate implanted in Temple's (P) back, was dismissed when Temple (P) failed to join the doctor and the hospital responsible for installing the plate.

RULE OF LAW

Joint tortfeasors are not necessary parties under Federal Rule of Civil Procedure 19.

FACTS: A plate and screw device implanted in Temple's (P) back malfunctioned. Temple (P) filed a federal court products liability action against Synthes Corporation, Ltd. (D), the manufacturer of the device. Temple (P) also filed a state court medical malpractice and negligence action against the doctor who implanted the device and the hospital where the operation was performed. Synthes (D) filed a motion to dismiss the federal lawsuit under Federal Rule of Civil Procedure 19 for Temple's (P) failure to join necessary parties. The district court agreed that the doctor and the hospital were necessary parties and gave Temple (P) 20 days to join them. When Temple (P) did not, the court dismissed the suit with prejudice. The court of appeals affirmed, finding that Rule 19 allowed the district court to order joinder in the interest of complete, consistent, and efficient settlement of controversies. It further found that overlapping, separate lawsuits would have prejudiced Synthes (D) because Synthes (D) might claim the device was not defective but that the doctor and the hospital were negligent, and the doctor and the hospital might claim the opposite. Temple (P) appealed, arguing that joint tortfeasors are not necessary parties under Rule 19.

ISSUE: Are joint tortfeasors necessary parties under Federal Rule of Civil Procedure 19?

HOLDING AND DECISION: (Per curiam) No. Joint tortfeasors are not necessary parties under Federal Rule of Civil Procedure 19. It has long been the rule that joint tortfeasors need not be named as defendants in a single lawsuit. Rule 19 does not change that principle. The Advisory Committee Notes to Rule 19(a) state that a tortfeasor with the usual joint and several liability is merely a permissive party. There is a public interest in avoiding multiple lawsuits. However, since the threshold requirements of Rule 19(a) have not been met, the district court had no authority to order dismissal. Reversed and remanded.

ANALYSIS

The function of compulsory joinder as codified in Federal Rule of Civil Procedure 19 is to bring all affected parties into the same lawsuit. Joinder is often required where the suit involves jointly held rights or liabilities, where more than one party claims the same property, or where granting relief necessarily would affect the rights of parties not in the lawsuit. Though there is a strong interest in "complete, consistent, and efficient settlement of controversies," compulsory joinder is limited. There is a strong tradition of allowing the parties themselves to determine who shall be a party, what claims shall be litigated, and what litigation strategies shall be followed.

Quicknotes

COMPULSORY JOINDER The joining of parties to a lawsuit that is mandatory if complete relief cannot be afforded to the parties in his absence or his absence will result in injustice.

INDISPENSABLE PARTY Parties whose joining in a lawsuit is essential for the adequate disposition of the action and without whom the action cannot proceed.

JOINDER The joining of claims or parties in one lawsuit.

JOINT TORTFEASORS Two or more parties that either in concert, or whose individual acts combine to cause a single injury, rendering them jointly and severally liable for damages incurred.

MEDICAL MALPRACTICE Conduct on the part of a doctor falling below that demonstrated by other doctors of ordinary skill and competency under the circumstances, resulting in damages.

PREJUDICE A preference of the court toward one party prior to litigation.

Daynard v. Ness, Motley, Loadholdt, Richardson & Poole, P.A.

Law professor (P) v. Law firms litigating against big tobacco (D)

184 F. Supp. 2d 55 (D. Mass. 2001)

NATURE OF CASE: Breach of contract.

FACT SUMMARY: A South Carolina law firm (D) argued that the breach of contract action brought by Daynard (P) should be dismissed for failure to join an indispensable party, a Mississippi law firm (D).

RULE OF LAW

A jointly and severally liable co-obligor under a verbal contract is not an indispensable party.

FACTS: Daynard (P), a law professor, was an advisor to two law firms that represented the state government in litigation against the tobacco industry (the State Tobacco Litigation). The defendant firms are Ness, Motley, Loadholdt, Richardson & Poole, P.A. from South Carolina (South Carolina defendants) (D) and Scruggs, Milette, Bozeman & Dent, P.A. from Mississippi (Mississippi defendants) (D). There was no written contract between Daynard (P) and either defendant, but Daynard (P) alleged that he and one of the partners from the Mississippi defendants (D) shook hands on a deal that would have paid Daynard (P) five percent of any attorneys' fees paid to either of the defendants. The Mississippi defendants (D) moved to dismiss for lack of personal jurisdiction, and the motion was granted. The South Carolina defendants (D) argued that the case should not proceed without the Mississippi defendants (D) because it was allegedly that firm that made the deal with Daynard (P). Daynard (P) argued that the two firms together agreed that he would be paid for his services, even though the handshake was with the partner of only one, and that under a theory of joint and several liability, only one defendant need be named in the complaint.

ISSUE: Is a jointly and severally liable co-obligor under a verbal contract an indispensable party?

HOLDING AND DECISION: (Young, C.J.) No. A jointly and severally liable co-obligor under a verbal contract is not an indispensable party. Determination of whether a party is "indispensable" requires two steps. The first step is to determine whether the party is "necessary" under Fed. R. Civ. P. 19(a). The second step is to determine whether the party is, in addition to being "necessary," also "indispensable" under Fed. R. Civ. P. 19(b). It is important to note that "indispensable" is a subset of "necessary," not a mutually exclusive category. A "necessary" party is one that should be joined to effect a just adjudication, while an "indispensable" party under Rule 19 (b) is a "necessary" party under Rule 19(a) who cannot be made a party and without whom the court determines the action cannot proceed. Under Rule 19(a)(1) and (2), the Mississippi defendants (D) are not a "necessary" party. First, Scruggs, Milette, Bozeman & Dent, P.A. from Mississippi (Mississippi defendants) (D) are not "necessary" under Rule 19(a)(1). Since Ness, Motley, Loadholdt, Richardson & Poole, P.A. from South Carolina (South Carolina defendants) (D) bear the burden of persuasion on their motion to dismiss, the court must draw inferences in Daynard's (P) favor and assume that the defendants are jointly and severally liable. Second, the Mississippi defendants (D) are not "necessary" under Rule 19(a)(2)(i). Any judgment against the South Carolina defendants (D) will not be binding against the Mississippi defendants (D), and any such judgment would not be "persuasive precedent" and thus impair the Mississippi defendants' (D) ability to protect their interests. Third, the possibility that the South Carolina defendants (D) may bear the entire bill unless the Mississippi defendants (D) are joined does not make the Mississippi defendants (D) "necessary" under 19(a)(2)(ii) because under the theory of joint and several liability, Daynard (P) has the right to satisfy his whole judgment by execution against any one of the multiple defendants who are liable to him. Fourth, under the traditional rule of thumb co-obligees are "indispensable" parties while co-obligors might not even be "necessary," the South Carolina defendants (D) tried to cast themselves as co-obligees under the alleged contract. The South Carolina defendants (D) argued that Daynard (P) still owes legal research and advice to them, even though the State Tobacco Litigation already settled. The facts do not support the conclusion that Daynard (P) still owes services to the South Carolina defendants (D). Finally, the South Carolina defendants (D) argued that a mutual release to which Daynard (P) allegedly agreed puts the validity and enforceability of the alleged contract into question, and thus requires joinder of all parties to the alleged contract, but this argument twists the traditional rule of thumb, which is that an action in equity to determine the rights under a contract requires joinder of all parties to the contract. This case concerns only money damages and does not concern rescission or specific performance. Thus, the traditional rule of thumb that rescission requires joinder of all parties must give way to the traditional rule of thumb that a plaintiff need not name all co-obligors as defendants. Therefore, it is not necessary for Daynard (P) to join the Mississippi defendants (D) in this action because they are jointly and severally liable as co-obligors. Since the Mississippi defendants (D) are not

Continued on next page.

a "necessary" party under Rule 19(a), then by definition, they cannot be "indispensable" under Rule 19(b).

ANALYSIS

The court notes that since Scruggs, Milette, Bozeman & Dent, P.A. from Mississippi (Mississippi defendants) (D) are not a "necessary" party, they cannot be "indispensable." That fact resolves the issue in the case. But the court went on to consider Ness, Motley, Loadholdt, Richardson & Poole, P.A. from South Carolina's (South Carolina defendants) (D) arguments under Fed. R. Civ. P. 19(b) anyway. The four factors to consider under Rule 19(b), which overlap with the factors enumerated in Rule 19(a), are: (1) To what extent might a judgment rendered in the person's absence be prejudicial to the person or those already parties? The court rejected the South Carolina defendants' (D) argument here, stating that (a) joint and several liability by definition includes the possibility that one defendant ends up footing the entire bill, (b) "persuasive precedent" alone cannot, as a practical matter, impair or impede the Mississippi defendants' (D) ability to defend themselves, and (c) Rule 19 is concerned with the risk of inconsistent obligations, not inconsistent adjudications. (2) To what extent can the prejudice be lessened or avoided by protective provisions in the judgment, by shaping the relief, or by other measures? (3) Would a judgment rendered in the person's absence be adequate? (4) Would the plaintiff have an adequate remedy if the action is dismissed for non-joinder? The court found that the first and third factors favor Daynard (P), the second factor is not relevant, and the fourth factor favors the South Carolina defendants (D). Even if the Mississippi defendants (D) were regarded as "necessary" parties, the court would allow the action to proceed against the South Carolina defendants (D). Given the significant overlap between the four factors in parts (a) and (b) of Rule 19, the difference between "necessary" and "indispensable" is that an "indispensable" party is also "necessary," whereas a "necessary" party is not always "indispensable." Where a "necessary" party cannot, for whatever reason, be made a party, the case must be dismissed. Note that if the Mississippi defendants had not been granted their motion to dismiss for lack of personal jurisdiction, they would have been able to be made party to the lawsuit and therefore may have been found to be "necessary." The court went on to show that even if that had been the case, they would not have been deemed "indispensable." The court probably dealt with the issue of "indispensable" in order to not have to deal with the issue in future litigation – the grant of the motion to dismiss was on appeal at the time of this decision.

Quicknotes

BREACH OF CONTRACT Unlawful failure by a party to perform its obligations pursuant to contract.

COMPLAINT The initial pleading commencing litigation that sets forth a claim for relief.

EXECUTION The full performance of an agreement's obligations.

INDISPENSABLE PARTY Party whose joining in a lawsuit is essential for the adequate disposition of the action and without whom the action cannot proceed.

JOINDER The joining of claims or parties in one lawsuit.

JOINT AND SEVERAL LIABILITY Liability amongst tortfeasors allowing the injured party to bring suit against any of the defendants, individually or collectively, and to recover from each up to the total amount of damages awarded.

PERSONAL JURISDICTION The court's authority over a person or parties to a lawsuit.

RESCISSION The canceling of an agreement and the return of the parties to their positions prior to the formation of the contract.

SPECIFIC PERFORMANCE An equitable remedy whereby the court requires the parties to perform their obligations pursuant to a contract.

United States v. Northern Indiana Public Service Co. et al.

Federal government (P) v. Landowner (D)

100 F.R.D. 78 (N.D. Ind. 1983)

NATURE OF CASE: Motion to intervene in a condemnation proceeding.

FACT SUMMARY: The Government (P) filed notice of condemnation against Northern Indiana Public Service Company (D). Save the Dunes Council filed a motion to intervene.

RULE OF LAW

A motion to intervene under Federal Rule of Civil Procedure 24(a)(2) must be denied where any of the four conditions of the rule are absent.

FACTS: The Government (P) filed its notice of condemnation affecting almost 40 acres of land owned by Northern Indiana Public Service Co. (NIPSCO) (D) on August 7, 1978. NIPSCO (D) filed objections to the notice on September 25, 1978. A hearing on NIPSCO's (D) objections was scheduled for February 8, 1982. The hearing was removed from the calendar on January 22, 1982. On April 4, 1982, the Save the Dunes Council filed a motion to intervene as a plaintiff under Federal Rule of Civil Procedure 24. NIPSCO (D) filed a motion to strike. On September 7, 1983, the Government (P) and NIPSCO (D) settled the case. Briefs were then filed on the issue of intervention.

ISSUE: Must a motion to intervene under Federal Rule of Civil Procedure 24(a)(2) be denied where any of the four conditions of the rule are absent?

HOLDING AND DECISION: (Sharp, C.J.) Yes. A motion to intervene under Federal Rule of Civil Procedure 24(a)(2) must be denied where any of the four conditions of the rule are absent. Fed. R. Civ. P. 24(a)(2) requires that four conditions be met by the proposed intervenor: (1) timely application, (2) an interest relating to the property or transaction that is the subject of the case, (3) that the disposition of the action may as a practical matter impair or impede his ability to protect that interest, and (4) that the interest is not adequately represented by existing parties. The Save the Dunes Council (the Council) satisfied the first condition by moving to intervene promptly after knowing or having reason to know its interest may be adversely affected by the outcome of the litigation. Northern Indiana Public Service Co. (NIPSCO) (D) argued that the Council should have moved to intervene prior to the time of the original parties' settlement. The case history shows that the first reference to a settlement was on January 12, 1982, and the Council filed its motion to intervene on April 2, 1982. The original parties did not settle and file to dismiss until over a year later. Additionally, from the institution of the action until early 1983, the Council had no reason to believe that intervention would be required, since Congress had expressed intent to preserve the land in question, which would have protected the Council's perceived interest. Thus, the timeliness condition is met. As to the second condition, the Council does not have an interest relating to the property. There is no consensus in case law as to what constitutes a litigable interest for purposes of intervention. However, cases in this circuit emphasize an interest that is legally protectable. NIPSCO (D) is the only party with a legal interest, as it is the sole owner of the property. The Council worked to preserve the development of the national lake shore but is essentially a private citizen with no interest in the property. The Council's motion to intervene is denied.

ANALYSIS

Although the court expressly stated in the opinion the Save the Dunes Council's (the Council's) motion fails on the second condition of Fed. R. Civ. P. 24(a), the language of the last paragraph of the opinion seems to imply that the court could have ruled in the Council's favor, notwithstanding its failure to meet the second condition of the rule. This is perhaps in response to Rule 24's language allowing intervention by discretion of the court.

Quicknotes

CONDEMNATION The taking of private property for public use so long as just compensation is paid therefor.

MOTION TO INTERVENE Method by which a party, not an initial party to the action, is admitted to the action, in order to assert an interest in the subject matter of a lawsuit.

Discovery

Quick Reference Rules of Law

Oxbow Carbon & Minerals LLC v. Union Pacific R.R. Co.

Coal and petroleum coke company (P) v. Railroad company (D)

322 F.R.D. 1 (D.D.C. 2017)

NATURE OF CASE: Motion to compel disclosure of discovery in private antitrust action brought under the Sherman Antitrust Act.

FACT SUMMARY: In a private antitrust action brought under the Sherman Antitrust Act by Oxbow Carbon & Minerals LLC and related companies (collectively, Oxbow) (P) against Union Pacific R.R. Co. (D) and BNSF Railway Co. (D), (collectively, the railroad companies (D)), the railroad companies (D) moved to compel Koch, Oxbow's (P) founder, owner, and CEO, to be added as a document custodian so his records could be searched for materials responsive to their discovery requests. Oxbow (P) opposed the motion to compel, asserting that the discovery sought was unduly burdensome and that many of Koch's documents would likely be duplicative of the other custodians' documents or only marginally responsive. The railroad companies (D) countered that Koch's records contained information that would, inter alia, show that market forces, as opposed to the railroad companies (D) alleged collusion, contributed to Oxbow's (P) increased freight costs and lost profits.

RULE OF LAW

(1) A motion to compel production of discovery may be granted where the requested discovery is undisputedly relevant and all the proportionality factors under Fed. R. Civ. P. 26(b)(1) weigh in favor of the motion.

(2) For purposes of discovery fee shifting, a producing party does not rebut the presumption under the Federal Rules of Civil Procedure that a producing party bears the costs of complying with a discovery request where the producing party fails to show that the payment of such costs will be unduly burdensome or expensive to it.

FACTS: Oxbow Carbon & Minerals LLC and related companies (collectively, Oxbow) (P), which mined and sold coal and petroleum coke (petcoke), brought suit under the Sherman Antitrust Act against Union Pacific R.R. Co. (UP) (D) and BNSF Railway Co. (BNSF) (D) (collectively, the railroad companies (D)), alleging that the railroad companies (D) had conspired and fixed coal and petcoke shipping prices, which resulted in Oxbow (P) overpaying fuel surcharges by over $50 million. Oxbow (P) sought treble damages as well as damages for lost profits that resulted from the alleged conspiracy. The railroad companies (D) moved for adding Koch—Oxbow's (P) founder, owner, and CEO—as a document custodian so his records could be searched pursuant to their discovery requests. The parties attempted to resolve the dispute between themselves, with Oxbow (P) conducting a search of a sample of Koch's documents using agreed-upon key search terms. Oxbow (P) determined that responsive documents constituted around 11.67 percent of all those sampled. The cost of conducting the search was around $57,000. Based on this, Oxbow (P) estimated that it would cost an additional $85,000 to process, review, and produce the remainder of Koch's documents. However, the sampling effort did not resolve the dispute without further court intervention, as Oxbow (P) believed that a complete production of Koch's documents would be an unnecessary burden and expense, particularly in light of the documents' low responsiveness rate to the search terms. The railroad companies (D), in turn, viewed the results of the sampling as proof of the existence of relevant and unique documents in Koch's records. Accordingly, the court considered the motion to compel. Oxbow (P) asked the court, in the event it granted the motion, to require the railroad companies (D) to bear the costs of production, in whole or in part.

ISSUE:

(1) May a motion to compel production of discovery be granted where the requested discovery is undisputedly relevant and all the proportionality factors under Fed. R. Civ. P. 26(b)(1) weigh in favor of the motion?

(2) For purposes of discovery fee shifting, does a producing party rebut the presumption under the Federal Rules of Civil Procedure that a producing party bears the costs of complying with a discovery request where the producing party fails to show that the payment of such costs will be unduly burdensome or expensive to it?

HOLDING AND DECISION: (Harvey, Mag. J.)

(1) Yes. A motion to compel production of discovery may be granted where the requested discovery is undisputedly relevant and all the proportionality factors under Fed. R. Civ. P. 26(b)(1) weigh in favor of the motion. Under Fed. R. Civ. P. 26, discovery must be relevant and proportional to the needs of the case. To determine whether a discovery request is proportional, courts weigh the following six factors: (1) the importance of the issues at stake in this action; (2) the amount in controversy; (3) the parties' relative access to relevant information; (4) the

Continued on next page.

parties' resources; (5) the importance of the discovery in resolving the issues; and (6) whether the burden or expense of the proposed discovery outweighs its likely benefit. No single factor outweighs the other factors in determining whether the discovery sought is proportional, and all proportionality determinations must be made on a case-by-case basis. Moreover, the objecting party bears the burden of showing that the requested discovery would impose an undue burden or would be otherwise objectionable. Here, it is undisputed that the requested discovery is relevant. Oxbow Carbon & Minerals LLC and related companies (collectively, Oxbow) (P) object to the request to review and produce discovery from Koch's remaining documents on the grounds that doing so would be unduly burdensome and because the benefit to Union Pacific R.R. Co. (D) and BNSF Railway Co. (D) (collectively, the railroad companies (D)) would not justify that effort and expense. However, Oxbow (P) has failed to address any of the other proportionality factors. Weighing these factors, however, demonstrates that the discovery request, in light of the facts of the case, will be neither unduly burdensome nor unreasonably expensive. The first factor, the importance of the issues at stake, as measured in philosophic, social, or institutional terms, favors a finding of proportionality, since the case has the potential to broadly impact a wide range of third parties not involved in the litigation, including, as Oxbow (P) has stated, all of America's shippers and consumers, saving billions of dollars a year in reduced rail freight charges in the United States. Under the second proportionality factor, courts compare the cost of discovery to the amount in controversy to determine the proposed discovery's proportionality. Here, Oxbow (P) is seeking to recover over $150 million, whereas the estimated cost of complying with the discovery request in total is $140,000. Given the ratio of the amount of recovery sought to the cost of discovery compliance, such cost is not excessive, and this factor, therefore, also weighs in favor of granting the motion to compel. Similarly, the third factor also weighs in favor of granting the motion. Under this factor, courts look for "information asymmetry" in determining the parties' relative access to the relevant information. Such asymmetry arises where one party has very little discoverable information whereas the other party has vast amounts of it. In such circumstances, the burden of production is heavier on the party that has more information. The fourth factor, the parties' resources, also weighs in favor of granting the motion to compel since Oxbow (P) has ability to pay for complying with the requested discovery. So, too, does the fifth factor—the importance of the discovery in resolving the issues. This requires an assessment of whether the issues at stake are at the very heart of the litigation. Although it may be too early in the production process to determine exactly how significant Koch's records are, it strains reason to suggest that the principal owner and CEO of a company, who has publicly commented on the importance and magnitude of litigation to which his company is a party and in which the financial health of his company is at issue, would have no unique information relevant to that litigation in his possession. The discovery request thus has merit and relates to the issues in litigation. The sixth and final factor is the only one that Oxbow (P) raised, claiming that its compliance with the discovery request will be prohibitively burdensome. This contention does not carry much weight in the face of the damages sought and the costs already incurred. Although the cost of compliance is high, it is not unreasonable or disproportionate. The projected number of responsive and unique documents in Koch's files is largely consistent with the number of responsive and unique documents produced by the other Oxbow (P) custodians, and the responsiveness rate of Koch's documents—11.67%—while low, is not the lowest among Oxbow's (P) custodians. For these reasons, the railroad companies' (D) request should not be denied, and it is therefore granted. Judgment for the railroad companies (D) as to this issue.

(2) No. For purposes of discovery fee shifting, a producing party does not rebut the presumption under the Federal Rules of Civil Procedure that a producing party bears the costs of complying with a discovery request where the producing party fails to show that the payment of such costs will be unduly burdensome or expensive to it. Although the presumption under the Federal Rules of Civil Procedure is that a producing party bears the costs of complying with a discovery request, a court may shift some of all of those costs in the event the court finds that the discovery request will unduly burden the producing party. However, it is clear such cost-shifting should not become a common practice. In making this determination, courts have applied the same factors they use to determine proportionality under Rule 26(b). The court's analysis of these factors in determining whether to deny the motion to compel confirms that the railroad companies' (D) proposed discovery request will not impose an undue burden or expense on Oxbow (P) that would warrant a reallocation of expenses. Therefore, Oxbow's (P) request for shifting costs is denied. Judgment for the railroad companies (D) as to this issue. Motion granted.

Continued on next page.

ANALYSIS

Rule 26 of the Federal Rules of Civil Procedure was amended in 2015 to read: "Unless otherwise limited by court order, the scope of discovery is as follows: Parties may obtain discovery regarding any nonprivileged matter that is relevant to any party's claim or defense and proportional to the needs of the case, considering the importance of the issues at stake in the action, the amount in controversy, the parties' relative access to relevant information, the parties' resources, the importance of the discovery in resolving the issues, and whether the burden or expense of the proposed discovery outweighs its likely benefit. Information within this scope of discovery need not be admissible in evidence to be discoverable." Fed. R. Civ. P. 26(b)(1). As this case illustrates, this amendment has brought to the forefront of Rule 26 the concept of proportionality—that is, the duty of the parties and the court to make a case-specific determination of the appropriate scope of discovery, considering the various factors set forth in the Rule. This concept was previously contained (some would say buried) in subsection (b)(2)(C)(iii), but it now enjoys a more prominent place in the amended Rule. Thus, Rule 26(b)(1), as amended, although not fundamentally different in scope from the previous version, constitutes a reemphasis on the importance of proportionality in discovery.

Quicknotes

DISCOVERY Pretrial procedure during which one party makes certain information available to the other.

REBUT A defendant's refuting of evidence that raises a presumption as to his liability.

UNDUE BURDEN A burden which is unlawfully oppressive or troublesome.

Alley v. MTD Products, Inc.

Snowblower user (P) v. Snowblower manufacturer (D)

2018 WL 4689112 (E.D. Pa. Sept. 28, 2018)

NATURE OF CASE: Motion for discovery and deposition protective order in products liability action.

FACT SUMMARY: In a products liability action brought by Alley (P) against MTD Products, Inc. (MTD) (D), a snowblower manufacturer, MTD (D) moved for a protective order against Alley's (P) deposition notice insofar as it sought information relating to MTD's (D) methodologies relating to electronically stored information, as well as against his request for documents from prior cases involving the MTD (D) snowblower used by Alley (P).

RULE OF LAW

(1) A court may grant a protective order against a deposition notice that seeks "discovery on discovery" by seeking information about the moving party's discovery process where the opposing party has not shown that the moving party has acted in bad faith or unlawfully withheld documents.

(2) A court may grant a protective order against a discovery request that is not proportional to the needs of the case.

FACTS: Alley (P) was injured when he was inflating the tire of a snowblower manufactured by MTD Products, Inc. (MTD) (D). He brought a products liability action in federal district court against MTD (D). In his Rule 30(b)(6) deposition notice, Alley (P) sought information relating to MTD's (D) methods for storing, creating, retrieving, and retaining electronically stored information that he sought in discovery. In his request for production of documents, Alley (P) sought all documents related to all prior litigation involving the snowblower model he had used, including all expert reports, deposition transcripts, and discovery responses. MTD (D) moved for a protective order, contending that Alley (P) was seeking improper "discovery on discovery" in his deposition notice, and that his discovery request for documents from prior litigation was not proportional. The district court considered the motion for a protective order.

ISSUE:

(1) May a court grant a protective order against a deposition notice that seeks "discovery on discovery" by seeking information about the moving party's discovery process where the opposing party has not shown that the moving party has acted in bad faith or unlawfully withheld documents?

(2) May a court grant a protective order against a discovery request that is not proportional to the needs of the case?

HOLDING AND DECISION: (Gibson, J.)

(1) Yes. A court may grant a protective order against a deposition notice that seeks "discovery on discovery" by seeking information about the moving party's discovery process where the opposing party has not shown that the moving party has acted in bad faith or unlawfully withheld documents. Courts will not compel a party to disclose its discovery process as a result of the opponent's mere suspicion that the party's process has not produced adequate documents, and a party cannot seek discovery of another party's discovery processes without any showing of bad faith or unlawful withholding of documents. Although Alley (P) argues that the requested information relates not only to MTD Products, Inc.'s (MTD's) (D) discovery processes (discovery on discovery) but also to MTD's (D) assertion of undue burden, the request is nevertheless an impermissible request for discovery on discovery. Accordingly, the protective order is granted with respect to that portion of Alley's (P) notice of deposition that requests discovery on discovery. Judgment for MTD (D) as to this issue.

(2) Yes. A court may grant a protective order against a discovery request that is not proportional to the needs of the case. Under Rule 26(b), parties may obtain discovery regarding any nonprivileged matter that is relevant to any party's claim or defense and proportional to the needs of the case considering (1) the importance of the issues at stake in the action, (2) the amount in controversy, (3) the parties' relative access to relevant information, (4) the parties' resources, (5) the importance of the discovery in resolving the issues, and (6) whether the burden or expense of the proposed discovery outweighs its likely benefit. As to the first factor, the issues in this action are important since the case involves an individual who sustained bodily injury due to an allegedly defective snowblower. Alley's (P) alleged injuries are serious, and companies producing defective products must be held responsible for injuries caused by their products. However, when considering the other factors in Rule

Continued on next page.

26(b), the importance of the issues at stake in this case alone does not justify the extensive production of discovery materials from prior litigation. Regarding the second factor, Alley's (P) requests for production of documents from prior litigation are not proportional to the amount in controversy in the case. The total amount in controversy is about $100,000, and Alley (P) incurred about $6,000 in medical bills. The total amount in controversy is roughly equivalent to the cost for MTD (D) to comply with Alley's (P) discovery requests based on the costs of locating and storing the responsive documents, reviewing these documents for privileged information and HIPPA compliance, and complying with protective orders from the prior lawsuits. Although Alley (P) disputes how much it would cost MTD (D) to comply with Alley's (P) discovery requests, a comparison of the amount in controversy to the cost of complying with Alley's (P) discovery requests weighs against production, and weighs in favor of granting MTD's (D) protective order. Even if MTD (D) overstated the cost of complying with Alley's (P) discovery request by several thousand dollars, the cost of producing these documents would still be disproportionately close to the amount in controversy. Therefore, Alley's (P) request for production of documents from prior cases is not proportional to the amount in controversy in this case. As to the third factor, although MTD (D) has greater access to the discovery documents that Alley (P) seeks, MTD (D) already produced considerable information on prior cases involving the snowblower model that allegedly injured Alley (P). MTD (D) produced the names of the plaintiffs in prior cases, the courts where those cases were filed, and the names of the plaintiffs' attorneys in those cases. Thus, although Alley's (P) counsel has sufficient information to seek out discovery materials from those prior cases on his own, he admitted that he had not investigated state court dockets to determine if he could obtain the sought-after documents through online document-filing systems. Respecting the fourth factor, MTD (D) likely has more resources than Alley (P). However, this factor is less important to the proportionality analysis here because, as noted in the discussion of the fifth factor, the discovery documents from prior litigation involving MTD's (D) snowblowers are not crucial to the resolution of this case. As to the fifth factor, Alley (P) argues that the requested documents are necessary to prove that he is entitled to punitive damages, which requires a showing that MTD (D) was aware of the risks of its defective product and consciously disregarded such risks. However, Alley (P) does not need discovery documents like expert reports, deposition transcripts, and responsive documents from prior cases to prove that MTD (D) was aware of defects in the snowblowers it produced. MTD (D) already provided Alley (P) with information on prior lawsuits involving the tire rims of the snowblower model that injured him, thereby admitting that MTD (D) was on notice of problems with the tire rims. MTD's (D) counsel stated that these prior lawsuits generally involved some version of putting air in the tire rims that then exploded, resulting in eye or face or hand injuries. Moreover, MTD (D) also provided Alley (P) with information on product recalls for the snowblower model that injured him, further acknowledging their knowledge of the defect. Thus, there is ample evidence that MTD (D) was on notice of the defective nature of the snowblower tires. Accordingly, discovery documents from prior litigation are not necessary for Alley (P) to pursue punitive damages or to resolve any other issues in this case. Finally, as to the sixth factor, the burden and expense of MTD's (D) production of these documents clearly outweighs the likely benefit. The estimated cost to MTD (D) of producing discovery documents from prior litigation is overly burdensome and unduly expensive, especially in light of the amount in controversy. Similarly, MTD's (D) production of discovery documents from prior litigation will not be beneficial to resolving the key issues in this case. Accordingly, MTD (D) has demonstrated that a protective order is necessary to protect it from unduly burdensome production of documents. Therefore, the protective order is granted with respect to Alley's (P) request for past litigation documents. Judgment for MTD (D) as to this issue. Motion granted.

ANALYSIS

As the court in this case noted, the sometimes-gargantuan repositories of electronically stored information (ESI) created by companies can give rise to complex mechanisms to store and retrieve huge amounts of information. Although such complexity alone cannot be used in and of itself as a shield to avoid discovery requests otherwise permitted under the Federal Rules of Civil Procedure, the court concluded that even if the cost of complying with the discovery requests in question were significantly lower than MTD (D) estimated, the burden in this case of accessing and retrieving relevant information from MTD's (D) ESI was still not proportional to the needs of the case.

Quicknotes

DEPOSITION A pretrial discovery procedure whereby oral or written questions are asked by one party of the opposing party or of a witness for the opposing party under oath in preparation for litigation.

DISCOVERY Pretrial procedure during which one party makes certain information available to the other.

Freedom's Path at Dayton v. Dayton Metro. Hous. Auth.

Developer of affordable housing for veterans (P) v. Public housing authority (D)

2018 WL 2948021 (S.D. Ohio, June 13, 2018)

NATURE OF CASE: Plaintiff's motion to compel, and defendant's motion for protective orders, in action for violation of the Americans with Disabilities Act of 1990, 42 U.S.C. § 12101, and the Fair Housing Act of 1968, 42 U.S.C. § 3601.

FACT SUMMARY: Freedom's Path at Dayton (Freedom's Path) (P), a developer of affordable housing for veterans, brought suit against Dayton Metropolitan Housing Authority (DMHA) (D) d/b/a Greater Dayton Premier Management (D), a public housing authority, under the Americans with Disabilities Act of 1990 (ADA), 42 U.S.C. § 12101, and the Fair Housing Act of 1968 (FHA), 42 U.S.C. § 3601, alleging that DMHA (D) impermissibly and discriminatorily blocked funding for and financing of 60 units of project-based funded affordable housing for veterans, most of whom were disabled. Freedom's Path (P) sought to depose a former DMHA (D) official as well as several other third-party witnesses. DMHA (D) moved for protective orders barring the depositions on the grounds of relevance and proportionality. In turn, Freedom's Path (P) moved to compel discovery and requested attorney's fees, seeking to compel the deposition testimony of DMHA's (D) CEO, Heapy, and to admonish defense counsel, Freudiger, to refrain from speaking and coaching objections, instructing witnesses not to answer questions, and making baseless objections.

RULE OF LAW

(1) A protective order barring discovery will not be granted where the information sought is relevant to the issues in the case and the discovery is proportional to the needs of the case.

(2) A motion to compel seeking to admonish an opposing party's attorney to refrain from speaking and coaching objections, instructing witnesses not to answer questions, and making baseless objections will be granted where the movant has shown that opposing counsel has engaged in such conduct.

(3) A corporation does not, as a matter of law, fail to comply with its Fed. R. Civ. P. 30(b)(6) obligation to prepare its deponent designee if that designee cannot answer every deposition question about a particular topic that has been designated as relevant and the proper subject of discovery.

(4) Under Fed. R. Civ. P. 30(d)(2), sanctions such as attorney's fees are not warranted where counsel's conduct has been improper at times, but such conduct has not ultimately prevented the deposing party from conducting a fair examination of deponents.

FACTS: Freedom's Path at Dayton (Freedom's Path) (P), a developer of affordable housing for veterans, sought to use Veterans Affairs Supportive Housing (VASH) project-based rental assistance to house veterans, most of whom were disabled, in a development in Dayton, Ohio. To reach this goal, Freedom's Path (P) needed the support of a public housing authority, because only such authorities may apply for a VASH allocation. In 2013, Dayton Metropolitan Housing Authority (DMHA) (D) d/b/a Greater Dayton Premier Management (GDPM) (D), a public housing authority, by a letter written by its interim CEO, Prude, extended support for 33 project-based vouchers, which Freedom's Path (P) understood as GDPM's (D) initial commitment to support Freedom's Path's (P) efforts to obtain VASH financing. However, after this initial commitment, GDPM (D) balked at providing continued support to Freedom's Path (P). In 2015, Freedom's Path (P) asked GDPM (D) to apply for project-specific, project-based VASH vouchers on Freedom's Path's (P) behalf, but GDPM (D) declined to do so and, instead, proposed applying for VASH Project-Based Rental Assistance on behalf of itself. Freedom's Path (P) alleged that GDPM (D) provided various inconsistent, mistaken, or shifting rationales for its indecision. In 2016, Freedom's Path (P), through its counsel, asked DMHA (D) for a reasonable accommodation to honor its request for support, but DMHA (D) denied the requested accommodation. Freedom's Path (P) brought suit in federal district court against DMHA (D), asserting that DMHA's (D) conduct violated the Americans with Disabilities Act of 1990 (ADA), 42 U.S.C. § 12101, and the Fair Housing Act of 1968 (FHA), 42 U.S.C. § 3601, because such conduct discriminated against disabled veterans. Freedom's Path (P) sought declaratory and injunctive relief as well as damages. As part of discovery, Freedom's Path (P) sought to depose several third-party witnesses, including Prude, the former interim CEO, Smith (a manager at the U.S. Dept. of Veterans Affairs (VA)), Smelkinson (a specialist at the U. S. Department of Housing and Urban Development (HUD)), and Keyser (General Counsel for HUD). DMHA (D) moved for protective orders barring the depositions on the grounds of

Continued on next page.

relevance and proportionality. In turn, Freedom's Path (P) moved to compel discovery and requested attorney's fees, seeking to compel the deposition testimony of DMHA's (D) current CEO, Heapy (an attorney), and to admonish defense counsel, Freudiger, to refrain from speaking and coaching objections, instructing witnesses not to answer questions, and making baseless objections. The federal district court considered the parties' respective motions.

ISSUE:

(1) Will a protective order barring discovery be granted where the information sought is relevant to the issues in the case and the discovery is proportional to the needs of the case?
(2) Will a motion to compel seeking to admonish an opposing party's attorney to refrain from speaking and coaching objections, instructing witnesses not to answer questions, and making baseless objections be granted where the movant has shown that opposing counsel has engaged in such conduct?
(3) Does a corporation, as a matter of law, fail to comply with its Fed. R. Civ. P. 30(b)(6) obligation to prepare its deponent designee if that designee cannot answer every deposition question about a particular topic that has been designated as relevant and the proper subject of discovery?
(4) Under Fed. R. Civ. P. 30(d)(2), are sanctions such as attorney's fees warranted where counsel's conduct has been improper at times but where such conduct has not ultimately prevented the deposing party from conducting a fair examination of deponents?

HOLDING AND DECISION: (Ovington, Mag. J.)

(1) No. A protective order barring discovery will not be granted where the information sought is relevant to the issues in the case and the discovery is proportional to the needs of the case. Under Fed. R. Civ. P. Rule 26(c), a "court may, for good cause, issue an order to protect a party or person from annoyance, embarrassment, oppression, or undue burden or expense. . . ." The party objecting to the discovery has the burden of showing that the requested discovery does not fall with Fed. R. Civ. P. 26(b)(1)'s scope of relevance or that a discovery request would impose an undue burden or expense or is otherwise objectionable. Here, the Dayton Metropolitan Housing Authority (DMHA) (D) asserted that the deposition of Prude, its former interim CEO who wrote the letter committing to assist Freedom's Path at Dayton (Freedom's Path) (P), was largely irrelevant since his involvement was limited to writing the letter in 2013. DMHA (D) also claimed that it was barred by law from satisfying Freedom's Path's (P) accommodation request based on the letter. In this regard, DMHA (D) asserted that under 24 C.F.R. § 983.51(b), there are two methods by which a public housing authority (PHA) can select project-based voucher (PBV) proposals: (1) request PBV proposals or (2) rely on previous competition. A PHA must have an administrative plan that describes the procedures for owner submission of PBV proposals and for PHA selection of PBV proposals. DMHA (D) argued that because its administrative plan at the time indicated that it could only select PBV proposals using the first method, and because the attempt to utilize Prude's letter to obtain vouchers for Freedom's Path's (P) housing project involved the issuance of vouchers through the second method in violation of the U.S. Department of Housing and Urban Development (HUD) regulations, the letter was completely irrelevant to the claim that DMHA (D) improperly refused to satisfy Freedom's Path's (P) accommodation request. Freedom's Path (P) countered that this was merely one of DMHA's (D) "various inconsistent, mistaken, or shifting rationales for its inactions" and argued that because DMHA's (D) administrative plan requires compliance with all HUD regulations and because HUD regulations permitted two methods of selection of PBV proposals, DMHA (D) could rely on the second method for selecting PBV proposals. Freedom's Path (P) further contended that because its previous competitive processes satisfied this second method, awarding it housing vouchers through Prude's letter would not violate HUD regulations. Moreover, if DMHA (D) could not—under its administrative plan at that time—select Freedom's Path's (P) PVB proposal, DMHA (D) could amend its administrative plan. In fact, DMHA (D) did so in 2016, with HUD approval. Because DMHA's (D) commitment to support Freedom's Path (P) is central to the case and because Prude was DMHA's (D) interim CEO at the time of this commitment, it is likely that Prude has relevant—and thus discoverable—information about Freedom's Path's (P) claims. Next, DMHA (D) contends the deposition of Smith is also largely irrelevant. Smith had corresponded with DMHA (D) and Freedom's Path's (P) representatives regarding the status of DMHA's response to Plaintiff's accommodation request. DMHA (D) argues that any testimony provided by Smith regarding her conversations and interactions with DMHA (D) would constitute inadmissible hearsay so could not be used to support Freedom's Path's (P) causes of action. Given that Freedom's Path's (P) central claim is that DMHA (D) improperly refused to satisfy its accommodation request, the deposition of Smith, who was involved with the accommodation request, seeks information relevant to that claim. Additionally,

Continued on next page.

DMHA's (D)'s argument that Smith's testimony is not relevant because it would constitute inadmissible hearsay lacks merit for discovery purposes, since under Fed. R. Civ. P. 26(b)(1) information that is within the scope of discovery need not be admissible in evidence to be discoverable.

Turning to the depositions of Smelkinson and Keyser, DMHA (D) asserts that those individuals lacked any personal knowledge regarding any facts underlying Freedom's Path's (P) suit. However, that assertion is contradicted by Freedom's Path (P), which alleges that Smelkinson reportedly told Smith that, contrary to DMHA's (D) assertion, Freedom's Path (P) was eligible to partner with DMHA (D). As to Keyser, HUD's general counsel, Heapy, stated that Keyser agreed with the opinion of Black, a HUD official who said that Heapy could not honor the voucher commitment made to Freedom's Path (P), whereas Freedom's Path's (P) attorney, Cabrera, indicated that Keyser had told Cabrera that there were a number of ways DMHA (D) could partner with Freedom's Paths (P), including amending its Administrative Plan. In other words, Smelkinson and Keyser were allegedly involved in the facts giving rise to the present lawsuit and, along with Smith, possess information regarding whether DMHA (D) could lawfully honor its initial voucher commitment and/or whether DMHA (D) could lawfully grant the request for reasonable accommodation. Therefore, their depositions search for relevant and discoverable information about Freedom's Path's (P) claims. Additionally, because Freedom's Path (P) alleges that the sequence of events reflect an intent to discriminate, the factual background—including Prude's initial commitment letter, the parties' respective consultations with HUD employees, and HUD employee's discussions with VA employees—might or might not shed light on the merits of Freedom's Path's (P) claims. Consequently, the information sought by deposing Prude, Smith, Smelkinson, and Keyser is discoverable as relevant.

However, that determination does not by itself resolve whether the protective orders should be granted, since discovery must be proportional to the needs of the case, considering the importance of the issues at stake in the action, the amount in controversy, the parties' relative access to relevant information, the parties' resources, the importance of the discovery in resolving the issues, and whether the burden or expense of the proposed discovery outweighs its likely benefit. Here, the issues at stake are important, as they involve housing for homeless veterans, many of whom are disabled, and implicate important national policies about eradicating homelessness, especially for veterans, and providing permanent housing for them as proposed by Freedom's Path (P). This factor weighs in favor of Freedom's Path (P). According to Freedom's Path (P), the amount in controversy is over $15 million in lost housing and services, an amount DMHA (D) does not controvert. Thus, this second factor also weighs in Freedom's Path's (P) favor. As to the third factor, which also weighs in favor of Freedom's Path (P), it is likely that DMHA (D) has, or has access to, most or all the information sought. The fourth factor is a draw, favoring neither party: DMHA (D) asserts that it is publicly funded and has limited resources, whereas Freedom's Path (P) contends that the parties' resources are the same since DMHA (D) is being defended by an insurance defense firm, has millions of dollars in potential coverage, and has an annual budget of $45 million. Without more information, this factor is neutral. As to the fifth factor, DMHA (D) argues that none of the depositions are necessary or important to resolving the key issue of whether it improperly declined to satisfy the accommodation request. Freedom's Path (P) disagrees and argues that all the witnesses have important information that is directly relevant to whether DMHA (D) used shifting rationales for denying Freedom's Path's (P) request for housing vouchers. As discussed in greater detail regarding the parties' relevancy arguments, it is clear the deponents do have such information. As to the sixth and final proportionality factor, DMHA (D) argues that permitting the four depositions would subject it to severe undue burden and expense in the form of transportation and overnight lodging costs, as well as substantial additional litigation expenses of preparing for and attending the depositions, without yielding much if any benefit to either party. On the other hand, Freedom's Path (P) points out that there are non-stop flights to and from the deponents' disparate locations, and that it scheduled two depositions on the same day in the same city, so that if DMHA (D) had agreed to that schedule, it would not have incurred significant additional expenses. DMHA (D) bears the burden of establishing good cause for a protective order. To show good cause, a movant for a protective order must articulate specific facts showing clearly defined and serious injury resulting from the discovery sought and cannot rely on mere conclusory statements. DMHA's (D) broad allegations of "significant travel expenses" and "substantial additional litigation expenses" are insufficient to show it will suffer undue burden or expense and do not establish good cause for a protective order. In sum, the balancing of these factors weighs in favor of allowing the depositions of Prude, Smith, Smelkinson, and Keyser. Additionally,

Continued on next page.

Freedom's Path (P) has shown that it seeks information from their depositions that is relevant to its claims and proportional to the needs of the case. Accordingly, DMHA's (D) motion for protective orders is denied. Judgment for Freedom's Path (P) as to this issue.

(2) Yes. A motion to compel seeking to admonish an opposing party's attorney to refrain from speaking and coaching objections, instructing witnesses not to answer questions, and making baseless objections will be granted where the movant has shown that opposing counsel has engaged in such conduct. Under Rule 30, an objection at the time of the examination—whether to evidence, to a party's conduct, to the officer's qualifications, to the manner of taking the deposition, or to any other aspect of the deposition—must be noted on the record, but the examination still proceeds; the testimony is taken subject to any objection. An objection must be stated concisely in a nonargumentative and nonsuggestive manner. A person may instruct a deponent not to answer only when necessary to preserve a privilege, to enforce a limitation ordered by the court, or to present a motion under Fed. R. Civ. P. 30(d)(3). Freedom's Path (P) points to at least 17 instances where Freudiger made speaking objections that suggested to his client how to answer questions and more than 20 instances where he instructed Heapy not to answer, even though no claim of privilege had been raised or was implicated. DMHA (D) contends that many of Freudiger's comments were made to remind witnesses that deponents should not guess or speculate as to matters as to which they have no personal knowledge, and that this practice is common in both state and federal courts. Although it is true that deponents should testify about their personal knowledge, even assuming the practice of reminding deponents of this is widespread, there is no valid reason for Freudiger to have repeatedly interrupted the deposition questioning of any individual and certainly not of Heapy, herself an attorney of many years. Instead, Freudiger should cease this practice. It is the attorney's job to make an objection and then stop talking. If the deponent does not know how to answer a question, the deponent may state as much, but it is not appropriate for the deponent's attorney to push the deponent in that direction. Freudiger also made multiple objections where he also suggested a response. Such comments are improper under Fed. R. Civ. P. 30(c)(2) because in so doing the attorney is interjecting a position into the course of the opposing party's deposition inquiry. Although an attorney may attempt to clarify the attorney's client's testimony, such an attempt must await the completion of the inquiry. Additionally, Freudiger incorrectly stated that under the Federal Rules of Civil Procedure he had the right to instruct his witness whether to answer or not. To the contrary, an attorney does not have the right to tell his witness that she can answer a question. Indeed, all he can do is state a concise, nonargumentative, and nonsuggestive objection on the record and instruct his witness not to answer in the limited circumstances laid out in Fed. R. Civ. P. 30(c)(2). This Rule has been said to allow non-examining counsel at a deposition to do one of two things: (1) listen and (2) make objections. Freedom's Path (P) also asserts that Freudiger improperly instructed Heapy not to respond to questions about Prude's application for unemployment benefits, which the court previously had ruled was relevant evidence and as to which the court had ordered production. Given that DMHA (D) neither produced that evidence nor certified that it could not be located, DMHA (D) failed to follow the court's instruction and is now ordered to produce the evidence. Freedom's Path (P) also faults Freudiger for instructing Heapy, on the grounds of "pending litigation," not to answer questions about why Heapy's predecessor CEOs (Wright and Rieck) left DMHA (D). Although DMHA (D) does not suggest that "pending litigation" is a valid ground for instructing a deponent not to answer, it insists that the questions were "wholly improper" because Wright's and Rieck's prior employment were "wholly irrelevant." This argument misses the mark: Fed. R. Civ. P. 30(c)(2) requires a deponent to continue her testimony over objection unless she has asserted a privilege, is enforcing a limitation ordered by the court, or presents a motion under Fed. R. Civ. P. 30(d)(3). Objecting on basis of relevance does not constitute one of these exceptions. Accordingly, Freedom's Path (P) is permitted to send written deposition questions to Heapy to which she must respond within two weeks after she receives them. Next, Freedom's Path (P) asserts that Freudiger improperly objected to questions concerning DMHA's (D) Administrative Plan and HUD regulations. On several occasions, Freudiger objected and instructed Heapy not to respond on the grounds that the question called for a legal conclusion or for her to interpret law. In some instances, he answered questions himself. Fed. R. Civ. P. 30 is clear about this: "An objection . . . must be noted on the record, but the examination still proceeds; the testimony is taken subject to any objection. . . . A person may instruct a deponent not to answer only when necessary to preserve a privilege, to enforce a limitation ordered by the court, or to present a motion under Rule 30(d)(3)." There is no indication

Continued on next page.

here that any of the exceptions apply. Accordingly, it was improper for Freudiger to instruct Heapy not to answer questions on the grounds that it called for a legal conclusion.

(3) No. A corporation does not, as a matter of law, fail to comply with its Fed. R. Civ. P. 30(b)(6) obligation to prepare its deponent designee if that designee cannot answer every deposition question about a particular topic that has been designated as relevant and the proper subject of discovery. Under Fed. R. Civ. P. 30(b)(6), "a party may name as the deponent a . . . corporation . . . and must describe with reasonable particularity the matters for examination. The named organization must then designate one or more . . . persons who consent to testify on its behalf. . . . The persons designated must testify about information known or reasonably available to the organization." A Fed. R. Civ. P. 30(b)(6) deponent testifies as to the knowledge of the corporation and to the corporation's subjective beliefs and opinions and interpretation of documents and events. The corporation has a duty to prepare the witness to answer all questions about the designated topics fully and without evasion. Here, Freedom's Path (P) contends that Heapy failed to adequately prepare as the Fed. R. Civ. P. 30(b)(6) designee regarding the circumstances of Prude's termination, which the court held was a relevant discovery topic, by failing to look for records concerning the reasons for Prude's termination, by failing to conduct a written review of documentation as to the reasons for the termination, and by speaking with only one member of her board. Heapy testified that, in preparation for her deposition, she spoke to one board member about Prude's termination and reviewed Prude's personnel file, which did not contain a record of the reasons for his termination. She did not, however, review Prude's "benefits file" because she does not consider it to be part of a personnel matter. She was able to answer many, but not all, questions related to this topic and was able to explain why her knowledge about certain questions was limited. Although Heapy could not answer every question concerning personnel or disciplinary reasons for Prude's termination, the inability of a designee to answer every question on a particular topic does not necessarily mean that the corporation has failed to comply with its obligations under the Rule. Here, it seems that Heapy did adequately prepare for her deposition and was able to provide the reasons for Mr. Prude's termination. Further, DMHA (D) provided a sworn affidavit from a board member indicating that the board discussed Prude's employment issues during an executive session where no meeting minutes were generated. Ideally, Heapy would have known those details during her deposition, but a 30(b)(6) witness is not expected to perform with absolute perfection. Judgment for DMHA (D) as to this issue.

(4) No. Under Fed. R. Civ. P. 30(d)(2), sanctions such as attorney's fees are not warranted where counsel's conduct has been improper at times, but such conduct has not ultimately prevented the deposing party from conducting a fair examination of deponents. A court has the discretion to impose an appropriate sanction on a person who impedes, delays, or frustrates the fair examination of a deponent. Here, Freedom's Path (P) seeks attorney's fees, at a rate of $500 per hour, for the time spent preparing the motion to compel. Although Freudiger's conduct during the deposition of Heapy was improper at times, the imposition of sanctions is presently unwarranted because Freedom's Path (P) was not ultimately prevented from conducting a "fair examination of the deponent." Judgment for DMHA (D) as to this issue. DMHA's (D) motion for protective orders is denied, and Freedom's Path's (P) motion to compel discovery and request for attorney's fees and expenses is granted in part and denied in part.

ANALYSIS

Under the Federal Rules of Civil Procedure, the scope of discovery is traditionally quite broad, but as this case illustrates, the desire to allow broad discovery is not without limits and a trial court is given wide discretion in balancing the needs and rights of both plaintiffs and defendants. For example, a party objecting to or desiring to restrict discovery on the grounds of harassment or oppression must show that the harassment or oppression are unreasonable, but discovery has limits and these limits grow more formidable as the showing of need decreases. In any event, the need for judicial intervention should be limited. In contentious cases, counsel for both parties should strive to be cooperative, practical, and sensible, and they should turn to the court only in extraordinary situations that implicate truly significant interests. The discovery provisions of the Federal Rules of Civil Procedure are meant to function without the need for constant judicial intervention, and thus they rely on the honesty and good faith of counsel in dealing with adversaries.

Quicknotes

DEPOSITION A pretrial discovery procedure whereby oral or written questions are asked by one party of the opposing party or of a witness for the opposing party under oath in preparation for litigation.

DISCOVERY Pretrial procedure during which one party makes certain information available to the other.

Hickman v. Taylor

Representative (P) v. Tug owner (D)

329 U.S. 495 (1947)

NATURE OF CASE: Action for damages for wrongful death.

FACT SUMMARY: Five crew members drowned when a tug sank. In anticipation of litigation, the attorney for Taylor (D), the tug owner, interviewed the survivors. Hickman (P), as representative of one of the deceased, brought this action and tried by means of discovery to obtain copies of the statements Taylor's (D) attorney obtained from the survivors.

RULE OF LAW

Material obtained by counsel in preparation of litigation is the work product of the lawyer, and while such material is not protected by the attorney-client privilege, it is not discoverable on mere demand without a showing of necessity or justification.

FACTS: When a tug sank, five of the nine crew members drowned. A public hearing was held at which the four survivors were examined. Their testimony was recorded and was made available to all interested parties. A short time later, Fortenbaugh, the attorney for Taylor (D), the tug owner, interviewed the survivors in preparation for possible litigation. He also interviewed other persons believed to have information on the accident. Ultimately, the representatives of the five deceased members brought claims. Four of the claims were settled. Hickman (P), the fifth claimant, brought this action. He filed interrogatories asking for any statements taken from crew members, as well as any oral or written statements, records, reports, or other memoranda made concerning any salvaging and repair of the tug and the death of the deceased. Taylor (D) refused to summarize or set forth the material on the ground that it was protected by the attorney-client privilege. The District Court held that the subjects of the requests were not privileged and ordered Fortenbaugh to answer the interrogatory and the supplemental interrogatories, produce all of the witnesses' statements, and state any facts concerning the case that the defendants learned through the witnesses, and to produce Fortenbaugh's memoranda containing statements of fact by witnesses or to submit these memoranda to the District Court for determination of those portions that should be revealed to Hickman (P). Upon their refusal, the court adjudged them in contempt and ordered them imprisoned until they complied. The Third Circuit Court of Appeals, also sitting en banc, reversed the judgment of the District Court. It held that the information sought was part of the "work product of the lawyer" and hence privileged from discovery under the Federal Rules of Civil Procedure. The importance of the problem, which had engendered a great divergence of views among district courts, led the United States Supreme Court to grant certiorari.

ISSUE: While material obtained by counsel in preparation of litigation is the work product of the lawyer, and while such material is not protected by the attorney-client privilege, is it discoverable on mere demand without a showing of necessity or justification?

HOLDING AND DECISION: (Murphy, J.) No. Material obtained by counsel in preparation of litigation is the work product of the lawyer, and while such material is not protected by the attorney-client privilege, it is not discoverable on mere demand without a showing of necessity or justification. The deposition-discovery rules are to be accorded a broad and liberal treatment since mutual knowledge of all the relevant facts gathered by both parties is essential to proper litigation. But discovery does have ultimate and necessary boundaries. Limitations arise upon a showing of bad faith or harassment or when the inquiry seeks material that is irrelevant or privileged. In this case, the material sought by Hickman (P) is not protected by the attorney-client privilege. However, such material as that sought here does constitute the work product of the lawyer. The general policy against invading the privacy of an attorney in performing his various duties is so well recognized and so essential to the orderly working of our legal system that the party seeking work-product material has a burden to show reasons to justify such production. Interviews, statements, memoranda, correspondence, briefs, mental impressions, etc., obtained in the course of preparation for possible or anticipated litigation fall within the work product. Such material is not free from discovery in all cases. Where relevant and nonprivileged facts remain hidden in an attorney's file and where production of those facts is essential to the preparation of one's case, discovery may be had. But there must be a showing of necessity and justification. In this case, Hickman (P) seeks discovery of oral and written statements of witnesses whose identity is well known and whose availability to Hickman (P) appears unimpaired. Here, no attempt was made to show why it was necessary for Taylor's (D) attorney to produce the material. No reasons were given to justify this invasion of the attorney's privacy. Hickman's (P) counsel, Fortenbaugh, admitted that he wanted the statements only to help him prepare for trial. That is insufficient to warrant an exception to

Continued on next page.

the policy of protecting the privacy of an attorney's professional activities. Affirmed.

CONCURRENCE: (Jackson, J.) The primary effect of the practice advocated would be to require attorneys to act as witnesses.

ANALYSIS

The *Hickman* decision left open a number of questions as to the scope of the work product doctrine and the showing needed to discover work product material. In 1970, Fed. R. Civ. P. 26(b)(3) was added to deal with the discovery of work product. It provides that documents and tangible things that were prepared in anticipation of litigation or for trial are discoverable only upon a showing that the party seeking such materials has substantial need of them and that he is unable without undue hardship to obtain the substantial equivalent of the materials by other means. The rule states that mental impressions, conclusions, opinions, or legal theories of an attorney or other representative of a party are to be protected against disclosure.

Quicknotes

ATTORNEY-CLIENT PRIVILEGE A doctrine precluding the admission into evidence of confidential communications between an attorney and his client made in the course of obtaining professional assistance.

DEPOSITION A pretrial discovery procedure whereby oral or written questions are asked by one party of a witness of the opposing party under oath in preparation for litigation.

DISCOVERY Pretrial procedure during which one party makes certain information available to the other.

INTERROGATORIES A method of pretrial discovery in which written questions are provided by one party to another who must respond in writing under oath.

WORK PRODUCT Work performed by an attorney in preparation of litigation that is not subject to discovery.

WORK PRODUCT RULE A doctrine excluding from discovery work performed by an attorney in preparation of litigation.

WRONGFUL DEATH An action brought by the beneficiaries of a deceased person, claiming that the deceased's death was the result of wrongful conduct by the defendant.

CHAPTER 5

The Right to Jury Trial and Judicial Control of Results

Quick Reference Rules of Law

Chauffeurs, Teamsters and Helpers, Local No. 391 v. Terry

Union (D) v. Union members (P)

494 U.S. 558 (1990)

NATURE OF CASE: Review of denial of motion to strike jury demand in action for breach of the duty of fair representation.

FACT SUMMARY: The Teamsters Union (D), subject to a suit for breach of fair representation, contended that Terry and others (P) were not entitled to a jury.

RULE OF LAW

A plaintiff in an action against a union for breach of duty of fair representation is entitled to a jury.

FACTS: Terry and other various members (P) of the Teamsters Union, Local 391 (the Union) (D) brought an action against the Union (D), contending that it did not represent them fairly in a grievance claim seeking back pay. The plaintiffs requested a jury. The Union (D) moved to strike the jury demand. The district court denied the motion and the Fourth Circuit affirmed. The United States Supreme Court granted certiorari.

ISSUE: Is a plaintiff in an action against a union for breach of a duty of fair representation entitled to a jury?

HOLDING AND DECISION: (Marshall, J.) Yes. A plaintiff in an action against a union for breach of representation is entitled to a jury. The Seventh Amendment guarantees a civil party a right to trial by jury in actions at law. Consequently, any decision as to whether a party is entitled to a jury depends on whether the issue being tried is legal or equitable, and whether the remedy sought is legal or equitable. Here, the action at issue is similar to action for breach of fiduciary duty, an equitable action. At the same time, the action has elements of breach of contract, as the plaintiffs must show that their employer breached the collective bargaining agreement. Thus, the issue being tried is both legal and equitable. However, the remedy sought, damages, is wholly legal. This being so, the action is more legal than equitable, and the right to a jury therefore exists. Affirmed.

CONCURRENCE: (Brennan, J.) The right to a jury should be determined only with reference to the remedy sought.

DISSENT: (Kennedy, J.) The action is most analogous to breach of fiduciary duty, an equitable action.

ANALYSIS

At common law, equity and law were separate. Their merger came after adoption of the Seventh Amendment. The radical transformation of forms of action since then has made Seventh Amendment jurisprudence often a confusing field.

Quicknotes

BREACH OF CONTRACT Unlawful failure by a party to perform its obligations pursuant to contract.

BREACH OF FIDUCIARY DUTY The failure of a fiduciary to observe the standard of care exercised by professionals of similar education and experience.

CERTIORARI A discretionary writ issued by a superior court to an inferior court in order to review the lower court's decisions; the Supreme Court's writ ordering such review.

COLLECTIVE BARGAINING Negotiations between an employer and employee that are mediated by a specified third party.

EQUITY Fairness; justice; the determination of a matter consistent with principles of fairness and not in strict compliance with rules of law.

SEVENTH AMENDMENT Provides that no fact tried by a jury shall be otherwise re-examined in any court of the United States, other than according to the rules of the common law.

Adickes v. S.H. Kress & Co.

Restaurant patron (P) v. Restaurant owner (D)

398 U.S. 144 (1970)

NATURE OF CASE: Appeal of summary judgment denying damages for civil rights violation.

FACT SUMMARY: In a civil rights action in which a conspiracy between the police and a S.H. Kress & Co. (D) was alleged, summary judgment was granted when Adickes (P) could not produce evidence to support a conspiracy.

RULE OF LAW

In an action based on conspiracy, summary judgment may not be granted unless a defendant can show that no evidence thereof exists.

FACTS: Adickes (P) was refused service at a restaurant owned by S.H. Kress & Co. (Kress) (D) and arrested for loitering. She then brought an action seeking damages under § 1983, alleging a conspiracy between Kress (D) and the police. Under the circumstances of the case, a conspiracy could have existed only if police had been present at the store before the arrest. When Adickes (P) could not show that police had earlier been present, Kress (D) moved for summary judgment. This was granted and affirmed on appeal. Adickes (P) appealed to the United States Supreme Court.

ISSUE: In an action based on conspiracy, may summary judgment be granted if a defendant has not shown that no evidence thereof exists?

HOLDING AND DECISION: (Harlan, J.) No. In an action based on conspiracy, summary judgment may not be granted unless a defendant can show that no evidence thereof exists. In a motion for summary judgment, the burden is on the moving party to affirmatively show the absence of a genuine issue as to any material fact. The fact that the burden would be on the other party on the same fact at trial is of no matter. Here, while at trial, Adickes (P) would have to prove the presence of police earlier in the day; at the summary judgment level, the burden was on S.H. Kress & Co. (D) to prove they were not. This it did not do. Reversed.

ANALYSIS

The present case's rule was modified by the Supreme Court 16 years later in *Celotex Corp. v. Catrett*, 477 U.S. 317 (1986). The Court in *Celotex* liberalized the burden on a moving party, holding that such a party, on an issue the opposing party has the ultimate burden of proving, could prevail on the basis that the nonmoving party could not produce evidence on the issue. This has made summary judgment a much easier procedure to obtain in federal courts than in most state courts, as most states' procedural rules are similar to that announced in the present action.

Quicknotes

42 U.S.C. § 1983 Provides that every person who under color of state law subjects or causes to be subjected any citizen of the United States or person within its jurisdiction to be deprived of rights, privileges, and immunities guaranteed by the federal Constitution and laws is liable to the injured party at law or in equity.

BURDEN OF PROOF The duty of a party to introduce evidence to support a fact that is in dispute in an action.

CONSPIRACY Concerted action by two or more persons to accomplish some unlawful purpose.

MATERIAL FACT A fact without the existence of which a contract would not have been entered.

SUMMARY JUDGMENT Judgment rendered by a court in response to a motion by one of the parties, claiming that the lack of a question of material fact in respect to an issue warrants disposition of the issue without consideration by the jury.

Celotex Corp. v. Catrett

Asbestos manufacturer (D) v. Widow (P)

477 U.S. 317 (1986)

NATURE OF CASE: Appeal from reversal of grant of summary judgment.

FACT SUMMARY: The court of appeals reversed summary judgment in favor of Celotex Corp. (D) on the basis that Celotex (D) had not offered sufficient evidence rebutting Catrett's (P) allegations.

RULE OF LAW

Summary judgment must be entered against a party who fails to make a showing sufficient to establish the existence of an element essential to his case and on which he bears the burden of proof at trial.

FACTS: Catrett's (P) husband died, and she sued several asbestos manufacturers, claiming the death resulted from exposure to their products. Celotex Corp. (D), one of the manufacturers, moved for summary judgment on the basis that no evidence existed that the decedent had been exposed to Celotex's (D) products. The district court granted the motion, and the court of appeals reversed, holding that Celotex (D) had not offered sufficient evidence to rebut Catrett's (P) allegations. The United States Supreme Court granted certiorari.

ISSUE: Must summary judgment be entered against a party who fails to make a showing sufficient to establish the existence of an element essential to his case and on which he bears the burden of proof at trial?

HOLDING AND DECISION: (Rehnquist, J.) Yes. Summary judgment must be entered against a party who fails to make a showing sufficient to establish the existence of an element essential to his case and on which he bears the burden of proof at trial. Catrett (P) had the burden of showing that Celotex (D) had some level of culpability in order to go forward on her claim. She thus bore the burden of proof on this issue. Her failure to meet this burden and thus establish a genuine issue of material fact justified entry of summary judgment. Reversed and remanded.

CONCURRENCE: (White, J.) The party moving for summary judgment must meet the burden placed upon him by the Federal Rules of Civil Procedure.

DISSENT: (Brennan, J.) Celotex Corp. (D) failed to meet its burden of production, and summary judgment was therefore improper. The party moving for summary judgment has the burden of establishing the nonexistence of a "genuine issue." This burden has two distinct components: an initial burden of production, which shifts to the nonmoving party if satisfied by the moving party; and an ultimate burden of persuasion, which always remains on the moving party. Here, Celotex (D) failed to discharge its initial burden of production. It chose to base its motion on the argument that there was no evidence in the record to support plaintiff's claim, and therefore was not free to ignore supporting evidence that the record clearly contained. Rather, Celotex (D) was required, as an initial matter, to attack the adequacy of this evidence. Celotex's (D) failure to fulfill this simple requirement constituted a failure to discharge its initial burden of production under Fed. R. Civ. P. 56, and thereby rendered summary judgment improper.

ANALYSIS

Summary judgment is a radical judicial tool that completely disposes of a case or issue prior to trial. The basis for the motion is the absence of a genuine issue of material fact. When such occurs, the only questions remaining are legal questions that are determined by the court. Because the result of a successful motion is the end of a case, the court exercises great restraint in granting them.

Quicknotes

BURDEN OF PROOF The duty of a party to introduce evidence to support a fact that is in dispute in an action.

CAUSE OF ACTION A fact or set of facts the occurrence of which entitle a party to seek judicial relief.

CERTIORARI A discretionary writ issued by a superior court to an inferior court in order to review the lower court's decisions; the Supreme Court's writ ordering such review.

ISSUE OF MATERIAL FACT A fact that is disputed between two or more parties to litigation that is essential to proving an element of the cause of action or a defense asserted or would otherwise affect the outcome of the proceeding.

SUMMARY JUDGMENT Judgment rendered by a court in response to a motion by one of the parties, claiming that the lack of a question of material fact in respect to an issue warrants disposition of the issue without consideration by the jury.

Galloway v. United States

Disabled veteran (P) v. Federal government (D)

319 U.S. 372 (1943)

NATURE OF CASE: Action to recover disability benefits under a government insurance policy.

FACT SUMMARY: Galloway (P) sued to prove that he was eligible for insurance benefits due to permanent disability that began before the date that his G.I. insurance policy lapsed. The lower court granted the Government's (D) motion for a directed verdict on the ground that the evidence introduced by Galloway (P) was legally insufficient to sustain a verdict in Galloway's (P) favor.

RULE OF LAW

The power of a judge to direct a verdict, thereby preventing the evidence from going to the jury, does not violate the constitutional guarantee of "trial by jury."

FACTS: In order to collect liability benefits under his G.I. policy, Galloway (P) had to prove that he had been totally and permanently disabled due to insanity since May 31, 1919, the date on which his policy lapsed for nonpayment of premiums. As supporting evidence, Galloway (P) introduced testimony of two fellow soldiers that he had done two "crazy" acts while on active duty in 1920, the testimony of an old friend that he was a "wreck" in 1919 to 1922, the testimony of a chaplain that a soldier with the same name as Galloway (P) was insane in 1920, the testimony of Galloway's (P) commanding officers that he had alternating periods of gaiety and depression in 1920 to 1922, a 1930 examination that showed permanent insanity, and expert testimony by a physician who first examined Galloway (P) in 1938, that he had been insane since 1918. Galloway (P) introduced no evidence covering the period from 1925 to 1930, and he gave no reason for this lack of evidence. In order to collect benefits, he had to prove that his disability began in 1919 and continued until the date of the trial. The lower court granted the Government's (D) request for a directed verdict because the evidence submitted by Galloway (P) was not sufficient to prove total and continuous disability from 1919.

ISSUE: Does the power of a judge to direct a verdict, thereby preventing the evidence from going to the jury, violate the constitutional right of a "trial by jury"?

HOLDING AND DECISION: (Rutledge, J.) No. The power of a judge to direct a verdict, thereby preventing the evidence from going to the jury, does not violate the constitutional guarantee of "trial by jury." The Seventh Amendment guarantees the right of trial by jury "in suits at common law," but this right does not prevent a court from relieving a jury of its function by directing it to return a verdict for one of the parties. Galloway (P) argues that since the directed verdict was not known at the time of the enactment of the Seventh Amendment, the procedure is therefore unconstitutional. This argument fails, because the Seventh Amendment served to preserve only the most fundamental elements of the institution of a jury trial and not all the procedural elements of a jury trial that existed at the time of its enactment. Also, even at the time of the adoption of the amendment, the judge could remove a case from jury consideration by the devices of a demurrer to the evidence or a motion for a new trial. By a demurrer to the evidence a party had to admit all the facts that his opponent sought to prove, and the judge would make final judgment on these facts; if the demurring party lost, he could not attempt to disprove the facts admitting by the demurrer. By a motion for a new trial after a verdict, the moving party was given another chance to prove his case in a second trial. Since these two devices produced such contradictory results (the demurrer ending all litigation without the demurring party being allowed to prove his case, and the motion for new trial allowing relitigation of all facts in dispute), it is obvious that the amendment did not enact any one specific device to allow a judge to remove a case from the jury. Therefore, courts have the power to direct a verdict for insufficiency of the evidence. The standard for determining whether proof is sufficient to allow submission of the evidence to the jury is that "mere speculation" can't take the place of probative facts, after making allowance for all reasonable inferences in the favor of the party whose case is attacked. Here, Galloway's (P) case failed, since he introduced no facts, only speculation, that his condition continued for the entire period in question. Affirmed.

DISSENT: (Black, J.) Granting a motion for a directed verdict is not appropriate in this case. The jury is the best judge of disputed facts. The majority's statement that a directed verdict serves the same function as a demurrer to the evidence is misleading. In the demurrer, the moving party undertook a great risk in admitting the facts that the opposing party's evidence tends to prove, so the device was not commonly used. There is no such risk in a directed verdict because if the motion is denied, the case then goes to the jury. The directed verdict is frequently used, and to prevent abuse of the procedure that would allow judges to decide cases that should go to the jury, it

Continued on next page.

should be used only where there is no room in the evidence for an honest difference of opinion. There is in this case sufficient evidence for dispute and the case should have gone to the jury.

ANALYSIS

The federal rules allow either party to move for a directed verdict after the presentation of the other party's evidence, and if the motion is denied, that party can still present his own evidence in rebuttal and the case will go to the jury. The device is used to test the sufficiency of the other party's evidence to prove a cause of action, and the judge must evaluate the evidence to see if it tends to prove the elements alleged by the party against whom the motion is made. The motion for directed verdict is granted if there is an absence of evidence or a defect of proof of a crucial element of the challenged claim or defense.

Quicknotes

CAUSE OF ACTION A fact or set of facts the occurrence of which entitle a party to seek judicial relief.

DEMURRER The assertion that the opposing party's pleadings are insufficient and that the demurring party should not be made to answer.

DIRECTED VERDICT A verdict ordered by the court in a jury trial.

PROBATIVE Tending to establish proof.

RIGHT TO TRIAL BY JURY The right guaranteed by the Sixth Amendment to the federal constitution that in all criminal prosecutions the accused has a right to a trial by an impartial jury of the state and district in which the crime was allegedly committed.

SEVENTH AMENDMENT Provides that no fact tried by a jury shall be otherwise re-examined in any court of the United States, other than according to the rules of the common law.

Brandon v. Chicago Board of Education

Disabled claimant (P) v. Board of Education (D)

143 F.3d 293 (7th Cir. 1998)

NATURE OF CASE: Action for relief from judgment for failure to prosecute.

FACT SUMMARY: A series of errors by the Clerk of the district court and by Brandon's (P) attorney resulted in judgment against Brandon (P) for failure to prosecute. Brandon (P) moved for relief from judgment under Federal Rule of Civil Procedure 60(b)(6).

RULE OF LAW

Federal Rule of Civil Procedure 60(b)(1) applies to errors by both the district court clerk and the parties' attorneys.

FACTS: Brandon (P) filed an Americans with Disabilities action against the Chicago Board of Education (the Board) (D). Due to repeated errors by the office of the Clerk of the United States District Court, Brandon's (P) attorneys did not receive notice of two different status hearings and failed to appear in court on Brandon's (P) behalf. After the second hearing, the court dismissed the case for want of prosecution. The order dismissing the case was sent to the wrong address. One year and three days after the dismissal, Brandon's (P) attorney filed a Rule 60 motion to vacate the judgment. Before the hearing, Brandon's (P) attorney received notice from the court that the motion was granted. As a courtesy, Brandon's (P) attorney sent to the Board's (D) attorney a letter stating that the motion had been granted, and that no appearance was necessary on the date set for hearing the motion. But the Board's (D) attorney appeared in court on the day of the hearing anyway, and he persuaded the court to vacate its order granting Rule 60 relief. After briefing on the motion, the court denied Rule 60 relief.

ISSUE: Does Federal Rule of Civil Procedure 60(b)(1) apply to errors by both the district court clerk and the parties' attorneys?

HOLDING AND DECISION: (Rovner, J.) Yes. Federal Rule of Civil Procedure 60(b)(1) applies to errors by the district court clerk and the parties' attorneys. Under Rule 60(b), the motion to vacate judgment pursuant to Rule 60(b)(1) must be brought within one year of the judgment. Here, the motion was brought by Brandon's (P) attorney one year and three days after judgment. The district court determined that Brandon's (P) attorney demonstrated a lack of due diligence that was not excusable neglect under Rule 60(b)(1) by failing to bring the motion in a timely fashion, and therefore denied Brandon's (P) motion. A trial court's denial of a Rule 60(b) motion cannot be reversed absent an abuse of discretion, and no abuse of discretion was found here. Since Rule 60(b)(1) applies, Rule 60(b)(6) does not. Therefore, the motion was correctly denied. Affirmed.

ANALYSIS

The district court narrowly construed the language of Federal Rule of Civil Procedure 60(b). If the Clerk's errors had not occurred, Brandon's (P) attorney's failure to bring the motion on time would undoubtedly be considered inexcusable neglect. Under the circumstances, however, Brandon's (P) attorney's neglect could be construed as excusable within the meaning of the Rule. The Clerk's errors continued, even after the attorney who was confused with Brandon's (P) attorney wrote to the Clerk to clear up the issue. The multiple errors by the Clerk could be construed as mitigating the error committed by Brandon's (P) attorney, thus making it excusable within the meaning of Rule 60(b)(1).

Quicknotes

ABUSE OF DISCRETION A determination by an appellate court that a lower court's decision was based on an error of law.

AMERICANS WITH DISABILITIES ACT Prohibits discrimination in employment, housing, transportation, and other services on the basis of an individual's physical or mental disabilities.

DUE DILIGENCE The standard of care as would be taken by a reasonable person in accordance with the attendant facts and circumstances.

WANT OF PROSECUTION Dismissal of an action where the prosecution fails to further the case toward final disposition or trial.

CHAPTER 6

Alternative Dispute Resolution

Quick Reference Rules of Law

PAGE

1. *Kindred Nursing Centers Limited Partnership v. Clark.* A "clear-statement rule," requiring that for a power of attorney to entitle its holder to bind a principal to an arbitration agreement, thereby depriving the principal of the right of access to the courts and trial by jury, the power of attorney must clearly and specifically so provide, violates the Federal Arbitration Act because such a clear-statement rule singles out arbitration agreements for disfavored treatment. *78*

Kindred Nursing Centers Limited Partnership v. Clark

Nursing home operator (D) v. Relative and representative of nursing home patient (P)

137 S. Ct. 1421 (2017)

NATURE OF CASE: Appeal from judgment of a state's highest court affirming the invalidation by the state's lower courts of an arbitration agreement.

FACT SUMMARY: Kindred Nursing Centers L.P. (D), a nursing home operator, contended that a "clear-statement rule," which requires that for a power of attorney to entitle its holder to bind a principal to an arbitration agreement, the power of attorney must clearly and specifically so provide, violates the Federal Arbitration Act because such a clear-statement rule singles out arbitration agreements for disfavored treatment.

RULE OF LAW

A "clear-statement rule," requiring that for a power of attorney to entitle its holder to bind a principal to an arbitration agreement, thereby depriving the principal of the right of access to the courts and trial by jury, the power of attorney must clearly and specifically so provide, violates the Federal Arbitration Act because such a clear-statement rule singles out arbitration agreements for disfavored treatment.

FACTS: Beverly Wellner (Beverly) (P) and Janis Clark (Janis) (P)—the wife and daughter, respectively, of Joe Wellner (Joe) and Olive Clark (Olive)—each held a power of attorney affording her broad authority to manage her family member's affairs. When Joe and Olive moved into a nursing home operated by Kindred Nursing Centers L.P. (Kindred) (D), Beverly (P) and Janis (P) used their powers of attorney to complete all necessary paperwork. As part of that process, each signed an arbitration agreement on her relative's behalf providing that any claims arising from the relative's stay at the facility would be resolved through binding arbitration. After Joe and Olive died, their estates (represented by Beverly (P) and Janis (P)) filed suits in state court alleging that Kindred's (D) substandard care had caused their deaths. Kindred (D) moved to dismiss the cases, arguing that the arbitration agreements prohibited bringing the disputes to court. The trial court denied Kindred's (D) motions, and the state's intermediate appellate court agreed that the suits could go forward. The state's highest court consolidated the cases and affirmed. The court held, inter alia, that both arbitration agreements were invalid because neither power of attorney specifically entitled the representative to enter into an arbitration agreement. Because the state's constitution declared the rights of access to the courts and trial by jury to be "sacred" and "inviolate," the court determined that an agent could deprive her principal of such rights only if expressly provided in the power of attorney (the "clear-statement rule"). Kindred (D) appealed, and the United States Supreme Court granted certiorari.

ISSUE: Does a "clear-statement rule," requiring that for a power of attorney to entitle its holder to bind a principal to an arbitration agreement, thereby depriving the principal of the right of access to the courts and trial by jury, the power of attorney must clearly and specifically so provide, violate the Federal Arbitration Act because such a clear statement rule singles out arbitration agreements for disfavored treatment?

HOLDING AND DECISION: (Kagan, J.) Yes. A "clear-statement rule," requiring that for a power of attorney to entitle its holder to bind a principal to an arbitration agreement, thereby depriving the principal of the right of access to the courts and trial by jury, the power of attorney must clearly and specifically so provide, violates the Federal Arbitration Act (FAA) because such a clear-statement rule singles out arbitration agreements for disfavored treatment. The FAA, which makes arbitration agreements "valid, irrevocable, and enforceable, save upon such grounds as exist at law or in equity for the revocation of any contract," establishes an equal-treatment principle: a court may invalidate an arbitration agreement based on generally applicable contract defenses but not on legal rules that apply only to arbitration or that derive their meaning from the fact that an agreement to arbitrate is at issue. The FAA thus preempts any state rule that discriminates on its face against arbitration or that covertly accomplishes the same objective by disfavoring contracts that have the defining features of arbitration agreements. Here, the clear-statement rule fails to put arbitration agreements on an equal plane with other contracts. By requiring an explicit statement before an agent can relinquish her principal's right to go to court and receive a jury trial, the state's highest court did exactly what is barred: adopt a legal rule hinging on the primary characteristic of an arbitration agreement. Beverly (P) and Janis (P) argue that the clear-statement rule affects only contract formation and that the FAA does not apply to contract formation questions. However, the FAA's text says otherwise. The FAA cares not only about the "enforce[ment]" of arbitration agreements, but also about their initial "valid[ity]"—that is, about what it takes to enter them. Precedent confirms the point, as the Court previously noted the impermissibility of applying

Continued on next page.

a contract defense like duress "in a fashion that disfavors arbitration." That point would make no sense if the FAA had nothing to say about contract formation, given that duress involves unfair dealing at the contract formation stage. Accordingly, the decision below is reversed, and the state's highest court must now enforce the arbitration agreement at issue. Reversed and remanded.

ANALYSIS

Justice Thomas, dissenting, expressed the view that the Federal Arbitration Act (FAA) does not apply to proceedings in state courts, so that in such proceedings the FAA does not displace a rule that requires express authorization from a principal before an agent may waive the principal's right to a jury trial.

Quicknotes

ARBITRATION An alternative resolution process where a dispute is heard and decided by a neutral third party, rather than through legal proceedings.

ARBITRATION AGREEMENT A mutual understanding entered by parties wishing to submit to the decisionmaking authority of a neutral third party, selected by the parties and charged with rendering a decision.

POWER OF ATTORNEY A written instrument that allows a person to appoint an agent and confer authority to perform certain specified acts on his behalf.

CHAPTER 7

The Choice of an Appropriate Court: Personal Jurisdiction, Notice, and Venue

Quick Reference Rules of Law

	PAGE
1. *Pennoyer v. Neff.* Where the object of the action is to determine the personal rights and obligations of the parties, service by publication against nonresidents is ineffective to confer jurisdiction on the court.	*83*
2. *Harris v. Balk.* A debtor's obligation to pay debt accompanies him wherever he goes, and the question of jurisdiction is not dependent on either the situs of the debt or the nature of the debtor's stay in a state.	*85*
3. *Hess v. Pawloski.* In advance of a nonresident's use of its highways, a state may require the nonresident to appoint one of the state's officials as his agent on whom process may be served in proceedings growing out of such highway use.	*86*
4. *International Shoe Co. v. State of Washington.* For a state to subject a nonresident defendant to in personam jurisdiction, due process requires that he have certain minimum contacts with it such that the maintenance of the suit does not offend traditional notions of fair play and substantial justice.	*87*
5. *World-Wide Volkswagen Corp. v. Woodson.* A state court may exercise personal jurisdiction over a nonresident defendant only so long as there exist sufficient "minimum contacts" between him and the forum state such that maintenance of the suit does not offend "traditional notions of fair play and substantial justice."	*89*
6. *Calder v. Jones.* A state court may exercise jurisdiction over an out-of-state party whose intentional conduct is calculated to cause, and does cause, injury to the complainant in the forum state.	*91*
7. *Walden v. Fiore.* A court sitting in one state may not exercise personal jurisdiction over a defendant who is in another state, where the only connection with the state in which the court sits is that the defendant commits an intentional tort that he knows will cause harm to an individual residing in that state.	*92*
8. *Asahi Metal Industry Co., Ltd. v. Superior Court of California, Solano County.* Minimum contacts sufficient to sustain jurisdiction are not satisfied simply by the placement of a product into the stream of commerce coupled with awareness that its product would reach the forum state.	*94*
9. *J. McIntyre Machinery, Ltd. v. Nicastro.* In products liability cases, the "stream-of-commerce" doctrine cannot displace the general rule that the exercise of judicial power is not lawful unless the defendant purposefully avails itself of the privilege of conducting activities within the forum state, thus invoking the benefits and protections of its laws.	*96*
10. *Bristol-Myers Squibb Co. v. Superior Court of California.* For a state court to exercise specific jurisdiction over a claim, the lawsuit must arise out of or relate to the defendant's contacts with the state.	*98*
11. *Ford Motor Co. v. Montana Eighth Judicial Dist. Ct.* In a products liability action, there is specific jurisdiction over a company whose product is claimed to be defective and to have caused in-state injury where, although the company did not design, manufacture, or first sell the product in the state where the injury occurred, the company did substantial business in the state, including advertising, selling, and servicing the type of product at issue.	*99*

Pennoyer v. Neff

Purchaser of property (D) v. Real property owner (P)

95 U.S. 714 (1877)

NATURE OF CASE: Action to recover possession of land.

FACT SUMMARY: Neff (P) alleged that Pennoyer's (D) deed from a sheriff's sale was invalid because the court ordering the sale had never obtained personal jurisdiction over Neff (P).

RULE OF LAW

Where the object of the action is to determine the personal rights and obligations of the parties, service by publication against nonresidents is ineffective to confer jurisdiction on the court.

FACTS: Neff (P) owned real property in Oregon. Mitchell brought suit in Oregon to recover legal fees allegedly owed him by Neff (P). Neff (P), a nonresident, was served by publication, and Mitchell obtained a default judgment. The court ordered Neff's (P) land sold at a sheriff's sale to satisfy the judgment. Pennoyer (D) purchased the property. Neff (P) subsequently learned of the sale and brought suit in Oregon to recover possession of his property. Neff (P) alleged that the court ordering the sale had never acquired in personam jurisdiction over him. Therefore, the court could not adjudicate the personal rights and obligations between Neff (P) and Mitchell, and the default judgment had been improperly entered. The court ruled for Neff (P).

ISSUE: Where the object of the action is to determine the personal rights and obligations of the parties, is service by publication against nonresidents ineffective to confer jurisdiction on the court?

HOLDING AND DECISION: (Field, J.) Yes. Where the object of the action is to determine the personal rights and obligations of the parties, service by publication against nonresidents is ineffective to confer jurisdiction on the court. Every state possesses exclusive jurisdiction and sovereignty over persons and property within its territory. Following from this, no state can exercise direct jurisdiction and authority over persons or property outside of its territory. These are two well-established principles of public law respecting the jurisdiction of an independent state over persons and property. However, the exercise of jurisdiction that every state possesses over persons and property within it will often affect persons and property outside of it. A state may compel persons domiciled within it to execute, in pursuance of their contracts respecting property situated elsewhere, instruments transferring title. Likewise, a state may subject property situated within it that is owned by nonresidents to the payment of the demands of its own citizens. Substituted service by publication or by other authorized means may be sufficient to inform the parties of the proceedings where the property is brought under the control of the court or where the judgment is sought as a means of reaching such property or effectuating some interest therein. That is, such service is effectual in proceedings in rem. The law assumes that property is always in the possession of its owner or an agent. It proceeds upon the theory that a seizure of the property will inform the owner that he must look to any proceedings upon such seizure for the property's condemnation or sale. But where the entire object of the action is to determine personal rights and obligations, the action is in personam, and service by publication is ineffectual to confer jurisdiction over the nonresident defendant upon the court. Process sent out of state to a nonresident is equally ineffective to confer personal jurisdiction. In an action to determine a defendant's personal liability, he must be brought within the court's jurisdiction by service of process within the state or by his voluntary appearance. Without jurisdiction, due process requirements are not satisfied. In the case herein, Neff (P) was not personally served and never appeared. Hence, the personal judgment obtained against Neff (P) was not valid, and the property could not be sold. Affirmed.

ANALYSIS

This is the leading case on the extent of the court's power to compel a defendant's attendance. At common law the presence of the defendant within the jurisdiction plus service while there were the indispensable ingredients for the acquisition of jurisdiction of the person of the defendant. It remains the basic method of acquiring jurisdiction over the defendant. It does not matter how transient the defendant's presence is if she is served within the jurisdiction. One case held that service on a defendant while he was in an airplane passing over a state is sufficient. Of course, a voluntary appearance by a defendant also gives the court jurisdiction over her.

Continued on next page.

Quicknotes

DEED A signed writing transferring title to real property from one person to another.

DEFAULT JUDGMENT A judgment entered against a defendant due to his failure to appear in a court or defend himself against the allegations of the opposing party.

DUE PROCESS CLAUSE Clauses, found in the Fifth and Fourteenth Amendments to the United States Constitution, providing that no person shall be deprived of "life, liberty, or property, without due process of law."

IN PERSONAM JURISDICTION The jurisdiction of a court over a person as opposed to his interest in property.

IN REM JURISDICTION A court's authority over a thing so that its judgment is binding in respect to the rights and interests of all parties in that thing.

SERVICE OF PROCESS The communication of reasonable notice of a court proceeding to a defendant in order to provide him with an opportunity to be heard.

Harris v. Balk

Debtor (D) v. Creditor (P)

198 U.S. 215 (1905)

NATURE OF CASE: Action to recover a debt.

FACT SUMMARY: In North Carolina, Harris (D) owed a debt to Balk (P), which was attached by Epstein in Maryland.

RULE OF LAW

A debtor's obligation to pay debt accompanies him wherever he goes, and the question of jurisdiction is not dependent on either the situs of the debt or the nature of the debtor's stay in a state.

FACTS: Harris (D) and Balk (P) were both North Carolina residents. Harris (D) owed Balk (P) $180. Balk (P) owed Epstein, a Maryland resident, $300. In 1896, while Harris (D) was temporarily in Maryland, Epstein brought suit and had issued a writ of attachment, attaching the debt Harris (D) owed Balk (P). Harris (D) did not contest the process issued to garnish the debt due Balk (P). Judgment was entered for Epstein for $180, which Harris (D) paid. One week later, Balk (P) brought this action against Harris (D) in North Carolina to recover the $180 owed him. Harris (D) answered with Epstein's recovery in Maryland. The lower court entered judgment for Balk (P) on the ground that the Maryland court obtained no jurisdiction to attach or garnish the debt due Balk (P) because Harris (D) was in Maryland only temporarily and the situs of the debt was in North Carolina.

ISSUE: Is the question of jurisdiction dependent upon either the situs of the debt or the nature of the debtor's stay in the state?

HOLDING AND DECISION: (Peckham, J.) No. A debtor's obligation to pay debt accompanies him wherever he goes, and the question of jurisdiction is not dependent on either the situs of the debt or the nature of the debtor's stay in a state. Power over the person of the garnishee (or debtor) confers jurisdiction on the courts of the state where a writ of attachment issues. Jurisdiction is not dependent upon the original situs of the debt or upon the character of the garnishee's stay in the state where attachment is issued. As for the situs, the obligation of the debtor to pay the debt accompanies him wherever he goes. He is as much bound to pay the debt in a foreign state when sued there by a creditor as he is in the state where the debt was contracted. Balk (P) had a right to sue Harris (D) in Maryland since as a citizen of North Carolina he is entitled to all the privileges and immunities of citizens of all the states. If the garnishee is found in a state and process is personally served on him there, the court thereby acquires jurisdiction over him, and he can garnish the debt due from him and condemn it, provided the garnishee could be sued by his creditor in that state. Hence, the judgment against Harris (D) in Maryland was valid because the court had jurisdiction over Harris (D) by personal service. Further, Balk (P) obviously had notice of the Maryland suit because he sued Harris (D) a few days later. He could have contested it in Maryland but did not. Judgment for Balk (P) is reversed, and the case is remanded.

ANALYSIS

This case demonstrates how a debt may be seized. Since, for the purposes of garnishment, a debt clings to the debtor, quasi-in-rem jurisdiction can be obtained over the debt by personal service of process on the debtor. The problem becomes more complex when the debtor goes into another state or country or is a corporation who might be sued in many states. In *Weitzel v. Weitzel,* 27 Ariz. 117, 230 P. 1106 (1924), the plaintiff had a judgment for alimony against her husband, who was working in Mexico for a railroad company. She served a garnishee summons on the railroad in Arizona to reach the debt it owed her husband in Mexico. The court did not allow the garnishment on the ground that it was probable the Mexican courts would not respect the quasi-in-rem judgment of the Arizona court.

Quicknotes

ATTACHMENT The seizing of the property of one party in anticipation of, or in order to satisfy, a favorable judgment obtained by another party.

QUASI-IN-REM JURISDICTION A court's authority over the defendant's property within a specified geographical area.

SITUS Location; in community property, the location of an asset.

Hess v. Pawloski

Nonresident driver (D) v. Accident victim (P)

274 U.S. 352 (1927)

NATURE OF CASE: Review of verdict in plaintiff's favor in action to recover damages for personal injuries.

FACT SUMMARY: A Massachusetts statute provided that nonresident motorists were deemed to have appointed a state official as their agent for service of process in cases growing out of accidents or collisions involving them. Pawloski (P) sued Hess (D), a nonresident, for damages due to an auto accident in Massachusetts.

RULE OF LAW

In advance of a nonresident's use of its highways, a state may require the nonresident to appoint one of the state's officials as his agent on whom process may be served in proceedings growing out of such highway use.

FACTS: Pawloski (P) alleged that Hess (D) negligently drove a car on a Massachusetts highway, thereby injuring Pawloski (P). Hess (D) was a nonresident of Massachusetts. No personal service was made on him, and no property belonging to him was attached. A Massachusetts statute provided that nonresident motorists were deemed to have appointed the registrar of motor vehicles as their agent for service of process in cases arising out of accidents or collisions in which nonresidents were involved. The statute also required that notice of such service and a copy of the process be sent by registered mail to the defendant. Hess (D) moved to dismiss on due process grounds, but the lower courts held the statute to be a valid exercise of the police power. The United States Supreme Court granted review.

ISSUE: Does a state statute by which nonresident motorists are deemed to have appointed a state official as their agent for service of process in cases arising out of accidents involving them violate due process?

HOLDING AND DECISION: (Butler, J.) No. In advance of a nonresident's use of its highways, a state may require the nonresident to appoint one of the state's officials as his agent on whom process may be served in proceedings growing out of such highway use. Motor vehicles are dangerous vehicles. In the public interest, the state may make and enforce regulations reasonably calculated to promote care on the part of all who use its highways. The statute involved in this case limits the nonresident's implied consent to proceedings growing out of accidents or collisions on a highway involving the nonresident. It requires that he receive notice of the service and a copy of the process. It makes no hostile discrimination against nonresidents. The state's power to regulate the use of its highways extends to its use by nonresidents as well as residents. In advance of the operation of a motor vehicle on its highway by a nonresident, the state may require him to appoint one of its officials as his agent on whom process may be served in proceedings growing out of such use. Affirmed.

ANALYSIS

Other states were quick to pass similar nonresident motorist statutes and thus provide their citizens with local forums for injuries caused by nonresident motorists. Some passed statutes subjecting nonresident boat and airplane owners to local forums also. Under the reasoning of *Hess,* it was thought that in order to subject the nonresident to local jurisdiction, the activity engaged in must be one subject to state regulations under its police power. Consequently, the first extensions of *Hess* were to such situations as the sale of securities, an industry subject to a high degree of regulation, and the ownership of local real estate.

Quicknotes

DUE PROCESS CLAUSE Clauses, found in the Fifth and Fourteenth Amendments to the United States Constitution, providing that no person shall be deprived of "life, liberty, or property, without due process of law."

IMPLIED CONSENT The manifestation by actions, or by the failure to act, of an agreement of the minds or of the acquiescence by one party to the will of another.

PLAINTIFF IN ERROR Appellant; a party that appeals from a lower court judgment.

POLICE POWERS Power of a state or local government to regulate private conduct for the health, safety and welfare of the general public.

SERVICE OF PROCESS The communication of reasonable notice of a court proceeding to a defendant in order to provide him with an opportunity to be heard.

STATUTE A law enacted pursuant to the legislature's power and consistent with specified procedure so that it regulates a particular activity.

International Shoe Co. v. State of Washington

Delaware corporation (D) v. State (P)

326 U.S. 310 (1945)

NATURE OF CASE: Proceedings to recover unemployment contributions.

FACT SUMMARY: A state statute authorized the mailing of notice of assessment of delinquent contributions for unemployment compensation to nonresident employers. International Shoe Co. (International) (D) is a nonresident corporation. Notice of assessment was served on one of its salespersons within the state and was mailed to International's (D) office.

RULE OF LAW

For a state to subject a nonresident defendant to in personam jurisdiction, due process requires that he have certain minimum contacts with it such that the maintenance of the suit does not offend traditional notions of fair play and substantial justice.

FACTS: A Washington statute set up a scheme of unemployment compensation that required contributions by employers. The statute authorized the commissioner of the State of Washington (Washington) (P), to issue an order and notice of assessment of delinquent contributions by mailing the notice to nonresident employers. International Shoe Co. (International) (D) was a Delaware corporation having its principal place of business in Missouri. International (D) employed 11 to 13 salespersons under the supervision of managers in Missouri. These salespeople resided in Washington and did most of their work there. They had no authority to enter contracts or make collections. International (D) did not have any office in Washington and made no contracts there. Notice of assessment was served upon one of International's (D) Washington salespersons, and a copy of the notice was sent by registered mail to International's (D) Missouri address. The state courts decided against International (D).

ISSUE: For a state to subject a nonresident defendant to in personam jurisdiction, does due process require that he have certain minimum contacts with it such that the maintenance of the suit does not offend notions of fair play and substantial justice?

HOLDING AND DECISION: (Stone, C.J.) Yes. For a state to subject a nonresident defendant to in personam jurisdiction, due process requires that he have certain minimum contacts with it such that the maintenance of the suit does not offend traditional notions of fair play and substantial justice. Historically, the jurisdiction of courts to render judgment in personam is grounded on their power over the defendant's person, and his presence within the territorial jurisdiction of a court was necessary to a valid judgment. But now, due process requires only that in order to subject a defendant to a judgment in personam, if he is not present within the territorial jurisdiction, he must have certain minimum contacts with the territory such that the maintenance of the suit does not offend traditional notions of fair play and substantial justice. The contacts must be such as to make it reasonable, in the context of our federal system, to require a defendant corporation to defend the suit brought there. An estimate of the inconveniences that would result to the corporation from a trial away from its "home" is relevant. To require a corporation to defend a suit away from home where its contact has been casual or isolated activities has been thought to lay too unreasonable a burden on it. However, even single or occasional acts may, because of their nature, quality, and circumstances, be deemed sufficient to render a corporation liable to suit. Hence, the criteria to determine whether jurisdiction is justified is not simply mechanical or quantitative. Satisfaction of due process depends on the quality and nature of the activity in relation to the fair and orderly administration of the laws. In this case, International Shoe Co.'s (D) activities were neither irregular nor casual. Rather, they were systematic and continuous. The obligation sued upon here arose out of these activities. They were sufficient to establish adequate contacts or ties to make it reasonable to permit the State of Washington (P) to enforce the obligations International (D) incurred there. Affirmed.

DISSENT: (Black, J.) The United States Constitution leaves to each state the power to tax and to open the doors of its courts for its citizens to sue corporations who do business in the state. It is a judicial deprivation to condition the exercise of this power on this Court's notion of "fair play."

ANALYSIS

Before this decision, three theories had evolved to provide for suits by and against foreign corporations. The first was the consent theory. It rested on the proposition that since a foreign corporation could not carry on its business within a state without the permission of that state, that state could require a corporation to appoint an agent to receive service of process within the state. However, it soon became established law that a foreign corporation could not be prevented by a state from

Continued on next page.

carrying on interstate commerce within its borders. The presence doctrine required that the corporation was "doing business" and "present" in the state. The third theory used either the presence or consent doctrine, and it was necessary to determine whether the corporation was doing business within the state either to decide whether its consent could properly be implied or to discover whether the corporation was present.

Quicknotes

CONSENT JURISDICTION The forum having jurisdiction over a lawsuit as agreed upon by the parties prior to litigation.

DUE PROCESS CLAUSE Clauses, found in the Fifth and Fourteenth Amendments to the United States Constitution, providing that no person shall be deprived of "life, liberty, or property, without due process of law."

FAIR PLAY NOTION Equitable notion that persons must deal with each other fairly and justly.

IN PERSONAM JURISDICTION The jurisdiction of a court over a person as opposed to his interest in property.

INTERSTATE COMMERCE Commercial dealings between two parties located in different states or located in one state and accomplished through a point in another state or a foreign country; commercial dealings transacted between two states.

MINIMUM CONTACTS The minimum degree of contact necessary in order to sustain a cause of action within a particular forum, consistent with the requirements of due process.

STATUTE A law enacted pursuant to the legislature's power and consistent with specified procedure so that it regulates a particular activity.

World-Wide Volkswagen Corp. v. Woodson

Automobile distributor (P) v. Court (D)

444 U.S. 286 (1980)

NATURE OF CASE: Petition for a writ prohibiting the exercise of in personam jurisdiction.

FACT SUMMARY: World-Wide Volkswagen Corp. (P) sought a writ of prohibition to keep district court Judge Woodson (D) from exercising in personam jurisdiction over it, alleging it did not have sufficient "contacts" with the forum state of Oklahoma to render it subject to such jurisdiction.

RULE OF LAW

A state court may exercise personal jurisdiction over a nonresident defendant only so long as there exist sufficient "minimum contacts" between him and the forum state such that maintenance of the suit does not offend "traditional notions of fair play and substantial justice."

FACTS: World-Wide Volkswagen Corp. (World-Wide) (P) was the regional distributor of Audi automobiles for the tristate area of New York, New Jersey, and Connecticut. It was the distributor of the particular Audi that the Robinsons purchased from a New York dealer and drove to Oklahoma, where three family members were severely burned when another car struck their Audi in the rear. The Robinsons brought a products liability action in an Oklahoma district court, suing the New York dealership and World-Wide (P) (a New York corporation). Claiming that no evidence showed it had any connection with Oklahoma whatsoever, World-Wide (P) sought a writ of prohibition to keep district court Judge Woodson (D) from exercising in personam jurisdiction. It argued that a lack of sufficient contacts with the forum state made assertion of such jurisdiction improper under the Due Process Clause. The Supreme Court of Oklahoma denied the writ, noting that World-Wide (P) could foresee that the automobiles it sold would be taken into other states, including Oklahoma. The United States Supreme Court granted certiorari.

ISSUE: Must a defendant have "minimum contacts" with the forum state before it can exercise in personam jurisdiction over him?

HOLDING AND DECISION: (White, J.) Yes. A state court may exercise personal jurisdiction over a nonresident defendant only so long as there exist sufficient "minimum contacts" between him and the forum state such that maintenance of the suit does not offend "traditional notions of fair play and substantial justice." Under the Due Process Clause, the exercise of in personam jurisdiction over a defendant is not constitutional unless he has sufficient "minimum contacts" with the forum state so that maintenance of the suit does not offend "traditional notions of fair play and substantial justice." Here, World-Wide Volkswagen Corp. (World-Wide) (P) had no "contacts, ties, or relations" with Oklahoma, so personal jurisdiction could not be exercised. As for the notion that it was foreseeable that cars sold in New York would wind up in Oklahoma, the foreseeability that is critical to due process analysis is not the mere likelihood that a product will find its way into the forum state. Rather, it is that the defendant's conduct and connection with the forum state are such that he should reasonably anticipate being hauled into court there. Such conduct and connection are simply missing in this case. Reversed.

DISSENT: (Brennan, J.) The automobile is designed specifically to facilitate travel from place to place, and the sale of one purposefully injects it into the stream of interstate commerce. Thus, this case is not unlike those where in personam jurisdiction is properly exercised over one who purposefully places his product into the stream of interstate commerce with the expectation it will be purchased by consumers in other states. Furthermore, a large part of the value of automobiles is the extensive, nationwide network of highways. State maintenance of such roads contributes to the value of World-Wide's (P) business. World-Wide (P) also participates in a network of related dealerships with nationwide service facilities. Having such facilities in Oklahoma also adds to the value of World-Wide's (P) business. Thus, it has the required minimum contacts with Oklahoma to render this exercise of personal jurisdiction constitutional.

DISSENT: (Marshall, J.) Reasonable minds may differ as to whether World-Wide (P) has sufficient minimum contacts with Oklahoma, but the majority reached its decision by taking an unnecessarily narrow view of World-Wide's (P) conduct, by focusing instead on the Robinsons' conduct. Thus, it determined that jurisdiction could not be asserted over World-Wide (P) because World-Wide (P) had no control over the Robinsons' unilateral decision to drive to Oklahoma. Jurisdiction is based on the deliberate and purposeful actions of World-Wide (P), and here, World-Wide (P) chose to engage in the global business of marketing and servicing automobiles. The product it sells has value only in the fact that it is mobile. People buy cars in order to make short and long trips. Local dealers derive a substantial portion of their revenues from their service operations and thereby

Continued on next page.

obtain a further economic benefit from the opportunity to service cars that were sold in other states. Even though World-Wide (P) could not know in advance that this particular automobile would be driven to Oklahoma, it must have anticipated that a substantial portion of the cars it sold would travel out of New York. Knowing that some of its cars would be driven in all of the 50 states should alert a reasonable businessman to the likelihood that a defect in the product might manifest itself in another state, in the normal course of the operation of the car for its intended purpose. Foreseeability alone is not the only determinant of issues of jurisdiction. World-Wide (P) knowingly reached out of state and received economic advantage from the fact that its product can be moved out of state, and from the activities of dealers and distributors in other states. It intentionally became part of an interstate economic network. Thus, World-Wide (P) had reason to expect that it could be brought before an Oklahoma court. The majority correctly states that if the product is purchased in the forum state, the forum state may assert jurisdiction over everyone in the chain of distribution. But jurisdiction is not necessarily lacking if the product enters the state, not through the channels of distribution, but in the course of its intended use by the consumer.

DISSENT: (Blackmun, J.) It is the mobile nature of automobiles that ought to be the focus of this litigation. It is reasonable and constitutional to uphold Oklahoma jurisdiction.

ANALYSIS

Over the years, modern transportation and communication have made foreign state suits much less of a burden to defendants. This resulted in a relaxing of the due process limits placed on state jurisdiction down to the "minimum contacts" concept. However, even if there were no inconvenience to the defendant, a state could not exercise personal jurisdiction over him if he had no "contacts, ties, or relations." This is true even if that state had a strong interest in applying its law to the controversy it was the most convenient location for litigation, etc. The reason is that the Due Process Clause serves two distinct functions: The first is as a guarantor against inconvenient litigation, but the second is as a guardian of interstate federalism. It is in this second capacity that the Due Process Clause would prevent assumption of jurisdiction in the aforementioned instance by recognizing the "territorial limitations on the power of the respective states."

Quicknotes

CERTIORARI A discretionary writ issued by a superior court to an inferior court in order to review the lower court's decisions; the Supreme Court's writ ordering such review.

DUE PROCESS CLAUSE Clauses, found in the Fifth and Fourteenth Amendments to the United States Constitution, providing that no person shall be deprived of "life, liberty, or property, without due process of law."

FAIR PLAY NOTION Equitable notion that persons must deal with each other fairly and justly.

FORUM STATE The state in which a court, or other location in which a legal remedy may be sought, is located.

IN PERSONAM JURISDICTION The jurisdiction of a court over a person as opposed to his interest in property.

INTERSTATE COMMERCE Commercial dealings between two parties located in different states or located in one state and accomplished through a point in another state or a foreign country; commercial dealings transacted between two states.

MINIMUM CONTACTS The minimum degree of contact necessary in order to sustain a cause of action within a particular forum, consistent with the requirements of due process.

WRIT OF PROHIBITION A writ issued by a superior court prohibiting a lower court from exceeding its jurisdiction or from usurping jurisdiction beyond that authorized by law.

Calder v. Jones

Magazine publisher (D) v. Libel complainant (P)

465 U.S. 783 (1984)

NATURE OF CASE: Appeal from reinstatement of complaint after it had been quashed for lack of personal jurisdiction.

FACT SUMMARY: Shirley Jones (P), a California resident, brought a libel suit against Calder (D) in a California court. Calder (D) was served with process by mail in Florida and moved to quash such service on jurisdictional grounds. The trial court granted the motion, and the state appellate court reversed.

RULE OF LAW

A state court may exercise jurisdiction over an out-of-state party whose intentional conduct is calculated to cause, and does cause, injury to the complainant in the forum state.

FACTS: Shirley Jones (P), who lived and worked in California, sued Calder (D) in California. Calder (D) was president and editor of a national magazine published in Florida (*The National Enquirer*). The magazine had a large circulation in California. Calder (D) was served with process by mail in Florida and caused a special appearance to be entered on his behalf, moving to quash such service on the grounds of lack of jurisdiction. The trial court granted the motion, and the state appellate court reversed, reinstating the complaint.

ISSUE: May a state court exercise jurisdiction over an out-of-state party whose intentional conduct in the second state is calculated to cause, and does cause, injury to the complainant in the forum state?

HOLDING AND DECISION: (Rehnquist, J.) Yes. A state court may exercise jurisdiction over an out-of-state party whose intentional conduct is calculated to cause, and does cause, injury to the complainant in the forum state. *The National Enquirer* is a Florida corporation with its principal place of business in Florida and publishes a national weekly newspaper with a circulation of over 5 million. 600,000 of those copies, almost twice the level of the next highest state, are sold in California. The Due Process Clause of the Fourteenth Amendment permits personal jurisdiction over a defendant in any state with which the defendant has "certain minimum contacts," such that the maintenance of the suit does not offend "traditional notions of fair play and substantial justice." Here, Jones (P), a resident of California, was the focus of the activities of Calder (D), the publisher, out of which the suit arose. Specifically, the allegedly libelous story concerned the California activities of a California resident and impugned the professionalism of an entertainer whose television career was centered in California. An individual injured in California need not go to Florida to seek redress from persons who, though remaining in Florida, knowingly cause the injury in California. Affirmed.

ANALYSIS

In reaching its decision, the Court noted that here the defendant newspaper wrote and published an article that it knew would have a potentially devastating impact upon Jones (P) and that the newspaper (D) knew also that the brunt of the injury would be felt by Jones (P) in the state in which she lived and worked (California) and in which the newspaper (D) had its largest circulation.

Quicknotes

COMPLAINT The initial pleading commencing litigation that sets forth a claim for relief.

DUE PROCESS CLAUSE Clauses, found in the Fifth and Fourteenth Amendments to the United States Constitution, providing that no person shall be deprived of "life, liberty, or property, without due process of law."

FAIR PLAY NOTION Equitable notion that persons must deal with each other fairly and justly.

FORUM STATE The state in which a court, or other location in which a legal remedy may be sought, is located.

JURISDICTION The authority of a court to hear and declare judgment in respect to a particular matter.

LIBEL A false or malicious publication subjecting a person to scorn, hatred, or ridicule, or injuring him or her in relation to his or her occupation or business.

MINIMUM CONTACTS The minimum degree of contact necessary in order to sustain a cause of action within a particular forum, consistent with the requirements of due process.

QUASH To vacate, annul, void.

Walden v. Fiore

Georgia police officer/DEA agent (D) v. Nevada resident (P)

134 S. Ct. 1115 (2014)

NATURE OF CASE: Appeal from reversal of dismissal for lack of jurisdiction of tort action based on *Bivens v. Six Unknown Fed. Narcotics Agents*, 403 U.S. 388 (1971).

FACT SUMMARY: Walden (D), a Georgia police officer and deputized Drug Enforcement Agency agent, contended his tortious conduct in Georgia, which caused a delay in the return of a significant amount of Fiore's (P) funds, did not support jurisdiction in Nevada for an action based on that conduct.

RULE OF LAW

A court sitting in one state may not exercise personal jurisdiction over a defendant who is in another state, where the only connection with the state in which the court sits is that the defendant commits an intentional tort that he knows will cause harm to an individual residing in that state.

FACTS: Walden (D), a Georgia police officer working as a deputized Drug Enforcement Administration agent at a Georgia airport, searched Fiore (P) and Gipson (P) and seized close to $100,000 in cash they were carrying. Fiore (P) and Gipson (P) explained the money was their gambling "bank" and winnings, as they were professional gamblers. After Fiore (P) and Gipson (P) returned to their Nevada residence, Walden (D) allegedly helped draft a false probable cause affidavit in support of the funds' forfeiture and forwarded it to a United States Attorney's Office in Georgia. In the end, no forfeiture complaint was filed, and the funds were returned. Fiore (P) and Gipson (P) filed a tort suit against Walden (D) in federal district court in Nevada, asserting numerous claims under *Bivens v. Six Unknown Fed. Narcotics Agents*, 403 U.S. 388 (1971). The district court dismissed the suit, finding the Georgia search and seizure did not establish a basis to exercise personal jurisdiction in Nevada. The court of appeals reversed, holding the district court could properly exercise jurisdiction because, although the search and seizure alone could not support jurisdiction, Walden (D) had submitted the false probable cause affidavit with the knowledge it would affect persons with significant Nevada connections. The United States Supreme Court granted certiorari.

ISSUE: May a court sitting in one state exercise personal jurisdiction over a defendant who is in another state, where the only connection with the state in which the court sits is that the defendant commits an intentional tort that he knows will cause harm to an individual residing in that state?

HOLDING AND DECISION: (Thomas, J.) No. A court sitting in one state may not exercise personal jurisdiction over a defendant who is in another state, where the only connection with the state in which the court sits is that the defendant commits an intentional tort that he knows will cause harm to an individual residing in that state. The Fourteenth Amendment's Due Process Clause constrains a state's authority to bind a nonresident defendant to a judgment of its courts and requires that the nonresident have "certain minimum contacts" with the forum state. The inquiry into the "minimum contacts" necessary to create specific jurisdiction focuses "on the relationship among the defendant, the forum, and the litigation." For a state to exercise jurisdiction consistent with due process, that relationship must arise out of contacts the "defendant himself" creates with the forum and must be analyzed with regard to defendant's contacts with the forum itself, not with persons residing there. The plaintiff cannot be the only link between the defendant and the forum. These same principles apply when intentional torts are involved. A forum state's exercise of jurisdiction over an out-of-state intentional tortfeasor must be based on intentional conduct by the defendant that creates the necessary contacts with the forum. Applying these principles here, Walden (D) lacks the "minimal contacts" with Nevada that are a prerequisite to the exercise of jurisdiction over him. No part of his course of conduct occurred in Nevada, and he formed no jurisdictionally relevant contacts with that forum. The court of appeals reached its contrary conclusion by improperly shifting the analytical focus from Walden's (D) contacts with the forum to his contacts with Fiore (P) and Gipson (P), obscuring the reality that none of Walden's (D) challenged conduct had anything to do with Nevada itself. Fiore (P) and Gipson (P) emphasize they suffered the "injury" caused by the delayed return of their funds while residing in Nevada, but precedent makes clear that mere injury to a forum resident is not a sufficient connection to the forum. The proper question is whether the defendant's conduct connects him to the forum in a meaningful way: Here, the claimed injury does not evince such a connection. The injury occurred in Nevada simply because that is where Fiore (P) and Gipson (P) chose to be when they desired to use the seized funds. Therefore, under well-established

Continued on next page.

principles of personal jurisdiction, there were insufficient contacts between Walden (D) and Nevada to support jurisdiction. Reversed.

ANALYSIS

The Court acknowledged its decision did not decide the question of jurisdiction in cases of intentional torts committed via the Internet or other electronic means, such as cases of fraudulent access of financial accounts or "phishing" schemes, saying "this case does not present the very different questions whether and how a defendant's virtual 'presence' and conduct translate into 'contacts' with a particular State." The Court did reiterate, however, that even in such cases the "minimum contacts" inquiry would serve to principally protect the liberty of the nonresident defendant, not the interests of the plaintiff.

Quicknotes

FORUM STATE The state in which a court, or other location in which a legal remedy may be sought, is located.

FOURTEENTH AMENDMENT DUE PROCESS CLAUSE Provides that protections mandated by the U.S. Constitution and observed by the federal government are equally applicable, and therefore must be observed by the States.

MINIMUM CONTACTS The minimum degree of contact necessary in order to sustain a cause of action within a particular forum, consistent with the requirements of due process.

Asahi Metal Industry Co., Ltd. v. Superior Court of California, Solano County

Tire valve manufacturer (P) v. Court (D)

480 U.S. 102 (1987)

NATURE OF CASE: Appeal from discharge of writ quashing service of summons.

FACT SUMMARY: Asahi Metal Industry Co., Ltd. (Ashai) (P) appealed from a decision of the California Supreme Court discharging a peremptory writ issued by the appeals court quashing service of summons in Cheng Shin's indemnity action, contending there did not exist minimum contacts between California and Asahi (P) sufficient to sustain jurisdiction.

RULE OF LAW

Minimum contacts sufficient to sustain jurisdiction are not satisfied simply by the placement of a product into the stream of commerce coupled with awareness that its product would reach the forum state.

FACTS: Asahi Metal Industry Co., Ltd. (Ashai) (P), a Japanese corporation, manufactured tire valve assemblies in Japan, selling some of them to Cheng Shin, a Taiwanese company, which incorporated them into the motorcycles it manufactured. Zurcher was seriously injured in a motorcycle accident and a companion was killed. He sued Cheng Shin, alleging the motorcycle tire manufactured by Cheng Shin was defective. Cheng Shin sought indemnity from Asahi (P), and the main action settled. Asahi (P) moved to quash service of summons, contending that jurisdiction could not be maintained by California, the state in which Zurcher filed his action, consistent with the Due Process Clause of the Fourteenth Amendment. The evidence indicated that Asahi's (P) sales to Cheng Shin took place in Taiwan, and shipments went from Japan to Taiwan. Cheng Shin purchased valve assemblies from other manufacturers. Sales to Cheng Shin never amounted to more than 1.5 percent of Asahi's (P) income. Approximately 20 percent of Cheng Shin's sales in the United States are in California. In declaration, an attorney for Cheng Shin stated he made an informal examination of tires in a bike shop in Solano County, where Zurcher was injured, finding approximately 20 percent of the tires with Asahi's (P) trademark (25 percent of the tires manufactured by Cheng Shin). The California Superior Court (D) denied the motion to quash, finding it reasonable that Asahi (P) defend its claim of defect in their product. The Court of Appeal of the State of California issued a peremptory writ commanding the Superior Court (D) to quash service of summons. The Supreme Court of the State of California reversed and discharged the writ, finding that Asahi's (P) awareness that some of its product would reach California by placing it in the stream of commerce satisfied minimum contacts sufficient to sustain jurisdiction. From this decision, Asahi (P) appealed.

ISSUE: Are minimum contacts sufficient to sustain jurisdiction satisfied by the placement of a product into the stream of commerce, coupled with the awareness that its product would reach the forum state?

HOLDING AND DECISION: (O'Connor, J.) No. Minimum contacts sufficient to sustain jurisdiction are not satisfied by the placement of a product in the stream of commerce, coupled with the awareness that its product would reach the forum state. To satisfy minimum contacts, there must be some act by which the defendant purposefully avails itself of the privilege of conducting activities within the forum state. Although the courts that have squarely addressed this issue have been divided, the better view is that the defendant must do more than place a product in the stream of commerce. The unilateral act of a consumer bringing the product to the forum state is not sufficient. Asahi Metal Industry Co., Ltd. (Ashai) (P) has not purposefully availed itself of the California market. It does not do business in the state, conduct activities, maintain offices or agents, or advertise. Nor did it have anything to do with Cheng Shin's distribution system, which brought the tire valve assembly to California. Assertion of jurisdiction based on these facts exceeds the limits of due process. [The Court went on to consider the burden of defense on Asahi (P) and the slight interests of the state and Zurcher, finding the assertion of jurisdiction unreasonable and unfair.] Reversed and remanded.

CONCURRENCE: (Brennan, J.) The state supreme court correctly concluded that the stream of commerce theory, without more, has satisfied minimum contacts in most courts that have addressed the issue, and it has been preserved in the decision of this Court.

CONCURRENCE: (Stevens, J.) The minimum contacts analysis is unnecessary; the Court has found by weighing the appropriate factors that jurisdiction under these facts is unreasonable and unfair.

Continued on next page.

ANALYSIS

Justice Brennan's concurrence is quite on point in criticizing the plurality for its characterization that this case involves the act of a consumer in bringing the product within the forum state. The argument presented in *World-Wide Volkswagen Corp. v. Woodson,* 444 U.S. 286 (1980), cited by the plurality, seems more applicable to distributors and retailers than to manufacturers of component parts.

Quicknotes

DUE PROCESS CLAUSE Clauses, found in the Fifth and Fourteenth Amendments to the United States Constitution, providing that no person shall be deprived of "life, liberty, or property, without due process of law."

FORUM STATE The state in which a court, or other location in which a legal remedy may be sought, is located.

INDEMNITY The duty of a party to compensate another for damages sustained.

MINIMUM CONTACTS The minimum degree of contact necessary in order to sustain a cause of action within a particular forum, consistent with the requirements of due process.

PEREMPTORY WRIT Writ directing the sheriff to have the defendant appear before the court so long as the plaintiff has provided adequate security in order to prosecute the action.

QUASH To vacate, annul, void.

J. McIntyre Machinery, Ltd. v. Nicastro

Product manufacturer (D) v. Injured worker (P)

131 S. Ct. 2780 (2011)

NATURE OF CASE: Appeal of judgment by state supreme court.

FACT SUMMARY: A person who was injured when he used a piece of heavy machinery sued the foreign manufacturer in New Jersey state court. The company disputed the state's jurisdiction.

RULE OF LAW

In products liability cases, the "stream-of-commerce" doctrine cannot displace the general rule that the exercise of judicial power is not lawful unless the defendant purposefully avails itself of the privilege of conducting activities within the forum state, thus invoking the benefits and protections of its laws.

FACTS: Robert Nicastro (P) injured his hand while using a metal-shearing machine that was manufactured by J. McIntyre Machinery, Ltd. (J. McIntyre) (D). The machine was manufactured in England, where J. McIntyre (D) is incorporated and operates, and the injury occurred in New Jersey. Nicastro (P) filed suit in New Jersey. The New Jersey Supreme Court found that it had jurisdiction over J. McIntyre (D) because J. McIntyre (D) machines were sold in the United States, the company attended annual conventions for the scrap recycling industry to advertise, four machines were identified in New Jersey, and J. McIntyre (D) guided advertising and sales efforts for the U.S. distributor. J. McIntyre (D) appealed.

ISSUE: In products liability cases, can the "stream-of-commerce" doctrine displace the general rule that the exercise of judicial power is not lawful unless the defendant purposefully avails itself of the privilege of conducting activities within the forum state, thus invoking the benefits and protections of its laws?

HOLDING AND DECISION: (Kennedy, J.) No. In products liability cases, the "stream-of-commerce" doctrine cannot displace the general rule that the exercise of judicial power is not lawful unless the defendant purposefully avails itself of the privilege of conducting activities within the forum state, thus invoking the benefits and protections of its laws. The Supreme Court of New Jersey held that New Jersey's courts can exercise jurisdiction over a foreign manufacturer of a product as long as the manufacturer knows or reasonably should know that its products are distributed through a nationwide distribution system that might lead to those products being sold in any of the fifty states. That rule is from *Asahi Metal Industry Co. v. Superior Court of Cal, Solano County*, 480 U.S. 102 (1987). Based on that test, the court concluded that the British manufacturer of scrap metal machines was subject to New Jersey jurisdiction, even though the company had at no time advertised in, sent goods to, or in any way targeted the state. Those who live or operate primarily outside a state have a due process right not to be subjected to judgment in its courts, as a general rule. Where the individual or corporation explicitly consents to jurisdiction, is present in a state at the time a suit starts, is a citizen or has a domicile within the state, or is incorporated in the state, jurisdiction is proper, because all of those situations indicate an intent to submit to the laws of the state. The stream-of-commerce exception to the general rule refers to the movement of goods from manufacturers through distributors to consumers, and advocates of the exception argue that the placement of goods into the stream of commerce with the expectation that they will be purchased by consumers indicates purposeful availment. But the exception only holds where the activities manifest an intention to submit to the power of the sovereign. In this case, J. McIntyre Machinery, Ltd. (J. McIntyre) (D) directed marketing and sales efforts at the United States but not directly to New Jersey, and because of that, a federal court might have jurisdiction, but a New Jersey state court does not. It is J. McIntyre's (D) purposeful contacts with New Jersey, not with the United States, that are relevant. Because J. McIntyre has not engaged in conduct purposefully directed at New Jersey, New Jersey state courts did not have jurisdiction to hear the case. Reversed.

CONCURRENCE: (Breyer, J.) The judgment is correct, but it is determined by precedent. There is no reason to construct new general rules that limit jurisdiction, since on basis of existing precedent the case can be decided. No precedent finds that a single isolated sale, even if accompanied by the sales here, is sufficient. Nicastro (P) failed to meet his burden of showing that it was constitutionally proper to exercise jurisdiction over petitioner J. McIntyre (D).

DISSENT: (Ginsburg, J.) J. McIntyre (D) wanted to establish a market for its product in the United States and took steps to do so. Where in the United States buyers of the product live or operate is irrelevant to the manufacturer. The company simply wants to sell its product in

Continued on next page.

the United States. Under *International Shoe*, 326 U.S. 310 (1945), personal jurisdiction is established.

ANALYSIS

The absence of a majority opinion makes it difficult to identify a reliable rule: Three justices voted to reverse on the basis of a new rule that limits jurisdiction more severely than precedent; three voted to reverse on the basis of precedent, with making a new rule; and three voted to affirm on the basis of precedent.

Quicknotes

FORUM STATE The state in which a court, or other location in which a legal remedy may be sought, is located.

JURISDICTION The authority of a court to hear and declare judgment in respect to a particular matter.

Bristol-Myers Squibb Co. v. Superior Court of California

Corporation (D) v. Class of individuals (P)

137 S. Ct. 1773 (2017)

NATURE OF CASE: Appeal from the California Supreme Court's decision in favor of the plaintiffs.

FACT SUMMARY: More than 600 plaintiffs alleged they suffered physical injuries caused by a drug, Plavix, manufactured by Bristol-Myers Squibb (D), including 592 residents of other states.

RULE OF LAW

For a state court to exercise specific jurisdiction over a claim, the lawsuit must arise out of or relate to the defendant's contacts with the state.

FACTS: More than 600 plaintiffs alleged they suffered physical injuries caused by a drug, Plavix, a blood thinning pharmaceutical, manufactured by Bristol-Myers Squibb (BMS) (D). The cases were all filed in California Superior Court. The plaintiffs included 86 residents of California and 592 residents of thirty-three other states. BMS (D) is incorporated in Delaware and headquartered in New York. BMS (D) does have 400 employees working in California, including 250 sales representatives. Between 2007 and 2012, BMS (D) took in over $900 million in sales from Plavix. Significantly, the 592 residents of the other states did not allege they obtained Plavix in California or from a source in California. They did not claim they were injured in California nor did they receive any medical treatment in the state. After initial proceedings at the lower court levels, the California Supreme Court eventually decided that the California courts had specific jurisdiction over the claims filed by the nonresidents. BMS (D) appealed to the United States Supreme Court.

ISSUE: For a state court to exercise specific jurisdiction over a claim, must the lawsuit arise out of or relate to the defendant's contacts with the state?

HOLDING AND DECISION: (Alito, J.) Yes. For a state court to exercise specific jurisdiction over a claim, the lawsuit must arise out of or relate to the defendant's contacts with the state. A state court with general jurisdiction may adjudicate any claim made against a defendant, even if all the claims arise in a different state. General jurisdiction typically applies when a corporation has its headquarters in a particular state. Conversely, specific jurisdiction over a claim only arises when there is a connection between the state and the underlying case, usually via an activity or occurrence that takes place within the state. When assessing personal jurisdiction, courts must consider several factors. These include the interests of the forum state and of the plaintiff in proceeding with the cause in the plaintiff's forum of choice, but the main concern is the burden upon the defendant. Personal jurisdiction is limited by the territorial limitations of the state. Here, the California Supreme Court improperly concluded that its courts had jurisdiction over the claims of the nonresidents simply because their claims were similar to that of the state residents. This appears to be a form of general jurisdiction that is not supported by any prior decisions of this Court. Here, there are no connections between California and the claims of the nonresidents. Those plaintiffs did not purchase the drug in California, did not take the drug there, and were not treated for any injuries in the state. Accordingly, there are no facts present to establish specific jurisdiction over the claims of the nonresidents. Reversed and remanded.

DISSENT: (Sotomayor, J.) The majority's decision will make it difficult for class actions to proceed in one particular state court. Defendant corporations will now be forced to litigate separate claims in multiple jurisdictions. Clearly Bristol-Myers Squibb (BMS) (D) availed itself of the protections of the state of California by employing 400 people in the state and selling over $900 million dollars of the product in the state. The claims of the nonresidents also relate to BMS's (D) in-state activities. The nonresidents' claims are materially identical to the actions of BMS (D) in California.

ANALYSIS

It is not yet apparent whether this decision has had a significant impact on the filing of class action lawsuits across the country. The decision clearly limits, if not bars, the ability of nonresident plaintiffs to file claims in a jurisdiction where specific jurisdiction will not be present over their claims.

Quicknotes

CLASS ACTION A suit commenced by a representative on behalf of an ascertainable group that is too large to appear in court, shares a commonality of interests, and will benefit from a successful result.

PERSONAL JURISDICTION The court's authority over a person or parties to a lawsuit.

Ford Motor Co. v. Montana Eighth Judicial Dist. Ct.

Motor vehicle manufacturer (D) v. Individuals injured or killed by defective motor vehicle (P)

141 S. Ct. 1017 (2021)

NATURE OF CASE: Appeals from judgments of two separate state supreme courts in products liability actions holding that a motor vehicle manufacturer's contacts with the respective states was sufficient to support specific jurisdiction over the manufacturer in actions brought by residents of the states alleging that defects in the manufacturer's vehicles caused in-state injury to the residents.

FACT SUMMARY: Ford Motor Company (Ford) (D), a global auto company, asserted that it had insufficient contacts with states to support specific jurisdiction over it in products liability actions involving state residents who were injured or killed by allegedly defective Ford (D) motor vehicles where, notwithstanding that Ford (D) did substantial business in the states, the particular vehicles involved had not been designed, manufactured, or first sold in the states.

RULE OF LAW

In a products liability action, there is specific jurisdiction over a company whose product is claimed to be defective and to have caused in-state injury where, although the company did not design, manufacture, or first sell the product in the state where the injury occurred, the company did substantial business in the state, including advertising, selling, and servicing the type of product at issue.

FACTS: Ford Motor Company (Ford) (D), a global auto company, is incorporated in Delaware and headquartered in Michigan. Ford (D) markets, sells, and services its products across the United States and overseas. Ford (D) also encourages a resale market for its vehicles. In each of two cases, a state court exercised jurisdiction over Ford (D) in a products liability suit stemming from a car accident that injured a resident in the state. The first suit alleged that a 1996 Ford Explorer had malfunctioned, killing Markkaya Gullett (Gullett) near her home in Montana. The representative (P) of Gullett's estate sued Ford (D) in Montana state court, bringing claims for design defect, failure to warn, and negligence. In the second suit, Adam Bandemer (Bandemer) (P) claimed that he was injured in a collision on a Minnesota road involving a defective 1994 (Ford) (D) Crown Victoria. Bandemer (P) asserted claims for products liability, negligence, and breach of warranty. Ford (D) moved to dismiss both suits for lack of personal jurisdiction. It argued that each state court had jurisdiction only if Ford's (D) conduct in the state had given rise to the plaintiff's claims. According to Ford (D), that causal link existed only if the company had designed, manufactured, or first sold in the state the particular vehicle involved in the accident. In neither suit could the plaintiff make that showing. The vehicles were designed and manufactured in other states, and Ford (D) had originally sold the cars at issue outside the forum states. Only later resales and relocations by consumers had brought the vehicles to Montana and Minnesota. Although Ford (D) had not designed, manufactured, or first sold the particular vehicles at issue in the forum states, Ford (D) did substantial business in the states, including advertising, selling, and servicing the model of vehicle the respective suits claimed was defective. Both the Minnesota and Montana supreme courts rejected Ford's (D) argument. Affirming lower courts in its state, each supreme court held that Ford's (D) activities in the state had the needed connection to the plaintiff's allegations that a defective Ford (D) caused in-state injury to support specific jurisdiction over Ford (D). Ford (D) appealed in each case, and the United States Supreme Court granted certiorari in each.

ISSUE: In a products liability action, is there specific jurisdiction over a company whose product is claimed to be defective and to have caused in-state injury where, although the company did not design, manufacture, or first sell the product in the state where the injury occurred, the company did substantial business in the state, including advertising, selling, and servicing the type of product at issue?

HOLDING AND DECISION: (Kagan, J.) Yes. In a products liability action, there is specific jurisdiction over a company whose product is claimed to be defective and to have caused in-state injury where, although the company did not design, manufacture, or first sell the product in the state where the injury occurred, the company did substantial business in the state, including advertising, selling, and servicing the type of product at issue. The Fourteenth Amendment's Due Process Clause limits a state court's power to exercise jurisdiction over a defendant. The canonical decision in this area remains *International Shoe Co. v. Washington*, 326 U.S. 310 (1945). There, the Court held that a tribunal's authority depends on the defendant's having such "contacts" with the forum state that "the maintenance of the suit" is "reasonable" and "does not offend traditional notions of fair play and substantial justice." In applying that formulation, the Court has long focused on the nature and extent of the defendant's relationship to the forum state. That focus

Continued on next page.

has led to the recognition of two types of personal jurisdiction: general and specific jurisdiction. A state court may exercise general jurisdiction only when a defendant is essentially at home in the state. Specific jurisdiction covers defendants less intimately connected with a state, but only as to a narrower class of claims. To be subject to specific jurisdiction, the defendant must take some act by which it purposefully avails itself of the privilege of conducting activities within the forum state. Additionally, as held in *Bristol-Myers Squibb Co.* v. *Superior Court of Cal., San Francisco Cty.*, 137 S. Ct. 1773 (2017), the plaintiff's claims must arise out of or relate to the defendant's contacts with the forum. Here, Ford (D) admits that it has purposefully availed itself of the privilege of conducting activities in both Minnesota and Montana. However, Ford (D) contends instead that those activities are insufficiently connected to the suits. In Ford's (D) view, due process requires a causal link locating jurisdiction only in the state where Ford (D) sold the car in question or in the states where Ford (D) designed and manufactured the vehicle. Therefore, according to Ford (D), because none of these things occurred in Montana or Minnesota, those states' courts have no power over these cases. Ford's (D) causation-only approach is unavailing, however, because it finds no support in the Court's requirement of a "connection" between a plaintiff's suit and a defendant's activities. The most common formulation of that rule, expressed in *Bristol-Meyer*, demands that the suit arise out of or relate to the defendant's contacts with the forum. The second half of that formulation, following the word "or," extends beyond causality. So the inquiry is not whether a causal test would put jurisdiction elsewhere, given that another state's courts could also have jurisdiction, because of a non-causal affiliation between the forum and the underlying controversy, principally, an activity or an occurrence involving the defendant that takes place within the state's borders. Moreover, the Court has stated that specific jurisdiction attaches in cases identical to this one— when a company cultivates a market for a product in the forum state and the product malfunctions there. Here, Ford (D) advertises and markets its vehicles in Montana and Minnesota, including the two models that allegedly malfunctioned in those states. Apart from sales, the company works hard to foster ongoing connections to its cars' owners. All such Montana- and Minnesota-based conduct relates to the claims in these cases brought by state residents in the states' courts. Thus, because Ford (D) had systematically served a market in Montana and Minnesota for the very vehicles that the plaintiffs allege malfunctioned and injured them in those states, there is a strong relationship among the defendant, the forum, and the litigation— the "essential foundation" of specific jurisdiction. Allowing jurisdiction in these circumstances both treats Ford (D) fairly and serves principles of "interstate federalism." *Bristol-Myers* and *Walden v. Fiore*, 571 U.S. 277 (2014) reinforce this conclusion. In *Bristol-Myers*, the Court found jurisdiction improper because the forum state, and the defendant's activities there, lacked any connection to the plaintiffs' claims. That is not true of these cases, where the plaintiffs are residents of the forum states, used the allegedly defective products in the forum states, and suffered injuries when those products malfunctioned there. Also, *Walden* does not show, as Ford (D) claims, that a plaintiff's residence and place of injury can never support jurisdiction because the defendant in *Walden* had never formed any contact with the forum state. Ford (D), by contrast, has a host of forum connections. The place of a plaintiff's injury and residence thus may be relevant in assessing the link between those connections and the plaintiff's suit. The judgments of the Montana and Minnesota Supreme Courts are therefore affirmed.

CONCURRENCE: (Alito, J.) The Court's case law on specific personal jurisdiction is suitable for settling the cases at bar without any modification. Since *International Shoe*, the rule has been that a state court can exercise personal jurisdiction over a defendant if the defendant has "minimum contacts" with the forum— which means that the contacts must be such that the maintenance of the suit does not offend traditional notions of fair play and substantial justice. That standard is easily met here, given that Ford (D) has long had a heavy presence in Minnesota and Montana, and spends billions on national advertising. Because it was Minnesota and Montana residents who were killed or injured in accidents involving Ford (D) vehicles purchased within those states' borders, on those states' roads, it cannot seriously be argued that it would be fundamentally unfair to require Ford (D) to litigate these cases in those states. Ford (D) asks the Court to adopt an unprecedented rule whereby a defendant's contacts with the forum state must be proven to have been a but-for cause of the tort plaintiff's injury. Although the Court appropriately rejects that request, in doing so it recognizes a new category of cases in which personal jurisdiction is permitted, i.e., those in which the claims do not "arise out of" (i.e., are not caused by) the defendant's contacts but nevertheless sufficiently "relate to" those contacts in some undefined way. This is unwise, because to say that the Constitution does not require the kind of proof of causation that Ford (D) would demand— what the majority describes as a "strict causal relationship"— is not to say that no causal link of any kind is needed. Here, there is a sufficient link. The common-sense relationship between Ford's (D) activities and the cases at bar is causal in a broad sense of the concept, and personal jurisdiction can rest on this type of link without strict proof of the type Ford (D) would require. When "arise out of" is understood in this way, it is apparent that "arise out

Continued on next page.

of" and "relate to" overlap and are not really two discrete grounds for jurisdiction; the phrase "arise out of or relate to" is simply a way of restating the basic "minimum contacts" standard adopted in *International Shoe.* However, recognizing "relate to" as an independent basis for specific jurisdiction, as the Court does here, risks needless complications since everything can be said to be related everything else.

CONCURRENCE: (Gorsuch, J.) The majority reaches the correct result in these cases but adds confusion to the Court's personal jurisdiction jurisprudence. *International Shoe* sought to provide a bright-line dichotomy between general jurisdiction and specific jurisdiction. For general jurisdiction to apply, the defendant must be "at home" in the forum state. To trigger specific jurisdiction, the defendant must have purposely availed itself of the opportunity to do business in the forum state, and the suit has to "arise out of or relate to" the defendant's contacts with the forum state. Typically, lower court have read the second part of the test for specific jurisdiction as requiring at least a but-for causal link between the defendant's local activities and the plaintiff's injuries. Now, however, the majority pivots away from this understanding. Focusing on the phrase "arise out of or relate to," it zeros in on the disjunctive conjunction "or" and proceeds to build its entire opinion around that linguistic feature. The majority admits that "arise out of" may connote causation but argues that "relate to" is an independent clause that does not. Although the majority says that for a case to "relate to" the defendant's forum contacts it is enough if an "affiliation" or "relationship" or "connection" exists between the defendant's contacts and the plaintiff's claims, the majority fails to elucidate what these concepts mean in practice. Because these new euphemisms are not fleshed out, the lower courts will be required to figure out in litigation what is required, with little guidance from the Court. Thus, the majority's approach raises more questions than it answers. For example, how much of an "affiliation" will suffice? Not only does the majority's new test risk adding new layers of confusion to the Court's personal jurisdiction jurisprudence, but the whole project seems unnecessary because the cases could have been decided using the *International Shoe* framework. Immediately after disavowing any need for a causal link between the defendant's forum activities and the plaintiffs' injuries, the majority proceeds to admit that such a link may be present here. The majority stresses that the Montana and Minnesota plaintiffs before us "might" have purchased their cars because of Ford's (D) activities in their home states, that they "may" have relied on Ford's (D) local advertising, and that they "may" have depended on Ford's (D) promise to furnish in-state servicers and dealers. If the majority is right about these things, that would be more than enough to establish a but-for causal link between Ford's (D) in-state activities and the plaintiffs' decisions to purchase their allegedly defective vehicles. Nor should that result come as a surprise: One might expect such causal links to be easy to prove in suits against corporate behemoths like Ford (D). All the new euphemisms— "affiliation," "relationship," "connection"— thus seem pretty pointless. *International Shoe* was driven at least in part by the rise of multistate and multinational corporations that could only be incorporated in one state. Corporations that did business in many states wanted to retain the privilege of sending their personnel and products to jurisdictions where they lacked a charter to do business. At the same time, when confronted with lawsuits in the second forum, they sought to hide behind their foreign charters and deny their presence. Really, their strategy was to do business without being seen to do business. At the turn of the twentieth century, the Court supported this growth of multi-jurisdictional corporations, perhaps because enough members of the Court thought doing so would promote economic growth. However, critics of this approach questioned its fidelity to the Constitution and traditional jurisdictional principles, noting that it often left injured parties with no practical forum for their claims as well. With International Shoe, the Court sought to start over and craft a test focused on traditional notions of fair play and substantial justice. It is unclear whether this new test has achieved what it set out to accomplish. Even today, the Court usually considers corporations "at home" and thus subject to general jurisdiction in only one or two states, all in a world where global conglomerates boast of their many "headquarters." The Court has issued these restrictive rulings, too, even though individual defendants remain subject to the old "tag" rule, allowing them to be sued on any claim anywhere they can be found. Thus, nearly 80 years removed from *International Shoe,* it seems corporations continue to receive special jurisdictional protections in the name of the Constitution. Less clear is why. In any event, it may be that *International Shoe* just does not work as it was intended to because the way of doing business has changed dramatically since it was decided. When a company "purposefully availed" itself of the benefits of another state's market in the 1940s, the period during which *International Shoe* was decided, it often involved sending in agents, advertising in local media, or developing a network of on-the-ground dealers, much as Ford (D) did in these cases. Today, however, individuals conducting very small businesses can "purposefully avail" themselves of the chance to do business all over the continent after drawing online orders to their e-Bay "stores" thanks to internet advertising with global reach. A test once aimed at keeping corporations honest about their out-of-state operations now seemingly risks hauling individuals to jurisdictions where they have never set foot. It may be the majority crafted its

Continued on next page.

decision here the way it did because the old test no longer serves as a reliable proxy for determining corporate presence, and the Court's new test is an attempt at trying to create a test in today's world that will reliably assess a corporate defendant's presence or consent, and thereby promote "traditional notions of fair play and substantial justice." The issue is not that the result reached here is erroneous— no one seriously questions that Ford (D), seeking to do business, entered Montana and Minnesota through the front door, or that, when faced with the process server, it should be allowed to escape out the back. Instead, the real struggle here is making sense of the Court's personal jurisprudence and *International Shoe's* increasingly doubtful dichotomy. Hopefully, future litigants and lower courts will help the Court face these tangles and sort out a responsible way to address the challenges posed by our changing economy in light of the Constitution's text and the lessons of history.

ANALYSIS

A key takeaway from this decision is that a defendant's showing that a plaintiff's claim does not arise out of or is not causally linked to the defendant's conduct in the forum state may not be enough to establish that a court lacks personal jurisdiction if a plaintiff can show that the claim sufficiently "relates to" the defendant's conduct in the state. The Court emphasized that when a company like Ford (D) serves a market for a product in a state and that product causes injury in the state to a state resident, the state's courts may entertain the resulting suit. What this might mean is that plaintiffs bringing claims in certain industries, such as pharmaceuticals and medical and health devices, who purchased and used medical devices outside a forum state can now rely on the Court's decision in *Ford* to suggest that in-state business activities other than a defendant's manufacture and sale of a product can support jurisdiction. Thus, for example, specific jurisdiction over brand-name manufacturers for alleged injuries caused by generic drugs could now be available in an action for innovator liability, on the theory that the Court has rejected a strict but-for causation requirement for relatedness. Although this may provide courts with jurisdiction over claims relating to such industries, or involving very large companies, the Court expressly limited the scope of its holding by disclaiming any intent to address e-commerce or internet contacts and noting that "[n]one of this is to say that any person using any means to sell any good in a State is subject to jurisdiction there if the product malfunctions after arrival."

Quicknotes

BREACH OF WARRANTY The breach of a promise made by one party to a contract on which the other party may rely, relieving that party from the obligation of determining whether the fact is true and indemnifying the other party from liability if that fact is shown to be false.

DEFECTIVE PRODUCTS Products that contain a weakness or flaw in manufacture that is responsible for damages or injuries.

DESIGN DEFECT A design that is inherently flawed so that it presents an unreasonable risk of injury.

FAILURE TO WARN The failure of an owner or occupier of land to inform persons present on the property of defects or active operations that may cause injury.

FORUM STATE The state in which a court, or other location in which a legal remedy may be sought, is located.

FOURTEENTH AMENDMENT DUE PROCESS CLAUSE Provides that protections mandated by the U.S. Constitution and observed by the federal government are equally applicable, and therefore must be observed by the states.

GENERAL JURISDICTION The authority of a court to hear and determine all cases of a particular type.

NEGLIGENCE Conduct falling below the standard of care that a reasonable person would demonstrate under similar conditions.

PERSONAL JURISDICTION The court's authority over a person or parties to a lawsuit.

Burger King Corp. v. Rudzewicz

Franchisor (P) v. Defaulting franchisee (D)

471 U.S. 462 (1985)

NATURE OF CASE: Appeal from dismissal for lack of personal jurisdiction.

FACT SUMMARY: Rudzewicz (D), a Michigan resident, contended the Florida court lacked personal jurisdiction over him even though he had long conducted business in Florida and his franchise contract provided for adjudication of disputes in Florida.

RULE OF LAW

A party who establishes purposeful minimum contacts with a state is subject to that state's exercise of personal jurisdiction over him.

FACTS: Rudzewicz (D) entered into a franchise agreement with Burger King Corp. (P). Burger King (P) was a Florida corporation, and the contract held that it was to be governed by Florida law. All periodic payments for licensing and franchising were sent to Florida. Rudzewicz (D) defaulted on the obligations, and Burger King (P) brought a diversity suit against Rudzewicz (D), a Michigan resident. Rudzewicz (D) moved to dismiss on the basis that personal jurisdiction was lacking. The trial court denied the motion, and the court of appeals reversed. Burger King (P) appealed.

ISSUE: Is a party who establishes purposeful minimum contacts with a state subject to that state's exercise of personal jurisdiction over him?

HOLDING AND DECISION: (Brennan, J.) Yes. A party who establishes purposeful minimum contacts with a state is subject to personal jurisdiction in that state. In this case, the franchise contract allowed Rudzewicz (D) to enjoy the advantages of an association with a Florida corporation. This advantage was protected and governed by the laws of Florida. Therefore, Rudzewicz (D) had purposeful minimum contacts with Florida and personal jurisdiction existed. Reversed and remanded.

DISSENT: (Stevens, J.) It is a violation of fundamental fairness to force a franchisee to litigate a claim in a forum chosen unilaterally by the franchisor.

ANALYSIS

The Court cites *McGee v. International Life Insurance Co.,* 355 U.S. 220 (1957), in support of its holding in this case. In *McGee,* personal jurisdiction was found based on the single transaction involved in the case. A single insurance policy was sufficient to find personal jurisdiction. The key was that the policy was the document being sued on.

Quicknotes

FRANCHISE An agreement whereby one party (the franchisor) grants another (the franchisee) the right to market its product or service.

MINIMUM CONTACTS The minimum degree of contact necessary in order to sustain a cause of action within a particular forum, consistent with the requirements of due process.

PERSONAL JURISDICTION The court's authority over a person or parties to a lawsuit.

Rao v. Era Alaska Airlines

Maryland airline passenger (P) v. Alaskan airline (D)

22 F. Supp. 3d 529 (D. Md. 2014)

NATURE OF CASE: Motion to dismiss for lack of personal jurisdiction in action for negligence and other claims.

FACT SUMMARY: Era Alaska Airlines (Era) (D) contended a Maryland court could not exercise personal jurisdiction over it merely because, Rao and a companion—Maryland residents—had purchased Era (D) airline tickets in Maryland over the Internet for use exclusively in Alaska.

RULE OF LAW

The mere purchase over the Internet in one state by residents of that state of airline tickets for use exclusively in a second state does not satisfy the minimum contacts requirements of due process necessary to confer personal jurisdiction over the out-of-state airline in an action brought in the first state for torts that allegedly occurred in the second state.

FACTS: Rao and a companion (collectively, Rao) (P), Maryland residents, purchased Era Alaska Airlines (Era) (D) tickets in Maryland over the Internet via the website expedia.com (Expedia). The tickets, which were for exclusive use in Alaska, were sold on Expedia through the global distribution system (GDS) known as Sabre, of which Era (D) was a member. Sabre had offices in Maryland. After Rao (P) went to Alaska and used the ticket on an Era (D) flight, Rao (P) discovered upon disembarking that Rao's (P) case containing valuables and cash was missing. Rao (P) brought suit in Maryland against Era (D) for negligence and other claims. Era (D) moved to dismiss for lack of personal jurisdiction.

ISSUE: Does the mere purchase over the Internet in one state by residents of that state of airline tickets for use exclusively in a second state satisfy the minimum contacts requirements of due process necessary to confer personal jurisdiction over the out-of-state airline in an action brought in the first state for torts that allegedly occurred in the second state?

HOLDING AND DECISION: (Grimm, J.) No. The mere purchase over the Internet in one state by residents of that state of airline tickets for use exclusively in a second state does not satisfy the minimum contacts requirements of due process necessary to confer personal jurisdiction over the out-of-state airline in an action brought in the first state for torts that allegedly occurred in the second state. For the court to be able to exercise specific jurisdiction over Era Alaska Airlines (Era) (D), it must consider (1) the extent to which Era (D) purposefully availed itself of the privilege of conducting activities in Maryland; (2) whether the claims of Rao and a companion (collectively, Rao) (P) arise out of those activities directed at the state; and (3) whether the exercise of personal jurisdiction would be constitutionally reasonable. In making this determination, the court looks to the state's long-arm statute to determine if Era's (D) acts arose from an act enumerated therein. Here, Rao (P) relies on § 6-103(b)(1), which applies to a defendant who "[t]ransacts any business or performs any character of work or service in the State," and § 6-103(b)(2), which applies to a defendant who "[c]ontracts to supply goods, food, services, or manufactured products in the State." As a preliminary matter, § 6-103(b)(2) is inapplicable because it is clear Era (D) did not contract to supply any goods or services in Maryland, even assuming arguendo Era (D) entered into a contract in Maryland with Rao (P) for the delivery of goods or services in Alaska. This section has not been read to cover contracts to supply goods or services outside of Maryland, regardless of where the contracts were negotiated. The analysis regarding § 6-103(b)(2) is thornier. Rao (P) contends this section encompasses Era's (D) business transactions, since business transactions over the Internet are mainstays of the modern tourism business and Era (D) utilized its membership in Sabre to locate customers, communicate with customers and confirm customer itineraries, make reservations, and issue tickets for travel. However, Rao's (P) cause of action did not arise out of the ticket sale itself, but out of events that took place in Alaska. Thus it is not entirely clear, and the parties did not address, whether the actions of Era (D) employees in Alaska constituted "transact[ing] any business. . .in the State" merely by virtue of the fact the tickets were purchased in Maryland. Even assuming they are, the requirements of due process must be satisfied, as it is well established Maryland's long-arm statute is coextensive with the limits of personal jurisdiction set by the due process clause of the Constitution. Therefore, if the contacts at issue are sufficient to satisfy due process requirements, they will be sufficient to satisfy the long-arm statute. Accordingly, the minimum contacts test for personal jurisdiction must be applied. That test requires the plaintiff to show that the defendant purposely directed his activities at the residents of the forum and that the plaintiff's cause of action arises out of those activities. In a case such as this, where the contacts arise from the plaintiff's use of the Internet, a "sliding scale" for defining when electronic contacts with a state are sufficient

Continued on next page.

has been developed, see *ALS Scan, Inc. v. Digital Service Consultants, Inc.*, 293 F.3d 707 (4th Cir. 2002). At one end of the scale are situations where a defendant clearly does business over the Internet. If the defendant enters contracts with residents of a foreign jurisdiction that involve the knowing and repeated transmission of computer files over the Internet, personal jurisdiction is proper. At the opposite end are situations where a defendant has simply posted information on an Internet website that is accessible to users in foreign jurisdictions. A passive website that does little more than make information available to those who are interested in it is not grounds for the exercise of personal jurisdiction. The middle ground is occupied by interactive websites where a user can exchange information with the host computer. In these cases, the exercise of jurisdiction is determined by examining the level of interactivity and commercial nature of the exchange of information that occurs on the site. Under this framework, jurisdiction extends to a person outside of the state when that person (1) directs electronic activity into the state, (2) with the manifested intent of engaging in business or other interactions within the state, and (3) that activity creates, in a person within the state, a potential cause of action cognizable in the state's courts. Cases in this circuit demonstrate that personal jurisdiction will not extend to out-of-state defendants based on little more than their presence on the Internet, or where the defendants have not deliberately directed the information or other related activities towards the state. Here, Era (D) did not manifest the intent of engaging in business or other interactions within Maryland, nor was it locating customers in Maryland; rather, Era (D) was advertising exclusively in Alaska for flights wholly within Alaska, and was making tickets on those flights available on the Internet in a manner that could be accessed by potential passengers anywhere, but used by those passengers only if they first came to Alaska to board their flight. Thus, it was Rao (P) who sought out Era (D), using the Internet to reach into Alaska from Maryland, not the other way around. For these reasons, the court lacks personal jurisdiction over Era (D). The motion to dismiss is denied and the case is ordered transferred to the District for Alaska.

ANALYSIS

Personal jurisdiction may be either general or specific. To exercise general jurisdiction over a defendant, the defendant's activities in the state must be "continuous and systematic." If the cause of action arises out of the defendant's minimum contacts with the forum, the court may exercise specific jurisdiction. Although less contact is required with the forum state for specific jurisdiction than for general jurisdiction, both forms of jurisdiction require the defendant purposefully avail itself of the privilege of conducting activities within the forum state. Here, Rao and a companion (P) did not assert jurisdiction was general, and therefore the court had to determine whether (1) the exercise of jurisdiction was authorized under the state's long-arm statute and (2) the exercise of jurisdiction comported with the due process requirements of the Fourteenth Amendment. Although the court analyzed both these elements, the outcome as to both rested on the analysis of whether Era Alaska Airlines (D) had sufficient minimum contacts to satisfy due process, so that the analysis of both elements effectively melded into one.

Quicknotes

ARGUENDO Hypothetical argument.

DUE PROCESS The constitutional mandate requiring the courts to protect and enforce individuals' rights and liberties consistent with prevailing principles of fairness and justice and prohibiting the federal and state governments from such activities that deprive its citizens of life, liberty, or property interest.

GENERAL JURISDICTION Refers to the authority of a court to hear and determine all cases of a particular type.

LONG-ARM STATUTE A state statute conferring personal jurisdiction to state courts over a defendant not residing in the state, when the cause of action arises as a result of activities conducted within the state or affecting state residents.

MINIMUM CONTACTS The minimum degree of contact necessary in order to sustain a cause of action within a particular forum, consistent with the requirements of due process.

PERSONAL JURISDICTION The court's authority over a person or parties to a lawsuit.

Shaffer v. Heitner

Corporation (D) and corporate officers (D) v. Nonresident shareholder (P)

433 U.S. 186 (1977)

NATURE OF CASE: Appeal from a finding of state jurisdiction.

FACT SUMMARY: Heitner (P) brought a derivative suit against Greyhound (D) directors for antitrust losses it had sustained in Oregon. The suit was brought in Delaware, Greyhound's (D) state of incorporation.

RULE OF LAW

Jurisdiction cannot be founded on property within a state unless there are sufficient contacts within the meaning of the test developed in *International Shoe*, 326 U.S. 310 (1945).

FACTS: Heitner (P) owned one share of Greyhound (D) stock. Greyhound (D) had been subjected to a large antitrust judgment in Oregon. Heitner (P), a nonresident of Delaware, brought a derivative suit in Delaware, the state of Greyhound's (D) incorporation. Jurisdiction was based on sequestration of Greyhound (D) stock that was deemed to be located within the state of incorporation. The Delaware sequestration statute allowed property within the state to be seized ex parte to compel the owner to submit to the in personam jurisdiction of the court. None of the stock was actually in Delaware, but a freeze order was placed on the corporate books. Greyhound (D) made a special appearance to challenge the court's jurisdiction to hear the matter. Greyhound (D) argued that the sequestration statute was unconstitutional under the line of cases beginning with *Sniadach v. Family Finance Corp.*, 395 U.S. 337 (1969). Greyhound (D) also argued that there were insufficient contacts with Delaware to justify an exercise of jurisdiction. The Delaware courts found that the sequestration statute was valid since it was not a per se seizure of the property and was merely invoked to compel out-of-state residents to defend actions within the state. Little or no consideration was given to the "contact" argument based on a finding that the presence of the stock within the state conferred quasi-in-rem jurisdiction.

ISSUE: May a state assume jurisdiction over an issue merely because defendant's property happens to be within the state?

HOLDING AND DECISION: (Marshall, J.) No. Mere presence of property within a state is insufficient to confer jurisdiction on a court absent independent contacts within the meaning of *International Shoe*, 326 U.S. 310 (1945), which would make acceptance constitutional. We expressly disapprove that line of cases represented by *Harris v. Balk*, 198 U.S. 215 (1905), that permits jurisdiction merely because the property happens to be within the state. If sufficient contacts do not exist to assume jurisdiction absent the presence of property within the state, it cannot be invoked on the basis of property within the court's jurisdiction. We base this decision on the fundamental concepts of justice and fair play required under the Due Process and Equal Protection Clauses of the Fourteenth Amendment. Here, the stock is not the subject of the controversy. There is no claim to ownership of it or injury caused by it. The defendants do not reside in Delaware or have any contacts there. The injury occurred in Oregon. No activities complained of were done within the forum. Finally, Heitner (P) is not even a Delaware resident. Jurisdiction was improperly granted. Reversed.

CONCURRENCE: (Powell, J.) Property permanently within the state, e.g., real property, should confer jurisdiction.

CONCURRENCE: (Stevens, J.) Purchase of stock in the marketplace should not confer in rem jurisdiction in the state of incorporation.

CONCURRENCE AND DISSENT: (Brennan, J.) The Delaware sequestration statute's sole purpose is to force in personam jurisdiction through a quasi-in-rem seizure. The opinion is purely advisory in that if the Court finds the statute invalid, the rest of the opinion is not required. Delaware never argued that it was attempting to obtain in rem jurisdiction. Further, a derivative suit may be brought in the state of incorporation. Greyhound's (D) choice of incorporation in Delaware is prima facie showing of submission to its jurisdiction.

ANALYSIS

While the corporation could be sued in its state of incorporation under the dissents' theory, the suit is against the directors and neither the site of the wrong nor the residence of a defendant is in Delaware. The decision will only have a major impact in cases such as herein where the state really has no reason to want to adjudicate the issue. Of course, real property would still be treated as an exception.

Continued on next page.

Quicknotes

ANTITRUST Body of federal law prohibiting business conduct that constitutes a restraint on trade.

DERIVATIVE SUIT Action asserted by a shareholder in order to enforce a cause of action on behalf of the corporation.

DUE PROCESS CLAUSE Clauses, found in the Fifth and Fourteenth Amendments to the United States Constitution, providing that no person shall be deprived of "life, liberty, or property, without due process of law."

EX PARTE A proceeding commenced by one party.

FAIR PLAY NOTION Equitable notion that persons must deal with each other fairly and justly.

FORUM STATE The state in which a court, or other location in which a legal remedy may be sought, is located.

IN PERSONAM JURISDICTION The jurisdiction of a court over a person as opposed to his interest in property.

IN REM JURISDICTION A court's authority over an object so that its judgment is binding in respect to the rights and interests of all parties in that object.

MINIMUM CONTACTS The minimum degree of contact necessary in order to sustain a cause of action within a particular forum, consistent with the requirements of due process.

PRIMA FACIE Action in which the plaintiff introduces sufficient evidence to submit an issue to the judge or jury for determination.

QUASI-IN-REM PROCEEDING Proceeding in order to determine the interest of a specified person in particular property.

SEQUESTRATION ORDER A court order requiring the attachment of property or funds, pending a final disposition in the action.

Burnham v. Superior Court of California

Husband (P) v. Court (D)

495 U.S. 604 (1990)

NATURE OF CASE: Review of order denying motion to quash service of summons.

FACT SUMMARY: Burnham (P) was personally served with process while temporarily in California on business, while visiting his children.

RULE OF LAW

The Fourteenth Amendment does not deny a state jurisdiction over a person personally served with process while temporarily in a state, in a suit unrelated to his activities in the state.

FACTS: The Burnhams lived in New Jersey. After they separated, the wife moved to California. Mrs. Burnham filed a divorce action in California. At one point, Mr. Burnham (P) came to California on business. He had no other contacts with California. On this trip, he was served with the divorce action papers. He moved to quash, contending that his contacts with California were insufficient to confer jurisdiction. The trial court denied the motion, and the state court of appeal denied his petition for mandamus. The United States Supreme Court granted review.

ISSUE: Does the Fourteenth Amendment deny a state jurisdiction over a person personally served with process while temporarily in a state, in a suit unrelated to his activities in the state?

HOLDING AND DECISION: (Scalia, J.) No. The Fourteenth Amendment does not deny a state jurisdiction over a person personally served with process while temporarily in a state, in a suit unrelated to his activities in the state. It is a firmly established principle of personal jurisdiction that courts of a state have jurisdiction over persons physically present in a state. The cases decided by this Court that raise Fourteenth Amendment due process considerations are those where a state attempts to exercise jurisdiction over a nonresident who is not physically present. In a situation where the nonresident is served while physically present, no due process implication is made by service of process, no matter what the reason for his presence may be. Affirmed.

CONCURRENCE: (White, J.) The rule here is so well established that no facial or as-applied challenge can be made.

CONCURRENCE: (Brennan, J.) The plurality incorrectly emphasizes the historical acceptance of the rule. This is an incorrect approach, as this Court may strike down a well-established rule it finds unconstitutional. Rather, in any fairness analysis, it does not offend notions of fair play and justice to subject a physically present nonresident to jurisdiction.

CONCURRENCE: (Stevens, J.) The various opinions give excessive analysis to a very easy case whose result was self-evident.

ANALYSIS

United States Supreme Court jurisprudence in this area goes back to 1877 with *Pennoyer v. Neff*, 95 U.S. 714. Since that case, the Court has fashioned a rule that out-of-state service may only be made on defendants having certain contacts with the state. The present case represents a total rejection of the notion of applying the same test to a physically in-state defendant.

Quicknotes

DUE PROCESS CLAUSE Clauses, found in the Fifth and Fourteenth Amendments to the United States Constitution, providing that no person shall be deprived of "life, liberty, or property, without due process of law."

FAIR PLAY NOTION Equitable notion that persons must deal with each other fairly and justly.

FOURTEENTH AMENDMENT No person shall be deprived of life, liberty, or property, without the due process of law.

PERSONAL JURISDICTION The court's authority over a person or parties to a lawsuit.

QUASH To vacate, annul, void.

WRIT OF MANDAMUS A court order issued commanding a public or private entity, or an official thereof, to perform a duty required by law.

Goodyear Dunlop Tires Operations, S.A., et al. v. Brown et ux., Co-Administrators of the Estate of Brown, et al.

Foreign subsidiaries of U.S. corporation (D) v. Decedents' parents (P)

564 U.S. 915 (2011)

NATURE OF CASE: Appeal of state court's assertion of jurisdiction.

FACTS SUMMARY: The parents of two American boys killed in a bus accident in France brought suit in North Carolina, where the boys lived, against the tire company.

RULE OF LAW

A state may not exercise general personal jurisdiction over a foreign subsidiary of a U.S. corporation where the subsidiary lacks continuous and systematic business contacts with the state.

FACTS: The parents (P) of two American boys who were killed in a bus accident in France brought suit in North Carolina state court against Goodyear Tire and Rubber Company (D) and three Goodyear subsidiaries (D) operating in Turkey, France, and Luxembourg. The parents (P) claimed that the accident resulted from a defective tire manufactured at the Turkish subsidiary's plant. Although Goodyear USA (D) operates in North Carolina, the three foreign subsidiaries (D) have no place of business, employees, or bank accounts in the state and neither solicit nor do business in the state. A small percentage of the subsidiaries' (D) tires were distributed in North Carolina by other Goodyear USA (D) affiliates, however. The subsidiaries (D) moved to dismiss the claims against them for lack of personal jurisdiction. The trial court denied the motion, and the North Carolina Court of Appeals affirmed, holding that the court had general jurisdiction over the subsidiaries (D) because their tires had reached the state through "the stream of commerce."

ISSUE: May a state exercise general personal jurisdiction over a foreign subsidiary of a U.S. corporation where the subsidiary lacks continuous and systematic business contacts with the state?

HOLDING AND DECISION: (Ginsburg, J.) No. A state may not exercise general personal jurisdiction over a foreign subsidiary of a U.S. corporation where the subsidiary lacks continuous and systematic business contacts with the state. As stated in *International Shoe Co. v. Washington*, 326 U. S. 310, 316 (1945), and its progeny, a distinction exists between general and specific personal jurisdiction. General personal jurisdiction arises from a defendant's "continuous and systematic" affiliation with a state and permits a state to exercise personal jurisdiction over the defendant for any claim, regardless of whether the claim itself has any connection to the defendant's activities in the state. Specific personal jurisdiction arises from a connection between the state and the underlying claim and permits a state to exercise jurisdiction only with respect to that claim. In this case, the North Carolina courts conflated the two types of jurisdiction, improperly using the isolated presence of the subsidiaries' products in the state as a result of others' actions to justify jurisdiction over the subsidiaries for claims having nothing to do with those products. Reversed.

ANALYSIS

Key to this case is the distinction between two types of personal jurisdiction: general and specific. General jurisdiction is all-purpose, in the sense that it allows any claim to be brought against a defendant so long as the defendant has "systematic and continuous" contacts with that forum. Specific jurisdiction exists where there is a connection between a forum and a particular controversy, and it is limited to that controversy. In this case, only general jurisdiction was in issue: The site of the accident and the factory where the tires were made were both outside of North Carolina, so there was no connection between the state and the controversy, and specific jurisdiction was therefore not properly at issue. As to whether general jurisdiction existed, the Court focused on "stream-of-commerce," and reached the conclusion that jurisdiction did not exist.

Quicknotes

FORUM A court or other location in which a legal remedy may be sought.

GENERAL JURISDICTION Refers to the authority of a court to hear and determine all cases of a particular type.

IN PERSONAM JURISDICTION The power of a court over a person, as opposed to a court's power over a person's interest in property.

PERSONAL JURISDICTION The court's authority over a person or parties to a lawsuit.

Daimler AG v. Bauman

Foreign corporation (D) v. Foreign residents (P)

134 S. Ct. 746 (2014)

NATURE OF CASE: Appeal from reversal of dismissal, for lack of personal jurisdiction, of action asserting claims under the Alien Tort Statute and the Torture Victim Protection Act of 1991, as well as under state and foreign law.

FACT SUMMARY: Argentinian residents (P) brought suit against Daimler AG (Daimler) (D) in U.S. federal district court, asserting various claims under the Alien Tort Statute and the Torture Victim Protection Act of 1991, as well as under state and foreign law, claiming Mercedes-Benz Argentina (MB Argentina), an Argentinian subsidiary of Daimler (D), collaborated with state security forces during Argentina's 1976–1983 "Dirty War" to kidnap, detain, torture, and kill certain MB Argentina workers, among them plaintiffs or persons closely related to the plaintiffs. Daimler (D) moved to dismiss for lack of personal jurisdiction, as none of MB Argentina's alleged actions occurred in the United States, because Daimler (D) had insufficient presence in the United States, and because jurisdiction could not be predicated on the presence in the United States of its indirect subsidiary, Mercedes-Benz USA, LLC.

RULE OF LAW

Notwithstanding significant contacts that may be imputed to a foreign corporation, the corporation is not subject to general jurisdiction in a state where the corporation is not at "home," i.e., where it is incorporated or has its principal place of business.

FACTS: Residents of Argentina (P) filed suit against Daimler AG (Daimler) (D) in California federal district court, alleging Mercedes-Benz Argentina (MB Argentina), an Argentinian subsidiary of Daimler, collaborated with state security forces during Argentina's 1976–1983 "Dirty War" to kidnap, detain, torture, and kill certain MB Argentina workers, among them plaintiffs or persons closely related to plaintiffs. Based on those allegations, plaintiffs asserted claims under the Alien Tort Statute and the Torture Victim Protection Act of 1991, as well as under California and Argentina law. Personal jurisdiction over Daimler (D) was predicated on the California contacts of Mercedes-Benz USA, LLC (MBUSA), an indirect Daimler (D) subsidiary, one incorporated in Delaware with its principal place of business in New Jersey. MBUSA, as an independent contractor, distributes Daimler (D)-manufactured vehicles to independent dealerships throughout the United States, including California. Daimler (D) moved to dismiss the action for want of personal jurisdiction. Opposing that motion, plaintiffs argued jurisdiction over Daimler (D) could be founded on the California contacts of MBUSA. The district court granted Daimler's (D) motion to dismiss, finding Daimler (D) itself has insufficient contacts with California to support jurisdiction, and MBUSA did not act as Daimler's (D) agent. Reversing, the court of appeals held MBUSA, which it assumed to fall within the California courts' all-purpose jurisdiction, was Daimler's (D) "agent" for jurisdictional purposes, so Daimler (D), too, should generally be answerable to suit in California. The United States Supreme Court granted certiorari.

ISSUE: Notwithstanding significant contacts that may be imputed to a foreign corporation, is the corporation subject to general jurisdiction in a state where the corporation is not at "home," i.e., where it is incorporated or has its principal place of business?

HOLDING AND DECISION: (Ginsburg, J.) No. Notwithstanding significant contacts that may be imputed to a foreign corporation, the corporation is not subject to general jurisdiction in a state where the corporation is not at "home," i.e., where it is incorporated or has its principal place of business. Since *International Shoe v. Washington*, 326 U.S. 310 (1945), specific jurisdiction has become the centerpiece of modern jurisdiction theory. This Court's general jurisdiction opinions, in contrast, have been few. As is evident from these post-*International Shoe* decisions, while specific jurisdiction has been cut loose from *Pennoyer*'s sway (*Pennoyer v. Neff*, 95 U.S. 714 (1877)), held that a tribunal's jurisdiction over persons reaches no farther than the geographic bounds of the forum), general jurisdiction has not been stretched beyond limits traditionally recognized. As the Court has increasingly focused on the relationship among the defendant, the forum, and the litigation, i.e., the attributes of specific jurisdiction, general jurisdiction has come to occupy a less dominant place in the contemporary scheme. Taking these trends into account, even assuming, arguendo, Mercedes-Benz USA, LLC (MBUSA) qualifies as at home in California, Daimler AG's (Daimler's) (D) affiliations with California are not sufficient to subject it to the general jurisdiction of California courts. Assuming MBUSA is at home in California and MBUSA's contacts are imputable to Daimler (D), nevertheless there would still be no basis to subject Daimler (D) to general jurisdiction in California. The paradigm all-purpose forums for general jurisdiction are a corporation's place of incorporation and principal place of business. Plaintiffs' reasoning,

Continued on next page.

however, would reach well beyond these exemplar bases to approve the exercise of general jurisdiction in every state in which a corporation "engages in a substantial, continuous, and systematic course of business." Instead, the proper inquiry is whether a foreign corporation's affiliations with the state are so continuous and systematic as to render it essentially at home in the forum state. Neither Daimler (D) nor MBUSA is incorporated in California, nor does either entity have its principal place of business there. If Daimler's (D) California activities sufficed to allow adjudication of this Argentina-rooted case in California, the same global reach would presumably be available in every other state in which MBUSA's sales are sizable. The Court has never before sanctioned a view of general jurisdiction so grasping. The court of appeals, therefore, had no warrant to conclude Daimler (D), even with MBUSA's contacts attributed to it, was at home in California, and hence subject to suit there on claims by foreign plaintiffs having nothing to do with anything that occurred or had its principal impact in California. Finally, the transnational context of this dispute bears attention. It is significant that the court of appeals paid little heed to the risks to international comity posed by its expansive view of general jurisdiction, which are not embraced by other nations. For these reasons, the exercise of personal jurisdiction over Daimler (D) would be inappropriate. Reversed.

CONCURRENCE: (Sotomayor, J.) The result of the Court's decision is correct, but not its approach. Here, Daimler (D) has conceded California courts may exercise general jurisdiction over MBUSA on the basis of its contacts with California, and the Court assumes MBUSA's contacts may be attributed to Daimler (D) for the purpose of deciding whether Daimler (D) is also subject to general jurisdiction. However, the Court errs in holding these contacts are insufficient to permit the exercise of general jurisdiction over Daimler (D)—not because the contacts are too few, but because Daimler's (D) contacts with other forums are too many. In other words, the Court does not dispute that the presence of multiple offices, the direct distribution of thousands of products accounting for billions of dollars in sales, and continuous interaction with customers throughout a state would be enough to support the exercise of general jurisdiction over some businesses. Daimler (D) is just not one of those businesses, the Court concludes, because its California contacts must be viewed in the context of its extensive "nationwide and worldwide" operations. Such an approach is wrong, as it ignores the lodestar of our personal jurisdiction jurisprudence: A state may subject a defendant to the burden of suit if the defendant has sufficiently taken advantage of the state's laws and protections through its contacts in the state; whether the defendant has contacts elsewhere is immaterial. The Court instead should have reached the conclusion that exercising jurisdiction over Daimler (D) in this case was inappropriate because, no matter how extensive Daimler's (D) contacts with California, that state's exercise of jurisdiction would be unreasonable given that the case involves foreign plaintiffs suing a foreign defendant based on foreign conduct and given that a more appropriate forum is available. The new rule announced by the majority is that in order for a foreign defendant to be subject to general jurisdiction, it must not only possess continuous and systematic contacts with a forum state, but those contacts must also surpass some unspecified level when viewed in comparison to the company's "nationwide and worldwide" activities. This approach unduly curtails the states' sovereign authority to adjudicate disputes against corporate defendants who have engaged in continuous and substantial business operations within their boundaries. This proportionality approach will also be unfair to smaller businesses that do not have extensive contacts outside the forum and will not be able to be immunized from jurisdiction by such contacts, as will multinational companies and conglomerates. Additionally, this approach will create the incongruous result that an individual defendant whose only contact with a forum state is a one-time visit will be subject to general jurisdiction if served with process during that visit, but a large corporation that owns property, employs workers, and does billions of dollars' worth of business in the state will not be, simply because the corporation has similar contacts elsewhere. Finally, the ultimate effect of the majority's approach will be to shift the risk of loss from multinational corporations to the individuals harmed by their actions, since such corporations would be immunized from suit in any state, even if—and possibly because—the corporation has a massive presence in multiple states.

ANALYSIS

This decision makes clear that even "substantial, continuous, and systematic" conduct does not equate with general jurisdiction, and that for there to be general jurisdiction a defendant's activities must be "so continuous and systematic as to render it essentially at home in the forum State." By so deciding, the Court seems to steer further away from general jurisdiction in favor of specific, conduct-based jurisdiction, since an entity that will satisfy the standard announced by the Court in the decision increasingly will be the exception rather than the norm in a global economy.

Quicknotes

GENERAL JURISDICTION Refers to the authority of a court to hear and determine all cases of a particular type.

PERSONAL JURISDICTION The court's authority over a person or parties to a lawsuit.

BNSF Railway Co. v. Tyrrell

Railroad company (D) v. Estate administrator of former railroad company employee (P)

137 S. Ct. 1549 (2017)

NATURE OF CASE: Appeal from judgment of a state's highest court that state courts could exercise general personal jurisdiction over railroad corporations either pursuant to the Federal Employers' Liability Act § 56, or pursuant to state law that conferred such jurisdiction over persons found within the state.

FACT SUMMARY: BNSF Railway Co. (BNSF) (D), a railroad company, contended that Montana could not exercise general personal jurisdiction over it in actions brought by employees or their estates for injuries allegedly incurred while working for BNSF (D), but that had not occurred in Montana, since BNSF (D) was neither incorporated nor headquartered in Montana and since the amount of its business in the state did not render it "at home" in Montana.

RULE OF LAW

(1) The Federal Employers' Liability Act does not authorize state courts to exercise personal jurisdiction over a railroad solely on the ground that the railroad does some business in their state but otherwise is not incorporated nor headquartered in the state.

(2) A state court may not exercise general personal jurisdiction over an out-of-state corporation where the business it conducts in the state is insufficiently substantial or of such a nature as to render the corporation "at home" in the state.

FACTS: The Federal Employers' Liability Act (FELA), 45 U.S.C. § 51 et seq., makes railroads liable in money damages to their employees for on-the-job injuries. Nelson (P), a North Dakota resident, brought a FELA suit against BNSF Railway Company (BNSF) (D) in a Montana state court, alleging that he had sustained injuries while working for BNSF (D). Similarly, Kelli Tyrrell (Tyrrell) (P), appointed in South Dakota as the administrator of her husband Brent Tyrrell's estate, also sued BNSF (D) under FELA in a Montana state court, alleging that Brent had developed a fatal cancer from his exposure to carcinogenic chemicals while working for BNSF (D). Neither worker was injured in Montana. BNSF (D) is neither incorporated nor headquartered in Montana, although it did business there. BNSF (D) maintains less than 5 percent of its work force and about 6 percent of its total track mileage in Montana. Contending that it is not "at home" in Montana, as required for the exercise of general personal jurisdiction, BNSF (D) moved to dismiss both suits. Its motion was granted in Nelson's (P) case and denied in Tyrrell's (P). After consolidating the two cases, the Montana Supreme Court held that Montana courts could exercise general personal jurisdiction over BNSF (D) because the railroad both "d[id] business" in Montana within the meaning of 45 U.S.C. § 56 and was "found within" the state within the compass of Mont. Rule Civ. Proc. 4(b)(1), thus satisfying the requirements of due process. The United States Supreme Court granted certiorari.

ISSUE:

(1) Does the Federal Employers' Liability Act authorize state courts to exercise personal jurisdiction over a railroad solely on the ground that the railroad does some business in their state but otherwise is not incorporated nor headquartered in the state?

(2) May a state court exercise general personal jurisdiction over an out-of-state corporation where the business it conducts in the state is insufficiently substantial or of such a nature as to render the corporation "at home" in the state?

HOLDING AND DECISION: (Ginsburg, J.)

(1) No. The Federal Employers' Liability Act (FELA) does not authorize state courts to exercise personal jurisdiction over a railroad solely on the ground that the railroad does some business in their state but otherwise is not incorporated nor headquartered in the state. Section 56's first relevant sentence provides that "an action may be brought in a district court of the United States," in, among other places, the district "in which the defendant shall be doing business at the time of commencing such action." This sentence is a venue prescription, not one governing personal jurisdiction. Congress generally uses the expression where suit "may be brought" to indicate the federal districts in which venue is proper, whereas it typically provides for the exercise of personal jurisdiction by authorizing service of process. The second § 56 sentence in point provides that "[t]he jurisdiction of the courts of the United States under this chapter shall be concurrent with that of the courts of the several States." Nelson (P) and Tyrrell (P) argue that this sentence extends to state courts the first sentence's alleged conferral of personal jurisdiction on federal courts. This cannot be however since, as just discussed, the first sentence concerns federal-court venue and confers

Continued on next page.

no personal jurisdiction on any court. Judgment for BNSF Railway Company (BNSF) (D) as to this issue.

(2) No. A state court may not exercise general personal jurisdiction over an out-of-state corporation where the business it conducts in the state is insufficiently substantial or of such a nature as to render the corporation "at home" in the state. Because FELA does not provide personal jurisdiction here, and because the injuries alleged by Nelson (P) and Tyrrell (P) did not occur in Montana, the only issue remaining is whether Montana's law in Mont. Rule Civ. Proc. 4(b)(1) comports with due process requirements. The Court has previously held that a state court may exercise general jurisdiction over out-of-state corporations when their affiliations with the state are so continuous and systematic as to render them essentially at home in the forum state. The paradigm forums in which a corporate defendant is "at home" are the corporation's place of incorporation and its principal place of business, but in an exceptional case, a corporate defendant's operations in another forum may be so substantial and of such a nature as to render the corporation at home in that state. That due process constraint applies to all state-court assertions of general jurisdiction over nonresident defendants; that constraint does not vary with the type of claim asserted or business enterprise sued. Here, BNSF (D) is not incorporated or headquartered in Montana and its activity there cannot be said to be so substantial and of such a nature as to render the corporation at home in that state. Judgment for BNSF (D) as to this issue. Reversed.

CONCURRENCE AND DISSENT: (Sotomayor, J.) The Court's "at home" test should have no place in personal jurisdiction jurisprudence. Instead, the Court would do well to adhere more faithfully to the direction from the seminal case of *International Shoe Co. v. Washington*, 326 U.S. 310 (1945), which instructed that general jurisdiction is proper when a corporation's continuous corporate operations within a state are so substantial and of such a nature as to justify suit against it on causes of action arising from dealings entirely distinct from those activities. Under *International Shoe*, in other words, courts were to ask whether the benefits a defendant attained in the forum state warranted the burdens associated with general personal jurisdiction. The at-home standard produces inequities insofar as it grants a jurisdictional windfall to large multistate or multinational corporations that operate across many jurisdictions. Under its reasoning, it is virtually inconceivable that such corporations will ever be subject to general jurisdiction in any location other than their principal places of business or of incorporation. Foreign businesses with principal places of business outside the United States may never be subject to general jurisdiction in this country even though they have continuous and systematic contacts within the United States. What was once a holistic, nuanced contacts analysis backed by considerations of fairness and reasonableness has now effectively been replaced by the rote identification of a corporation's principal place of business or place of incorporation. The unjust result is that individual plaintiffs, harmed by the actions of a far-flung foreign corporation, will have to bear the brunt of the majority's approach and be forced to sue in distant jurisdictions with which they have no contacts or connections. Moreover, under *International Shoe*, there is no comparative contacts test that compares the percentage of a corporation's contacts in one state to its contacts in another state. Such comparison should be irrelevant, and the focus should be solely on the quality and quantity of the defendant's contacts in the forum state. Further, the court, although purporting to reserve the possibility of an "exceptional case," practically forecloses such a possibility where any large or multinational corporation is involved. Such a result is perverse. Worse, the majority reaches its conclusion by departing from the Court's normal practice. Had it remanded to the Montana Supreme Court to reevaluate the due process question under the correct legal standard, that court could have examined whether this is such an "exceptional case." Instead, with its ruling today the Court unnecessarily sends a signal to the lower courts that the exceptional-circumstances inquiry is all form, no substance.

ANALYSIS

As this case illustrates, the use by the Court of the "at home" test deprives courts of general personal jurisdiction over corporations that do business in the state where the amount and nature of such business is a small part of the corporation's entire business – as measured from the corporation's point of view. Here, for example, BNSF Railway Company (BNSF) (D) had over 2,000 employees and over 2,000 miles of track with Montana and earned around $1.75 million in annual revenue from the state, which when compared to the amount of business conducted by other companies in the state could be considered "substantial." Whereas the majority makes much of the fact that BNSF's (D) contacts in Montana were only a percentage of its contacts with other jurisdictions, Justice Sotomayor objects on the grounds that such comparison – or proportionality analysis – should have no place in personal jurisdiction jurisprudence. In any event, the holding is limited to general personal jurisdiction; had the consolidated cases arisen out of events occurring in or significantly related to Montana, the business BNSF (D) conducted in Montana would have been sufficient to subject it to specific personal jurisdiction in those cases.

Continued on next page.

Quicknotes

FORUM STATE The state in which a court, or other location in which a legal remedy may be sought, is located.

PERSONAL JURISDICTION The court's authority over a person or parties to a lawsuit.

VENUE The specific geographic location over which a court has jurisdiction to hear a suit.

Carnival Cruise Lines, Inc. v. Shute

Cruise line (D) v. Passenger (P)

499 U.S. 585 (1991)

NATURE OF CASE: Appeal from reversal of a grant of defendant's motion for summary judgment in an admiralty case.

FACT SUMMARY: After being injured while on a Carnival Cruise Lines (D) cruise, Shute (P) brought this action in the state of Washington, despite a forum-selection clause in the tickets providing for litigation only in Florida.

RULE OF LAW

A forum-selection clause in a form ticket contract will be reasonable and fair so long as it does not limit all liability of the carrier or avoid the right of any claimant to a trial by a court of competent jurisdiction.

FACTS: While on a Carnival Cruise Lines, Inc. (Carnival) (D) cruise off the western coast of Mexico, Shute (P) sustained an injury when she slipped on a deck mat. She filed suit in her home state of Washington, claiming that her injuries had been caused by the negligence of Carnival (D) and its employees. The passage contract tickets contained a forum-selection clause stipulating that any disputes would be litigated only in a court in the state of Florida, where Carnival's (D) principal place of business was located. The district court granted Carnival's (D) motion for summary judgment, holding its contacts with Washington constitutionally insufficient to support the exercise of personal jurisdiction. The court of appeals reversed, concluding that Carnival's (D) solicitation of business in Washington constituted sufficient contacts within the state. Carnival (D) appealed.

ISSUE: Will a forum-selection clause in a form ticket contract be reasonable and fair so long as it does not limit all liability of the carrier or avoid the right of any claimant to a trial by a court of competent jurisdiction?

HOLDING AND DECISION: (Blackmun, J.) Yes. A forum-selection clause in a form ticket contract will be reasonable and fair so long as it does not limit all liability of the carrier or avoid the right of any claimant to a trial by a court of competent jurisdiction. Without a reasonable forum clause, a cruise line could be subjected to litigation in several different fora. Additionally, such a clause dispels any confusion about where suits arising from the contract must be brought and defended. Passengers also benefit from reduced fares reflecting the savings that the cruise line enjoys by limiting the fora in which it may be sued. Finally, because the clause allows for judicial resolution of claims against Carnival Cruise Lines, Inc. (Carnival) (D) without limiting Carnival's (D) liability for negligence, it does not violate 46 U.S.C. App. § 183c. Reversed.

DISSENT: (Stevens, J.) The fact that the cruise line (D) can reduce its litigation costs, and therefore its liability insurance premiums, by forcing this choice on its passengers does not suffice to render the provision reasonable. Long before the turn of the century, courts consistently held such clauses unenforceable under federal admiralty law.

ANALYSIS

Both parties argued vigorously that the Court's opinion in *The Bremen v. Zapata Off-Shore Co.,* 407 U.S. 1 (1972), governed this case. However, the Court noted that in *The Bremen,* the Court addressed the enforceability of a forum-selection clause in a contract between two business corporations of different nations for the towing of an extremely costly piece of equipment. It was entirely reasonable to have expected the parties in that case to negotiate with care the selection of a forum for the resolution of disputes arising from their towing contract. In contrast, the passage contract at issue here was routine and nearly identical to every commercial passage contract issued by Carnival Cruise Lines, Inc. (D) and most other cruise lines.

Quicknotes

ADMIRALTY Area of law pertaining to navigable waters.

PERSONAL JURISDICTION The court's authority over a person or parties to a lawsuit.

SUMMARY JUDGMENT Judgment rendered by a court in response to a motion by one of the parties, claiming that the lack of a question of material fact in respect to an issue warrants disposition of the issue without consideration by the jury.

Mullane v. Central Hanover Bank & Trust Co.

Guardian of trust beneficiaries (P) v. Bank (D)

339 U.S. 306 (1950)

NATURE OF CASE: Challenge to state law.

FACT SUMMARY: Under a state statute, the rights of out-of-state residents who are beneficiaries of a common trust fund could be conclusively determined.

RULE OF LAW

A state may determine the rights of nonresident beneficiaries in the settlement of trust accounts if the notice provided is constitutionally adequate.

FACTS: New York allowed institutions to adopt common trust funds under which many small trusts could be combined for efficient administration. Notice of the new law to beneficiaries was by publication and by mail of the initial decision. Notice of the filing of accountings was by publication. Acceptance of the accounting by the court was a nonappealable final determination of rights. An administrator was appointed to represent the interests of all beneficiaries. Mullane (P) challenged the validity of the statute to bind out-of-state beneficiaries.

ISSUE: May a state determine the rights of nonresident beneficiaries in the settlement of trust accounts if the notice provided is constitutionally adequate?

HOLDING AND DECISION: (Jackson, J.) Yes. A state may determine the rights of nonresident beneficiaries in the settlement of trust accounts if the notice provided is constitutionally adequate. Trusts are created and administered pursuant to state law. Supervision by state courts is so rooted in customs to establish beyond doubt the right to determine the interests of all claimants, provided the procedure provides adequate due process procedures. It is immaterial whether the accounting procedure is deemed in rem, quasi in rem, etc. The paramount state interest in finally determining rights and interests in its trusts is sufficiently great as to overcome any due process challenges. The statute is valid as applied to nonresidents. However, publication alone is a reliable means of acquainting interested parties with the fact that their rights are before the courts only with respect to those beneficiaries whose interests or whereabouts could not with due diligence be ascertained. As to them, the statutory notice is sufficient. However great the odds that publication will never reach such unknown parties, it is not much more likely to fail than any of the other methods for providing notice open to legislators who try to prescribe the best notice practicable. The constitutional objections to published notice are overruled insofar as they are urged on behalf of any beneficiaries whose interests or addresses are unknown to the trustee. As to known present beneficiaries of known place of residence, however, notice by publication stands on a different footing. Even though there are exceptions, the rule is that within the limits of practicability, notice must be reasonably calculated to reach interested parties. Where the names and post office addresses of those affected by a proceeding are at hand, the reasons disappear for resorting to means less likely than the mails to apprise them of them. Reversed and remanded.

ANALYSIS

It is typical that a state may decide in rem proceedings even though it may not have personal jurisdiction over some claimants or parties. The power inheres in the concept of state sovereignty. Without the ability to render such a final determination of rights in property in the state, the integrity of state court judgments would be threatened, and no judgments would be certain.

Quicknotes

COMMON TRUST FUND Trust fund managed by a financial institution as trustee wherein funds of many estates are commingled for purposes of efficient administration.

DUE PROCESS CLAUSE Clauses, found in the Fifth and Fourteenth Amendments to the United States Constitution, providing that no person shall be deprived of "life, liberty, or property, without due process of law."

IN REM An action against property.

PERSONAL JURISDICTION The court's authority over a person or parties to a lawsuit.

QUASI IN REM A court's authority over the defendant's property within a specified geographical area.

Piper Aircraft Co. v. Reyno

Aircraft company (D) v. Crash victims' representative (P)

454 U.S. 235 (1981)

NATURE OF CASE: Appeal of reversal of order of dismissal.

FACT SUMMARY: Reyno (P) sought to prevent transfer of this action from the district court in Pennsylvania to the courts of Scotland on the ground that the law of Scotland was less favorable to Reyno (P) than the law of Pennsylvania.

RULE OF LAW

Dismissal may not be barred solely because of the possibility of an unfavorable change in law.

FACTS: In July 1976, a small commercial aircraft, which had been manufactured by Piper Aircraft Co. (Piper) (D), crashed in the Scotland highlands, instantly killing the pilot and the plane's five passengers. The airplane's propellers had been manufactured in Ohio by Hartzell Propeller, Inc. (Hartzell) (D), and it was registered in Great Britain but operated by a Scottish air taxi service. In July 1977, a California probate court appointed Reyno (P) administratrix of the estates of the passengers, and she then commenced several wrongful death actions on behalf of the respective estates in the California Superior Court. Subsequently, Piper (D) successfully moved to have the case transferred to the United States District Court for the Middle District of Pennsylvania. In May 1978, both Hartzell (D) and Piper (D) moved to dismiss the action on the grounds of forum non conveniens. The district court granted these motions after applying a balancing test and determining that Scotland was the proper locus for the trial. The court of appeals reversed, after noting that the doctrine of strict liability was not applicable in the Scottish courts. The appellate panel held that dismissal is automatically barred where the law of the alternative forum is less favorable to a plaintiff than the law of the forum chosen by the plaintiff. Piper (D) and Hartzell (D) then brought this appeal.

ISSUE: May dismissal be barred solely because of the possibility of an unfavorable change in law?

HOLDING AND DECISION: (Marshall, J.) No. Dismissal may not be barred solely because of the possibility of an unfavorable change in law. Dismissal will ordinarily be appropriate where trial in the plaintiff's chosen forum imposes a heavy burden on the defendant or the court and where the plaintiff is unable to offer any specific reasons of convenience supporting his choice. The possibility of a change in substantive law should ordinarily not be given conclusive or even substantial weight in the forum non conveniens inquiry. A plaintiff's choice of forum is entitled to greater deference when the plaintiff has chosen a home forum. Because the central purpose of any forum non conveniens inquiry is to ensure that the trial is convenient, a foreign plaintiff's choice deserves less deference. Here, although the relatives of the decedents may not be able to rely on a strict liability theory, and although their potential damage award may be smaller, there is no danger that they will be deprived of any remedy or treated unfairly. Scotland has a very strong interest in litigation. The accident occurred in its airspace. All the decedents were Scottish. Apart from Piper (D) and Hartzell (D), all potential plaintiffs and defendants are either Scottish or British. Reversed.

ANALYSIS

As the Court noted in this case, at the outset of any forum non conveniens inquiry, the court must determine whether there exists an alternative forum. Ordinarily, this requirement will be satisfied if the defendant is amenable to process in the other jurisdiction. The court must then balance the competing factors, and if the balance of conveniences suggests that trial in the chosen forum would be unnecessarily burdensome for the defendant or the court, dismissal is proper.

Quicknotes

FORUM NON CONVENIENS An equitable doctrine permitting a court to refrain from hearing and determining a case when the matter may be more properly and fairly heard in another forum.

MOTION TO DISMISS Motion to terminate a trial based on the adequacy of the pleadings.

STRICT LIABILITY Liability for all injuries proximately caused by a party's conducting of certain inherently dangerous activities without regard to negligence or fault.

WRONGFUL DEATH An action brought by the beneficiaries of a deceased person, claiming that the deceased's death was the result of wrongful conduct by the defendant.

CHAPTER 8

The Choice of an Appropriate Court: Subject Matter Jurisdiction and Removal

Quick Reference Rules of Law

Louisville & Nashville Railroad Co. v. Mottley

Railroad (D) v. Injured passenger (P)

211 U.S. 149 (1908)

NATURE OF CASE: Appeal of a decision overruling a demurrer in an action for specific performance of a contract.

FACT SUMMARY: Mottley (P) was injured on a train owned by Louisville & Nashville Railroad Co. (D) and he was granted a lifetime free pass by the railroad, which he sought to enforce.

RULE OF LAW

Alleging an anticipated constitutional defense in the complaint does not give a federal court jurisdiction if there is no diversity of citizenship between the litigants.

FACTS: In 1871, Mottley (P) and his wife were injured while riding on the Louisville & Nashville Railroad. (D). The Mottleys (P) released their claims for damages against the Louisville & Nashville Railroad Co. (D) upon receiving a contract granting free transportation during the remainder of their lives. In 1907, the Louisville & Nashville Railroad (D) refused to renew the Mottleys' (P) passes, relying upon an act of Congress that forbade the giving of free passes or free transportation. The Mottleys (P) filed an action in a circuit court of the United States for the western district of Kentucky. The Mottleys (P) and the Louisville & Nashville Railroad (D) were both citizens of Kentucky. Therefore, the Mottleys (P) attempted to establish federal jurisdiction by claiming that the Louisville & Nashville Railroad (D) would raise a constitutional defense in their answer, thus raising a federal question. The Louisville & Nashville Railroad (D) filed a demurrer to the complaint for failing to state a cause of action. The demurrer was denied. On appeal, the United States Supreme Court did not look at the issue raised by the litigants but on their own motion raised the issue of whether the federal courts had jurisdiction to hear the case.

ISSUE: Does alleging an anticipated constitutional defense in the complaint give a federal court jurisdiction if there is no diversity of citizenship between the litigants?

HOLDING AND DECISION: (Moody, J.) No. Alleging an anticipated constitutional defense in the complaint does not give a federal court jurisdiction if there is no diversity of citizenship between the litigants. The Supreme Court reversed the lower court's ruling and remitted the case to that court with instructions to dismiss the suit for want of jurisdiction. Neither party to the litigation alleged that the federal court had jurisdiction in this case, and neither party challenged the jurisdiction of the federal court to hear the case. Because the jurisdiction of the circuit court is defined and limited by statute, the Supreme Court stated that it is their duty to see that such jurisdiction is not exceeded. Both parties to the litigation were citizens of Kentucky, and so there was no diversity of citizenship. The only way that the federal court could have jurisdiction in this case would be if there was a federal question involved. Mottley (P) did allege in his complaint that the Louisville & Nashville Railroad (D) based its refusal to renew the free pass on a federal statute. Mottley (P) then attempted to allege information that would defeat the defense of the Louisville & Nashville Railroad (D). This is not sufficient. The plaintiff's complaint must be based upon the federal laws of the Constitution to confer jurisdiction on the federal courts. Mottley's (P) cause of action was not based on any federal laws or constitutional privileges; it was based on a contract. Even though it is evident that a federal question will be brought up at the trial, plaintiff's cause of action must be based on a federal statute or the Constitution in order to have a federal question that would grant jurisdiction to the federal courts. Reversed and remanded.

ANALYSIS

If Mottley (P) could have alleged that he was basing his action on a federal right, it would have been enough to give the federal court jurisdiction. The federal court would have had to exercise jurisdiction at least long enough to determine whether there actually was such a right. If the federal court ultimately concludes that the claimed federal right does not exist, the complaint would be dismissed for failure to state a claim upon which relief can be granted rather than for lack of jurisdiction. The court has the power to determine the issue of subject matter jurisdiction on its own motion, as it did in this case. Subject matter jurisdiction can be challenged at any stage of the proceeding.

Quicknotes

DEMURRER The assertion that the opposing party's pleadings are insufficient and that the demurring party should not be made to answer.

DIVERSITY OF CITIZENSHIP Parties are citizens of different states, or one party is an alien; a factor, along with a

Continued on next page.

statutorily set dollar value of the matter in controversy, that allows a federal district court to exercise its authority to hear a lawsuit based on diversity jurisdiction.

JURISDICTION The authority of a court to hear and declare judgment in respect to a particular matter.

SPECIFIC PERFORMANCE An equitable remedy whereby the court requires the parties to perform their obligations pursuant to a contract.

Gunn v. Minton

Attorney (D) v. Client (P)

568 U.S. 251 (2013)

NATURE OF CASE: Appeal from a state supreme court decision finding a state law attorney malpractice case involving a question of federal patent law belonged in federal court as opposed to state court.

FACT SUMMARY: Minton (P) sued Gunn (D) in state court alleging Gunn (D) committed attorney malpractice while representing Minton (P) in a prior patent lawsuit.

RULE OF LAW

A state-law claim may be adjudicated in federal court if the state-law claim necessarily raises a stated federal issue that is actually disputed and substantial, and the federal court's hearing of the case does not disturb the congressionally mandated balance of federal and state judicial responsibilities.

FACTS: Minton (P) sued Gunn (D) in state court, alleging Gunn (D) committed legal malpractice while representing Minton (P) in a prior patent lawsuit in federal court. The specific claim was that Gunn (D) failed to raise an "experimental use" exception under federal patent law. In that prior case, Minton's (P) patent was found invalid. In the legal malpractice action, the state trial court and an intermediate state appellate court found the case involved only a state law issue. The Texas Supreme Court reversed on the ground the case belonged in federal court because it involved a determination of a federal patent law issue. The United States Supreme Court granted Gunn's (D) petition for review.

ISSUE: May a state law claim be adjudicated in federal court if the state-law claim necessarily raises a stated federal issue that is actually disputed and substantial, and the federal court's hearing of the case does not disturb the congressionally mandated balance of federal and state judicial responsibilities?

HOLDING AND DECISION: (Roberts, C.J.) Yes. A state-law claim may be adjudicated in federal court if the state-law claim necessarily raises a stated federal issue that is actually disputed and substantial, and the federal court's hearing of the case does not disturb the congressionally mandated balance of federal and state judicial responsibilities. Typically, cases arise under federal law when federal law creates the cause of action being adjudicated. Here, Minton's (P) malpractice claim does not arise under federal law. However, resolution of federal patent law issues is necessary to resolution of the malpractice action. Also, an issue of federal law, whether Gunn (D) could have argued the experimental use exception, is an actually disputed issue in this case. That particular determination will resolve the state law legal malpractice claim. However, the federal issue presented is not substantial in the relevant sense. The issue must not be substantial just to the parties involved in the case but to the federal system as a whole. Here, because of the hypothetical nature of the legal malpractice case, the outcome of that state law claim will not change the real world result that Minton's (P) patent was found invalid. In addition, a state court's determination of the case within a case, i.e., the federal patent law question, will carry little precedential value in a federal forum. It follows from the foregoing that Minton (P) does not meet the necessary fourth requirement, which is concerned with the appropriate federal-state balance. There is no reason to suppose Congress meant to bar from state courts state legal malpractice claims simply because they require resolution of a hypothetical patent issue. Moreover, state courts have a special interest in maintaining the professional levels of their licensed professional attorneys. Accordingly, because there is no substantial federal issue involved, the state court should retain subject matter jurisdiction over this case. Reversed and remanded.

ANALYSIS

Any time a federal court is presented with a case involving only a state law claim, the judge will review the case carefully to determine if subject matter jurisdiction is appropriate. In this case, there was no dispute the legal malpractice case turned on the determination of the federal patent law issue. The United States Supreme Court found the federal issue was not substantial because the outcome of the case would not overturn the prior federal court's decision regarding Minton's (P) patent. Federal courts are also not bound by state court decisions arising from attorney malpractice cases involving federal patents.

Quicknotes

CAUSE OF ACTION A fact or set of facts the occurrence of which entitles a party to seek judicial relief.

FEDERAL COURT JURISDICTION The authority of the federal courts to hear and determine in the first instance matters pertaining to the federal Constitution, federal law, or treaties of the United States.

Ceglia v. Zuckerberg

Alleged contracting party (P) v. Alleged contracting party (D)

772 F. Supp. 2d 453 (W.D.N.Y. 2011)

NATURE OF CASE: Motion to remand breach of contract action from federal court to state court.

FACT SUMMARY: Ceglia (P), who brought a breach of contract action against Zuckerberg (D) and Facebook, Inc. (D) that had been removed to federal court, moved to remand the action to state court, contending that he and Zuckerberg (D) were both domiciled in New York so there was no diversity jurisdiction. Zuckerberg (D) asserted that, in fact, he was a California domiciliary.

RULE OF LAW

For diversity jurisdiction purposes, the presumption that a party's prior domicile will continue until a change has occurred is rebutted where there is ample evidence that the party has changed domicile.

FACTS: In 2010, Ceglia (P), a New York domiciliary, brought a breach of contract action in New York state court against Facebook, Inc. (D), a Delaware corporation with its principal place of business in Palo Alto, California, and Zuckerberg (D), the company's founder, chairman, and CEO. The defendants removed the action to federal district court on the basis of diversity jurisdiction. Ceglia (P) moved to remand, alleging that diversity was lacking because, he alleged, Zuckerberg (D) was domiciled in New York, where his parents reside. In a prior unrelated proceeding, Zuckerberg (D) had asserted New York domicile as of 2004 when that action was filed. At the time, Zuckerberg (D) had just completed his sophomore year at Harvard University, had spent the summer of 2004 in California, and had decided to take a temporary leave of absence from Harvard. At the time, he represented to the court that, despite his temporary residency in California, he intended to return to New York after graduating from Harvard. Based upon those representations, the court determined that Zuckerberg's (D) domicile was New York. However, as a result of Facebook's (D) immense and extremely rapid growth from a start-up to a multi-billion-dollar global company, Zuckerberg (D) never returned to Harvard or New York. Instead, he remained in California and has never left, and he provided a sworn affidavit that he intends to live in California indefinitely. Ceglia (P) countered that Zuckerberg (D) had failed to show his intent to be a California domiciliary, and therefore the law presumed he was still a New York domiciliary. Alternatively, Ceglia (P) argued that jurisdictional discovery and a hearing were necessary to ascertain Zuckerberg's (D) true domicile.

ISSUE: For diversity jurisdiction purposes, is the presumption that a party's prior domicile will continue until a change has occurred be rebutted where there is ample evidence that the party has changed domicile?

HOLDING AND DECISION: (Arcara, J.) Yes. For diversity jurisdiction purposes, the presumption that a party's prior domicile will continue until a change has occurred is rebutted where there is ample evidence that the party has changed domicile. Diversity jurisdiction exists where the parties are citizens of different states and the amount in controversy exceeds $75,000. There must be complete diversity, which means that each plaintiff's citizenship must be different from the citizenship of each defendant. Thus, if Zuckerberg (D) is a citizen of New York, as Ceglia (P) contends, then diversity would be lacking because both the plaintiff and one of the defendants would be from the same state. A person's citizenship for purposes of diversity is based upon his domicile, which is determined as of the date the complaint is filed. Domicile is the place where a person has his true fixed home and principal establishment and to which, whenever he is absent, he has the intention of returning. A person can have multiple residences but only one domicile. A person's domicile, once established, is presumed to continue absent evidence that it has been changed. Courts consider the following, non-exhaustive, objective indicators to ascertain domiciliary intent: current residence; voting registration and voting practices; location of personal and real property; location of brokerage and bank accounts; membership in unions, fraternal organizations, churches, clubs, and other associations; place of employment or business; driver's license and automobile registration; and payment of taxes. Here, those objective indicators support Zuckerberg's (D) claim of California domicile. He currently resides in California and has done so continuously since the summer of 2004. He has no other residences. He does not own real property in New York, California, or elsewhere. In 2007, he purchased and registered a vehicle in California. He does not own or lease any other vehicles. He has paid California resident income taxes since 2004. He lists his California residence on his federal income tax returns. He has not filed taxes in any state other than California since 2004. Since at least 2007, he has been registered to vote in California and has voted in California. He possesses a valid California driver's license issued in 2006. His bank and brokerage accounts

Continued on next page.

list his California residence and his investment advisors are located in California. Zuckerberg (D) receives his mail at a California post office box and at his Facebook office. Most significantly, however, he is the owner, founder, and CEO of a multibillion-dollar corporation with over 1,600 employees and a principal place of business within walking distance to his current residence in Palo Alto, California. Together, these facts overwhelmingly show that as of the date Ceglia (P) filed his complaint, Zuckerberg (D) had changed his domicile to California and intends to remain there indefinitely. To support his motion, Ceglia (P) cites what he perceives as a "dizzying array of zip codes" used by Zuckerberg (D). However, that Zuckerberg (D) may use different addresses for different purposes provides no support for that position where, as here, each zip code begins with a Northern California prefix. Moreover, Ceglia (P) also claims that Zuckerberg's (D) assertion of California domicile is not credible in light of his prior claim of New York domicile. Merely because Zuckerberg (D) was domiciled in New York in 2004 does not preclude a finding of California domicile as of 2010. In 2004, Zuckerberg (D) was a 20–year old college student from New York who had decided to spend the summer of his sophomore year in California. Although he had originally intended to return to Harvard at the end of that summer, events occurred causing him to alter that plan. By August 2004, Facebook experienced significant growth and a $500,000 investment. At that point, Zuckerberg (D) decided to take a temporary leave of absence from Harvard. Even then, however, he ultimately intended to return to Harvard to obtain his undergraduate degree. Over the next year, Facebook (D) grew rapidly and by 2005, it had received $12.7 million in funding and had over 5 million users. That growth continued. In 2006, it had grown to 12 million users and had raised $27.5 million. Zuckerberg (D) claims that at some point in 2006, he decided not to return to Harvard or to New York. Instead, he decided to remain in California to run Facebook (D). By 2007, Facebook (D) had grown to over 50 million users. As of 2010, when Ceglia's (D) action was filed, Facebook (D) had over 500 million active users and employed over 1,600 people. It is simply incomprehensible to believe that Zuckerberg (D) intends to abandon his life, friends, and daily management of his multibillion-dollar company to return to New York and live near his parents. Although the law presumes that a prior domicile will continue until a change has occurred, there is ample evidence of Zuckerberg's (D) change in domicile. The evidence of this change is so overwhelming that there is no need for a hearing on the issue. Motion denied.

ANALYSIS

As this case illustrates, to effect a change in domicile, two elements are required: (1) residence in a new domicile and (2) the intention to remain there indefinitely. A person asserting a change in domicile bears the burden of proving it by clear and convincing evidence. In determining whether that burden has been met, a court will consider the totality of the circumstances. Here, based on all the evidence and circumstances, it seems the evidence was indeed overwhelming that Zuckerberg (D) had, in fact, changed his domicile.

Quicknotes

BREACH OF CONTRACT Unlawful failure by a party to perform its obligations pursuant to contract.

DIVERSITY JURISDICTION The authority of a federal court to hear and determine cases involving parties who are of different states and an amount in controversy greater than a statutorily set amount.

DOMICILE A person's permanent home or principal establishment to which he has an intention of returning when he is absent therefrom.

Hicks v. Leslie Feely Fine Arts, LLC and John Doe

Art painter (P) v. Art gallery (D) and painting purchaser (D)

1:20-cv-1991(ER) (S.D.N.Y. March 16, 2021)

NATURE OF CASE: Motion pursuant to Fed. R. Civ. P. 12(b)(1) for lack of subject matter in action for conversion and replevin.

FACT SUMMARY: Marianne Hicks (P), an abstract painter, alleged that she was the painter of a painting (the Painting) sold by Leslie Feely Fine Art, LLC (the Gallery) to a buyer, John Doe (D), as a work of the renowned artist Friedel Dzubas. Accordingly, she brought suit for conversion and replevin against these parties, seeking the return of the Painting to her. The Gallery (D) moved to dismiss under Fed. R. Civ. P. 12(b)(1) for lack of subject matter jurisdiction, contending that Hicks (P) could not satisfy the over $75,000 jurisdictional amount.

RULE OF LAW

Where asserted damages in a federal diversity action relate to sui generis property that is claimed to be worth more than $75,000, thus meeting the jurisdictional amount, and it cannot be determined with certainty that the property does not have such value, it is not proper to dismiss the action on a motion under Fed. R. Civ. P. 12(b)(1) for lack of subject matter jurisdiction.

FACTS: Friedel Dzubas was a renowned abstract expressionist painter whose award-winning work was widely celebrated in the 1950s and 1960s and whose paintings sold for hundreds of thousands of dollars. Marianne Hicks (P) met Dzubas when he was 65 years old and Hicks (P) was 26 years old, and they entered a romantic relationship that would span 11 years. When they met, Hicks (P) was an art student, and later became an abstract painter. In 1981, Hicks (P) allegedly created a painting (the Painting), and around a year later the couple began living together in Cambridge, Massachusetts. Hicks (P) brought the Painting, which they hung near the entrance of their home. Beginning in approximately 1990, Dzubas's health began to deteriorate, and with his worsening condition, Dzubas's adult children became increasingly involved in his financial and personal affairs, encouraging him to end his relationship with Hicks (P) and pursue a relationship with another partner. In 1991, Hicks (P) was driven out of the home she shared with Dzubas by his children and new partner. According to Hicks (P), she was not given the opportunity to retrieve the Painting, and, thus, the Painting remained in the house following her departure. When Dzubas died, the Painting was included among Dzubas's artwork as part of Dzubas's estate. In 2005, Hicks (P) filed for bankruptcy, and among her listed assets were 28 of her own paintings. The market value of those paintings was listed as "unknown." In 2017, the Painting was eventually acquired by Leslie Feely Fine Art, LLC (the Gallery) and sold to John Doe (D) for $40,000. In 2020, Hicks (P) filed suit against the Gallery (D) and John Doe (D) asserting two causes of action: (1) conversion against the Gallery (D) and Doe (D) and (2) replevin against Doe (D). In support of her action, Hicks (P) adduced the attestation of Dzubas's studio assistant, Wesley Frantz, stating that the Painting could not have been painted by Dzubas in 1951 because of the type of paint used and the specific technique used to apply the paint to the canvas. Hicks (P) further alleged that she at no point relinquished ownership of the Painting to Dzubas, his children, or any other entity. The Gallery (D) moved to dismiss, inter alia, under Fed. R. Civ. P. 12(b)(1) for lack of subject matter jurisdiction, claiming that Hicks (P) could not satisfy the over $75,000 jurisdictional amount. The federal district court considered the motion.

ISSUE: Where asserted damages in a federal diversity action relate to sui generis property that is claimed to be worth more than $75,000, thus meeting the jurisdictional amount, and it cannot be determined with certainty that the property does not have such value, is it proper to dismiss the action on a motion under Fed. R. Civ. P. 12(b)(1) for lack of subject matter jurisdiction?

HOLDING AND DECISION: (Ramos, J.) No. Where asserted damages in a federal diversity action relate to sui generis property that is claimed to be worth more than $75,000, thus meeting the jurisdictional amount, and it cannot be determined with certainty that the property does not have such value, it is not proper to dismiss the action on a motion under Fed. R. Civ. P. 12(b)(1) for lack of subject matter jurisdiction. Here, Leslie Feely Fine Art, LLC (the Gallery) (D) maintains that Marianne Hicks (P) cannot satisfy the jurisdictional amount required for diversity jurisdiction because she has failed to present competent evidence that she has ever sold a painting, let alone sold one for an amount over $75,000. In opposition, Hicks (P) argues that the court cannot determine to a legal certainty that her damages amount to less than the jurisdictional minimum. Given the sui generis nature of the property at issue, the court agrees that it cannot determine to a legal certainty that the value of the Painting does not amount to $75,000 as a matter of law. Although a plaintiff bears the burden of demonstrating a reasonable probability that his or

Continued on next page.

her claim exceeds the jurisdictional amount of $75,000, there is a rebuttable presumption that that the face of the complaint is a good faith representation of the actual amount in controversy. To rebut this presumption, the defendant must demonstrate to a legal certainty that the plaintiff cannot recover the alleged amount, or that the damages alleged were feigned to satisfy the jurisdictional amount. Legal certainty in this context means that the legal impossibility of recovery must be so certain as virtually to negate the plaintiff's good faith in asserting the claim. If the right of recovery is uncertain, the doubt should be resolved in favor of the plaintiff's subjective good faith. Although ordinarily the value of goods is generally determined at the time of conversion, where the property converted is unique and irreplaceable, such as works of art, the value of damages is measured at the time of trial. Here, the Gallery (D) emphasizes that there is no evidence that Hicks (P) ever sold a painting, that in her bankruptcy filings she averred that her pieces of artwork were of "unknown" value, and that the Painting sold for only $40,000. However, although the Gallery (D) shows a lack of evidence of the Painting's value as a work by Hicks (P), the Gallery's (D) showing is not enough to rebut the presumption of good faith to a legal certainty. The artwork at issue is not one of the 28 pieces referenced in Hicks's (P) bankruptcy filing, and a 15-year-old statement alleging unknown value to artworks not at issue is largely irrelevant. Furthermore, stating that the value is "unknown" is not the same as asserting that the value is zero; a lack of evidence showing value is not dispositive of a lack of value. This approach has been taken in other cases involving unique artwork and supports the court's conclusion. In contrast, the cases relied on by the Gallery (D) are inapposite. For these reasons, as a result of the sui generis nature of the property at issue and the impossibility of determining to a legal certainty that the Painting will not meet the jurisdictional minimum at trial, the Gallery's (D) motion to dismiss for lack of subject matter jurisdiction is denied.

ANALYSIS

Federal Rule of Civil Procedure 12(b)(1) requires that an action be dismissed for lack of subject matter jurisdiction when the district court lacks the statutory or constitutional power to adjudicate the case. The party asserting subject matter jurisdiction—here Hicks (P)—carries the burden of establishing, by a preponderance of the evidence, that jurisdiction exists. On a Rule 12(b)(1) motion challenging the district court's subject matter jurisdiction, evidence outside of the pleadings may be considered by the court to resolve the disputed jurisdictional fact issues. Additionally, when evaluating a motion to dismiss for lack of subject matter jurisdiction, the court accepts all material factual allegations in the complaint as true but does not necessarily draw inferences from the complaint favorable to the plaintiff. As this case illustrates, to meet his or her burden, a plaintiff in a case involving sui generis, unique art does not necessarily have to establish that the value of the property meets the jurisdictional amount, only that it cannot be determined with legal certainty that it doesn't.

Quicknotes

CONVERSION The act of depriving an owner of his or her property without permission or justification.

DIVERSITY OF CITIZENSHIP Parties are citizens of different states, or one party is an alien; a factor, along with a statutorily set dollar value of the matter in controversy, that allows a federal district court to exercise its authority to hear a lawsuit based on diversity jurisdiction.

DIVERSITY JURISDICTION The authority of a federal court to hear and determine cases involving parties who are of different states and an amount in controversy greater than a statutorily set amount.

FED. R. CIV. P. 12(B)(1) Defense for "lack of jurisdiction over the subject matter," which defense can never be waived.

REPLEVIN An action to recover personal property wrongfully taken.

United Mine Workers of America v. Gibbs

International union (D) v. Threatened superintendent (P)

383 U.S. 715 (1966)

NATURE OF CASE: Review of award of damages for violation of § 303 of the Labor Management Relations Act and for interference with a business interest.

FACT SUMMARY: Gibbs (P) lost his job as superintendent of a coal mining company because of alleged unlawful influence of United Mine Workers (D).

RULE OF LAW

Under pendent jurisdiction, federal courts may decide state issues that are closely related to the federal issues being litigated.

FACTS: There was a dispute between United Mine Workers (D) and the Southern Labor Union over who should represent the coal miners in that area. Tennessee Consolidated Coal Company closed a mine where over 100 men belonging to United Mine Workers (D) were employed. Later, Grundy Company, a wholly owned subsidiary of Tennessee Consolidated Coal Company, hired Gibbs (P) to open a new mine using members of the Southern Labor Union. Gibbs (P) was also given a contract to haul the mine's coal to the nearest railroad loading point. Members of Local 5881 of the United Mine Workers (D) forcibly prevented the opening of the mine. Gibbs (P) lost his job and never entered performance of his haulage contract. He soon began to lose other trucking contracts and mine leases he held in the area. Gibbs (P) claimed this was a result of a concerted union plan against him. He filed suit in the United States District Court for the Eastern District of Tennessee for violation of § 303 of the Labor Management Relations Act and a state law claim, based on the doctrine of pendent jurisdiction, that there was an unlawful conspiracy and boycott aimed at him to interfere with his contract of employment and with his contract of haulage. The jury's verdict was that the United Mine Workers (D) had violated both § 303 and the state law. On motion, the trial court set aside the award of damages for the haulage contracts and entered a verdict for United Mine Workers (D) on the issue of violation of § 303, which was the federal claim. The award as to the state claim was sustained. The Sixth Circuit Court of Appeals affirmed. The United States Supreme Court granted certiorari.

ISSUE: Can federal courts decide state issues that are closely related to the federal issues being litigated?

HOLDING AND DECISION: (Brennan, J.) Yes. Under pendent jurisdiction, federal courts may decide state issues that are closely related to the federal issues being litigated. When there are both state and federal claims involved in the same set of facts and the claims are such that the plaintiff would ordinarily be expected to try them all in one judicial proceeding, the federal court has the power to hear both the state and the federal claims. The federal claims must have substance sufficient to confer subject matter jurisdiction on the court. This is the doctrine of pendent jurisdiction. The court isn't required to exercise this power in every case. It has consistently been recognized that pendent jurisdiction is a doctrine of discretion, not of plaintiff's right. The court should look at judicial economy, convenience, and fairness to litigants in deciding whether to exercise jurisdiction over the state claims. If the factual relationship between the state and federal claims is so close that they ought to be litigated at the same trial, the court ought to grant pendent jurisdiction in order to save an extra trial. If the issues are so complicated that they are confusing to the jury, then the court probably should dismiss the state claims. The issue of whether pendent jurisdiction has been properly assumed is one that remains open throughout the litigation. If, before the trial, the federal claim is dismissed, then the state claim should also be dismissed. The court went on to hold that the plaintiff could not recover damages for conspiracy under the state claim. Reversed.

ANALYSIS

This case helped clarify the law that had been established by the case of *Hurn v. Oursler*, 289 U.S. 238 (1933). That case set the rule for determining if a federal court could hear the state claim. If a case had two distinct grounds in support of a single cause of action, one of which presents a federal question, then the court could hear the state claim. But if a case had two separate and distinct causes of action and only one was a federal question, then the court could not hear the state claim. Now, the state and federal claims can state separate causes of action so long as they are factually closely related.

Quicknotes

BOYCOTT A concerted effort to refrain from doing business with a particular person or entity.

Continued on next page.

CONSPIRACY Concerted action by two or more persons to accomplish some unlawful purpose.

LABOR MANAGEMENT RELATIONS ACT Federal law prohibiting secondary boycotts.

PENDENT JURISDICTION A doctrine granting authority to a federal court to hear a claim that does not invoke diversity jurisdiction if it arises from the same transaction or occurrence as the primary action.

Owen Equipment and Erection Company v. Kroger

Crane company (D) v. Wife of electrocuted decedent (P)

437 U.S. 365 (1978)

NATURE OF CASE: Appeal from an action for damages for wrongful death.

FACT SUMMARY: Kroger (P), the widow of decedent, filed a wrongful death action against Omaha Public Power District after her husband was electrocuted when a steel crane hit a power line.

RULE OF LAW

In an action in which federal jurisdiction is based on diversity, a plaintiff may not assert a claim against a third-party defendant when there is no independent basis for federal jurisdiction over that claim.

FACTS: James Kroger was electrocuted when the boom of a steel crane next to which he was walking came too close to a high-tension electric power line. Kroger (P), the decedent's widow, filed a wrongful death action in the U.S. District Court for Nebraska against Omaha Public Power District (Omaha). Kroger's (P) complaint alleged that Omaha's negligence had caused her husband's death. Federal jurisdiction was based on diversity, since Kroger (P) was a citizen of Iowa and Omaha was a Nebraska corporation. Omaha then filed a third-party complaint pursuant to Rule 14 against Owen Equipment and Erection Company (Owen) (D), alleging that the crane was owned and operated by Owen (D) and that Owen's (D) negligence had been the proximate cause of Kroger's (P) death. While a motion for summary judgment on the part of Omaha was pending, Kroger (P) was granted leave to file an amended complaint naming Owen (D) as an additional defendant. Omaha's motion was granted, and the case went to trial between Kroger (P) and Owen (D). At trial, it was disclosed that Owen (D) was an Iowa corporation and not a Nebraska corporation as was alleged and that Kroger (P) and Owen (D) were, thus, both citizens of Iowa. Owen (D) moved to dismiss the complaint for lack of jurisdiction. The court reserved decision on the motion, and the jury returned a verdict in favor of Kroger (P). Then the court denied the motion to dismiss. The judgment was affirmed on appeal. The Eighth Circuit Court of Appeals held that the district court had power to adjudicate the claim because it arose from the core of operative facts giving rise to both Kroger's (P) claim against Omaha and Omaha's claim against Owen (D). Owen (D) appealed.

ISSUE: In an action in which federal jurisdiction is based on diversity, may the plaintiff assert a claim against a third-party defendant when there is no independent basis for federal jurisdiction over that claim?

HOLDING AND DECISION: (Stewart, J.) No. In an action in which federal jurisdiction is based on diversity, the plaintiff may not assert a claim against a third-party defendant when there is no independent basis for federal jurisdiction over that claim. Section 1332 confers upon federal courts jurisdiction over civil actions where the matter in controversy exceeds the sum of $10,000 and is between citizens of different states. Thus, it is clear James Kroger (P) could not originally have brought suit in federal court naming Owen Equipment and Erection Company (Owen) (D) and Omaha Public Power District (Omaha) as codefendants, since citizens of Iowa would have been on both sides of the litigation. Yet the identical lawsuit resulted when Kroger (P) amended her complaint. Complete diversity was destroyed just as surely as if Kroger (P) had sued Owen (D) initially. If, as the court of appeals thought, a common nucleus of operative fact were the only requirement for ancillary jurisdiction in a diversity case, there would be no principled reason why Kroger (P) could not have joined her cause of action against Owen (D) in her original complaint as ancillary to her cause against Omaha. Congress's requirement of complete diversity would thus have been evaded completely. Reversed.

ANALYSIS

The court of appeals relied upon the doctrine of ancillary jurisdiction as enunciated in *United Mine Workers of America v. Gibbs*, 383 U.S. 715 (1966). However, the *Gibbs* case differed from this one in that it involved pendent jurisdiction, which concerns the resolution of a plaintiff's federal and state law claims against a single defendant in one action. In this claim, there was no claim based on substantive federal law.

Quicknotes

28 U.S.C. § 1332 Provides for original jurisdiction in federal district court for all civil actions between citizens of different states.

ANCILLARY JURISDICTION Authority of a federal court to hear and determine issues related to a case over which it

Continued on next page.

has jurisdiction, but over which it would not have jurisdiction if such claims were brought independently.

DIVERSITY OF CITIZENSHIP Parties are citizens of different states, or one party is an alien; a factor, along with a statutorily set dollar value of the matter in controversy, that allows a federal district court to exercise its authority to hear a lawsuit based on diversity jurisdiction.

PENDENT JURISDICTION A doctrine granting authority to a federal court to hear a claim that does not invoke diversity jurisdiction if it arises from the same transaction or occurrence as the primary action.

SUMMARY JUDGMENT Judgment rendered by a court in response to a motion by one of the parties, claiming that the lack of a question of material fact in respect to an issue warrants disposition of the issue without consideration by the jury.

WRONGFUL DEATH An action brought by the beneficiaries of a deceased person, claiming that the deceased's death was the result of wrongful conduct by the defendant.

Finley v. United States

Federal Tort Claims Act claimant (P) v. Federal government (D)

490 U.S. 545 (1989)

NATURE OF CASE: Appeal from denial of pendent-party jurisdiction.

FACT SUMMARY: Finley's (P) husband and children were killed in a plane crash. In her federal suit under the Federal Tort Claims Act against the Federal Aviation Administration, she sought to include claims against certain state defendants on basis of pendent-party jurisdiction.

RULE OF LAW

The Federal Tort Claims Act does not permit the assertion of pendent-party jurisdiction over additional parties.

FACTS: Finley's (P) husband and children were killed in a plane crash that Finley (P) believed resulted from the negligence of a power company against which she brought suit in state court, alleging the negligent illumination of runway lights and negligent positioning of electric transmission lines of the power company. Subsequently, Finley (P) learned that the party responsible for maintaining runway lights was the Federal Aviation Administration, and she filed a Federal Tort Claims Act suit against the United States (D) in federal district court. A year later, Finley (P) moved to amend the federal complaint to include claims against the original state-court defendants, as to which no independent basis for federal jurisdiction existed. The United States District Court for the Southern District of California granted the motion. The Ninth Circuit Court of Appeals reversed, and the United States Supreme Court affirmed the reversal.

ISSUE: Does the Federal Tort Claims Act permit the assertion of pendent-party jurisdiction over additional parties?

HOLDING AND DECISION: (Scalia, J.) No. The Federal Tort Claims Act does not permit the assertion of pendent-party jurisdiction over additional parties. The added claims in this case involve added parties over whom no independent basis of jurisdiction exists. The relationship between the added claims and the original complaint is one of mere "factual similarity," which is of no consequence, as neither the convenience of the litigants nor considerations of judicial economy can suffice to justify extension of the doctrine of ancillary jurisdiction. The Federal Tort Claims Act confers jurisdiction over "civil actions on claims against the United States," but the Act does *not* say "civil actions on claims that include requested relief against the United States" or "civil actions in which there is a claim against the United States." The latter would be formulations one might expect if the presence of a claim against the United States constituted merely a minimum jurisdictional requirement, rather than a definition of the permissible scope of Federal Tort Claims Act actions. Affirmed.

DISSENT: (Blackmun, J.) Because congressional preference here made the federal forum the only possible one in which to hear the constitutional case as a whole, pendent-party jurisdiction should be permitted.

DISSENT: (Stevens, J.) The congressional grant of jurisdiction to hear "civil actions on claims against the United States" authorizes the federal courts to hear state-law claims against a pendent party. Forcing a federal plaintiff to litigate a case in both federal and state courts impairs the ability of the federal court to grant full relief and imparts a fundamental bias against utilization of the federal forum owing to the deterrent effect imposed by the needless requirement of duplicate litigation if the federal forum is chosen.

ANALYSIS

The Court majority made clear that due regard for the rightful independence of state governments requires that federal courts scrupulously confine their own jurisdiction to the precise limits that a federal statute (in this case the Federal Tort Claims Act) has defined. Subsequent to *Finley,* Congress enacted a new supplemental jurisdiction statute that allows for pendent-party jurisdiction unless a federal statute specifically precludes it.

Quicknotes

ANCILLARY JURISDICTION Authority of a federal court to hear and determine issues related to a case over which it has jurisdiction, but over which it would not have jurisdiction if such claims were brought independently.

FEDERAL TORT CLAIMS ACT (FTCA) Legislation that provides a limited waiver of the federal government's sovereign immunity when its employees are negligent within the scope of their employment. The government is liable if a law enforcement officer commits assault, battery, false imprisonment, false arrest, abuse of process, or malicious prosecution. The government is not liable if the claim against law enforcement officers is for libel, slander,

Continued on next page.

misrepresentation, deceit, or interference with contract. Congress has not waived the government's sovereign immunity against all law enforcement acts or omissions.

JURISDICTION The authority of a court to hear and declare judgment in respect to a particular matter.

PENDENT JURISDICTION A doctrine granting authority to a federal court to hear a claim that does not invoke diversity jurisdiction if it arises from the same transaction or occurrence as the primary action.

Exxon Mobil Corp. v. Allapattah Services, Inc.

Class members (P) v. Corporations (D)

545 U.S. 546 (2005)

NATURE OF CASE: Appeal of judgment regarding supplemental jurisdiction.

FACT SUMMARY: [Only some members of a class met the amount-in-controversy requirement to establish diversity jurisdiction, and the circuit courts were split as to whether each member's claim must meet the requirement in order for their claims to go forward, if the claims of other members of the class meet the requirement.]

RULE OF LAW

Where one plaintiff's claim satisfies the minimum amount-in-controversy requirement for federal diversity jurisdiction and another plaintiff's related claim does not, 28 U.S.C. § 1367 allows federal courts to exercise supplemental jurisdiction over the claim that is less than the required amount.

FACTS: Two cases were consolidated, and the United States Supreme Court granted certiorari to resolve a circuit split over the federal supplemental jurisdiction statute, 28 U.S.C. § 1367. The plaintiffs in the *Exxon* case are a class of approximately 10,000 gas dealers (P) who claimed that Exxon (D) overcharged them for fuel purchases. The Eleventh Circuit Court of Appeals affirmed the district court's verdict for the dealers (P) and held the federal supplemental jurisdiction statute allows a district court in a class-action lawsuit to exercise supplemental jurisdiction over class members whose claims do not meet the jurisdictional minimum amount. In *Ortega v. Star-Kist Foods, Inc.*, 370 F.3d 124 (1st Cir. 2004), a nine-year-old girl injured her finger on a can of Star-Kist tuna. The girl (P) and her family (P) sued in federal court on the basis of diversity jurisdiction. The district court dismissed the claims for lack of jurisdiction, holding that the girl's (P) and family members' (P) claims did not meet the minimum amount for jurisdiction. The First Circuit Court of Appeals reversed as to the girl (P) but upheld the district court's conclusion that none of the family members (P) satisfied the amount-in-controversy requirement.

ISSUE: Where one plaintiff's claim satisfies the minimum amount-in-controversy requirement for federal diversity jurisdiction and another plaintiff's related claim does not, does 28 U.S.C. § 1367 allow federal courts to exercise supplemental jurisdiction over the claim that is less than the required amount?

HOLDING AND DECISION: (Kennedy, J.) Yes. Where one plaintiff's claim satisfies the minimum amount-in-controversy requirement for federal diversity jurisdiction and another plaintiff's related claim does not, 28 U.S.C. § 1367 allows federal courts to exercise supplemental jurisdiction over the claim that is less than the required amount. Courts need to determine only whether they have original jurisdiction over one of the claims in a case. If they do, courts can then decide to extend supplemental jurisdiction to the other related claims. The indivisibility and contamination theories are easily dismissed. The indivisibility theory is inconsistent with the whole notion of supplemental jurisdiction, and the contamination theory is inconsistent with the amount-in-controversy requirement. The unambiguous text of the statute indicates that jurisdiction should extend to the other plaintiffs, regardless of legislative history or other extrinsic material. Judgment of the court of appeals for the Eleventh Circuit affirmed, and judgment of the court of appeals for the First Circuit reversed.

DISSENT: (Ginsburg, J.) The majority's reading of the statute is plausible, but broad. It should be read as instructing that the district court have original jurisdiction over the action first, before supplemental jurisdiction can attach. This would be a less disruptive reading of the statute.

ANALYSIS

The Court's holding greatly expands the limits of diversity jurisdiction. This case overrules *Zahn v. International Paper*, 414 U.S. 291 (1973), which held that in order for a federal court to exercise diversity jurisdiction, all plaintiffs in the case had to satisfy 28 U.S.C. § 1332's amount-in-controversy requirement. The courts of appeal had divided on the question, and the United States Supreme Court had previously failed to resolve the issue in the 2000 case *Free v. Abbott Laboratories, Inc.*, 529 U.S. 333 (2000).

Quicknotes

AMOUNT IN CONTROVERSY The value of a claim sought by a party to a lawsuit.

CLASS ACTION A suit commenced by a representative on behalf of an ascertainable group that is too large to

Continued on next page.

appear in court, shares a commonality of interests, and will benefit from a successful result.

DIVERSITY JURISDICTION The authority of a federal court to hear and determine cases involving parties who are of different states and an amount in controversy greater than a statutorily set amount.

ORIGINAL JURISDICTION The power of a court to hear an action upon its commencement.

SUPPLEMENTAL JURISDICTION A doctrine granting authority to a federal court to hear a claim that does not invoke diversity jurisdiction if it arises from the same transaction or occurrence as the primary action.

CHAPTER 9

Choice of Federal or State Law—The *Erie* Doctrine

Quick Reference Rules of Law

Erie Railroad Co. v. Tompkins

Railroad (D) v. Injured (P)

304 U.S. 64 (1938)

NATURE OF CASE: Action to recover damages for personal injury allegedly caused by negligent conduct.

FACT SUMMARY: In a personal injury suit, federal district court trial judge refused to apply applicable state law because such law was "general" (judge-made) and not embodied in any statute.

RULE OF LAW

Although the 1789 Rules of Decision Act left federal courts unfettered to apply their own rules of procedure in common-law actions brought in federal court, state law governs substantive issues. State law includes not only statutory law but case law as well.

FACTS: Tompkins (P) was walking in a right-of-way parallel to some railroad tracks when an Erie Railroad Co. (Erie) (D) train came by. Tompkins (P) was struck and injured by what he would, at trial, claim to be an open door extending from one of the railcars. Under Pennsylvania case law (the applicable law since the accident occurred there), state courts would have treated Tompkins (P) as a trespasser in denying him recovery for other than wanton or willful misconduct on Erie's (D) part. Under "general" law, recognized in federal courts, Tompkins (P) would have been regarded as a licensee and would only have been obligated to show ordinary negligence. Because Erie (D) was a New York corporation, Tompkins (P) brought suit in a federal district court in New York, where he won a judgment for $30,000. Upon appeal to a federal circuit court, the decision was affirmed.

ISSUE: Although the 1789 Rules of Decision Act left federal courts unfettered to apply their own rule of procedure in common-law actions brought in federal court, does state law govern substantive issues?

HOLDING AND DECISION: (Brandeis, J.) Yes. Although the 1789 Rules of Decision Act left federal courts unfettered to apply their own rules of procedure in common-law actions brought in federal court, state law governs substantive issues. State law includes not only statutory law but case law as well. The Court's opinion is in four parts: (1) *Swift v. Tyson,* 41 U.S. (16 Pet.) 1 (1842), which held that federal courts exercising jurisdiction on the ground of diversity of citizenship need not, in matters of general jurisprudence, apply the unwritten law of the state as declared by its highest court, is overruled. Section 34 of the Federal Judiciary Act of 1789, c. 20, 28 U.S.C. § 725, requires that federal courts, in all matters except those where some federal law is controlling, apply as their rules of decision the law of the state, unwritten as well as written. Up to this time, federal courts had assumed the power to make "general law" decisions even though Congress was powerless to enact "general law" statutes. (2) *Swift* had numerous political and social defects. The hoped-for uniformity among state courts had not occurred; there was no satisfactory way to distinguish between local and general law. On the other hand, *Swift* introduced grave discrimination by noncitizens against citizens. The privilege of selecting the court for resolving disputes rested with the noncitizen who could pick the more favorable forum. The resulting far-reaching discrimination was due to the broad province accorded "general law" in which many matters of seemingly local concern were included. Furthermore, local citizens could move out of the state and bring suit in a federal court if they were disposed to do so; corporations, similarly, could simply reincorporate in another state. More than statutory relief is involved here; the unconstitutionality of *Swift* is clear. (3) Except in matters governed by the federal Constitution or by acts of Congress, the law to be applied in any case is the law of the state. There is no federal common law. The federal courts have no power derived from the Constitution or by Congress to declare substantive rules of common law applicable in a state whether they are "local" or "general" in nature. (4) The federal district court was bound to follow the Pennsylvania case law, which would have denied recovery to Tompkins (P). Reversed.

CONCURRENCE: (Reed, J.) It is unnecessary to go beyond interpreting the meaning of "laws" in the Rules of Decision Act. Article III and the Necessary and Proper Clause of Article I of the Constitution might provide Congress with the power to declare rules of substantive law for federal courts to follow.

ANALYSIS

Erie can fairly be characterized as the most significant and sweeping decision on civil procedure ever handed down by the United States Supreme Court. As interpreted in subsequent decisions, *Erie* held that while federal courts may apply their own rules of procedure, issues of substantive law must be decided in accord with the applicable state law – usually the state in which

Continued on next page.

the federal court sits. Note, however, how later Supreme Court decisions have made inroads into the broad doctrine enunciated here.

Quicknotes

DIVERSITY OF CITIZENSHIP Parties are citizens of different states, or one party is an alien; a factor, along with a statutorily set dollar value of the matter in controversy, that allows a federal district court to exercise its authority to hear a lawsuit based on diversity jurisdiction.

FEDERAL JUDICIARY ACT § 34 The laws of the states shall be regarded as rules of decisions in trials at common law in the federal courts.

JURISDICTION The authority of a court to hear and declare judgment in respect to a particular matter.

NECESSARY AND PROPER CLAUSE, ACT I, § 8 OF THE CONSTITUTION Enables Congress to make all laws that may be "necessary and proper" to execute its other, enumerated powers.

NEGLIGENCE Conduct falling below the standard of care that a reasonable person would demonstrate under similar conditions.

PERSONAL INJURY Harm to an individual's person or body.

RULES OF DECISION ACT Provides that the laws of the several states shall be regarded as rules of decisions in civil action, except where the Constitution, treaties, or acts of Congress otherwise provide.

Guaranty Trust Co. v. York

Trust company (D) v. Injured class members (P)

326 U.S. 99 (1945)

NATURE OF CASE: Class action suit for breach of trust.

FACT SUMMARY: York (P) brought a class action suit against Guaranty Trust Co. (D) in federal court on diversity jurisdiction. The action was barred in the state courts by the statute of limitations, and summary judgment was granted to Guaranty Trust (D) on that basis.

RULE OF LAW

In all cases where a federal court is exercising diversity jurisdiction, the outcome of the case should be substantially the same, so far as legal rules determine outcome, as it would be if tried in state court.

FACTS: York (P) brought suit in federal district court in New York on behalf of a class of persons allegedly damaged by Guaranty Trust Co.'s (D) breach of trust. The suit was brought in 1942 but complained of transactions occurring in 1931. Guaranty Trust (D) was granted a summary judgment on the grounds that the action was barred by the New York statute of limitations and that this suit being heard on diversity jurisdiction was governed by the statute. The Second Circuit Court of Appeals reversed, stating that suits in equity were not controlled by the state statute of limitations.

ISSUE: In all cases where a federal court is exercising diversity jurisdiction, should the outcome of the case be substantially the same, so far as legal rules determine outcome, as it would be if tried in state court?

HOLDING AND DECISION: (Frankfurter, J.) Yes. In all cases where a federal court is exercising diversity jurisdiction, the outcome of the case should be substantially the same, so far as legal rules determine outcome, as it would be if tried in state court. Since this Court's decision in *Erie Railroad Co. v. Tompkins,* 304 U.S. 64 (1938), a considerable amount of divergence has developed over what matters are procedural and what are substantive. Since these two concepts are fluid and situation-controlled in most instances, the debate misses the underlying rationale of *Erie.* When sitting in diversity jurisdiction, a federal court is but another state court. The controlling factor is whether, by reason of application of differing federal rules, an outcome substantially different would result than if the case were brought in state court. The rules of law applied to the case cannot allow or bar recovery in the federal court where an opposite result would occur in the state court. For that reason, the summary judgment granted by the trial court is sustained. Reversed and remanded.

ANALYSIS

Guaranty Trust, which clarified *Erie,* may itself be in the process of being slowly eroded by modern courts. *Hanna v. Plumer,* 380 U.S. 460 (1965), held that where state law conflicts with the Federal Rules of Civil Procedure, the latter prevails regardless of the effect on outcome of the litigation. And in *Byrd v. Blue Ridge Rural Electric Cooperative, Inc.,* 356 U.S. 525 (1958), the Court suggested that some constitutional doctrines (there, the right to a jury trial in federal court) are so important as to be controlling over state law—once again, the outcome notwithstanding.

Quicknotes

CLASS ACTION SUIT A suit commenced by a representative on behalf of an ascertainable group that is too large to appear in court, who shares a commonality of interests, and who will benefit from a successful result.

DIVERSITY JURISDICTION Authority of a federal court to hear and determine cases involving parties who are from different states and an amount in controversy greater than a statutorily set amount.

STATUTE OF LIMITATIONS A law prescribing the period in which a legal action may be commenced.

SUMMARY JUDGMENT Judgment rendered by a court in response to a motion by one of the parties, claiming that the lack of a question of material fact in respect to an issue warrants disposition of the issue without consideration by the jury.

Byrd v. Blue Ridge Rural Electric Cooperative, Inc.

Employee of subcontractor (P) v. General contractor (D)

356 U.S. 525 (1958)

NATURE OF CASE: Negligence action for damages.

FACT SUMMARY: Byrd (P) was injured while connecting power lines for a subcontractor of Blue Ridge Rural Electric Cooperative, Inc. (D).

RULE OF LAW

The *Erie* doctrine requires that federal courts in diversity cases must respect the definitions of rights and obligations created by state courts, but state laws cannot alter the essential characteristics and functions of the federal courts, and the jury function is such an essential function (provided for in the Seventh Amendment).

FACTS: Byrd (P) was injured while connecting power lines as an employee of a subcontractor of Blue Ridge Rural Electric Cooperative, Inc. (Blue Ridge) (D). He sued Blue Ridge (D) in federal court on a negligence theory. Because he was a citizen of North Carolina and Blue Ridge (D) was a South Carolina corporation, jurisdiction was grounded in diversity of citizenship. At trial, Blue Ridge (D) offered an affirmative defense based on a South Carolina law that would limit Byrd (P) to workmen's compensation benefits by defining him as a statutory employee of Blue Ridge (D) as well as the subcontractor (thereby precluding any collateral negligence action). The trial court refused to allow the defense to be offered, but the United States Supreme Court reversed and remanded the case to the trial court for a new trial allowing the defense. Under South Carolina law, however, the issue of immunity from negligence was to be tried by a judge. Blue Ridge (D) claimed that despite the *Erie* doctrine, South Carolina law cannot be allowed to preclude his right to a jury.

ISSUE: Do *Erie* doctrine considerations require that all state determinations of rights be upheld regardless of their intrusions into federal determinations?

HOLDING AND DECISION: (Brennan, J.) No. The *Erie* doctrine requires that federal courts in diversity cases must respect the definitions of rights and obligations created by state courts, but state laws cannot alter the essential characteristics and functions of the federal courts, and the jury function is such an essential function (provided for in the Seventh Amendment). The South Carolina determination here that immunity is a question of law to be tried by a judge is merely a determination of the form and mode of enforcing immunity. It does not involve any essential relationship or determination of right created by the state. Of course, the *Erie* doctrine will reach even such form and mode determinations where no affirmative countervailing considerations can be found. Here, however, the Seventh Amendment makes the jury function an essential factor in the federal process protected by the Constitution. Reversed and remanded.

ANALYSIS

This case points up a major retreat by the Court in its interpretation of the *Erie* doctrine. The *Guaranty Trust* case, 326 U.S. 99 (1945), had stated that the *Erie* doctrine required that federal courts not tamper with state remedies for violations of state-created rights. In *Byrd*, the Court retreats, stating that questions of mere "form and mode" of remedy (i.e., trial by jury or judge) are not necessarily the province of the states where essential federal rights (i.e., Seventh Amendment) are involved. Note that the Court does not abandon the *Guaranty Trust* rationale, however (that the outcome of a case should not be affected by the choice of court in which it is filed). The Court expresses doubt that the permitting of trial by jury here will make any difference in the final argument here, since the Court first states that trial by jury is an essential right, and then states that it is really insignificant after all.

Quicknotes

DIVERSITY OF CITIZENSHIP Parties are citizens of different states, or one party is an alien; a factor, along with a statutorily set dollar value of the matter in controversy, that allows a federal district court to exercise its authority to hear a lawsuit based on diversity jurisdiction.

IMMUNITY Exemption from a legal obligation.

NEGLIGENCE Conduct falling below the standard of care that a reasonable person would demonstrate under similar conditions.

SEVENTH AMENDMENT Provides that no fact tried by a jury shall be otherwise re-examined in any court of the United States, other than according to the rules of the common law.

Hanna v. Plumer

Injured (P) v. Estate executor (D)

380 U.S. 460 (1965)

NATURE OF CASE: Appeal of summary judgment in federal diversity tort action.

FACT SUMMARY: Hanna (P) filed tort action in federal court in Massachusetts, where Plumer (D) resided, for an auto accident that occurred in South Carolina.

RULE OF LAW

The *Erie* doctrine mandates that federal courts are to apply state substantive law and federal procedural law, but where matters fall roughly between the two and are rationally capable of classification as either, the Constitution grants the federal court system the power to regulate their practice and pleading (procedure).

FACTS: Hanna (P), a citizen of Ohio, filed a tort action in federal court in Massachusetts against Plumer (D), the executor of the estate of Louise Plumer Osgood, a Massachusetts citizen. It was alleged that Mrs. Osgood caused injuries to Hanna (P) in an auto accident in South Carolina. Service on Plumer (D) was accomplished pursuant to Fed. R. Civ. P. 4(d)(1) by leaving copies of the summons with Plumer's (D) wife. At trial, motion for summary judgment should have been accomplished pursuant to Massachusetts law (by the *Erie* doctrine), which requires service by hand to the party personally. On appeal, Hanna (P) contended Federal Rules of Civil Procedure apply to this case. Plumer (D), however, contended that: (1) a substantive law question under *Erie* is any question in which permitting application of federal law would alter the outcome of the case (the so-called outcome determination test); (2) the application of federal law here i.e., 4[d][1] will necessarily affect the outcome of the case (from a necessary dismissal to litigation); and so therefore (3) *Erie* requires that the state substantive law requirement of service by hand be upheld along with the trial court's summary judgment.

ISSUE: Does the *Erie* doctrine classification of "substantive law questions" extend to embrace questions involving both substantive and procedural considerations merely because such a question might have effect on the determination of the substantive outcome of the case?

HOLDING AND DECISION: (Warren, C.J.) No. The *Erie* doctrine mandates that federal courts are to apply state substantive law and federal procedural law, but where matters fall roughly between the two and are rationally capable of classification as either, the Constitution grants the federal court system the power to regulate their practice and pleading (procedure). It is well settled that the Enabling Act for the Federal Rules of Civil Procedure requires that a procedural effect of any rule on the outcome of a case be shown to actually "abridge, enlarge or modify" the substantive law in a case for the *Erie* doctrine to come into play. Where, as here, the question only goes to procedural requirements (e.g., service of summons), a dismissal for improper service here would not alter the substantive right of Hanna (P) to serve Plumer (D) personally and refile or effect the substantive law of negligence in the case. Article III and the Necessary and Proper Clause provide that the Congress has a right to provide rules for the federal court system such as Fed. R. Civ. P. 4(d)(1). "Outcome determination analysis was never intended to serve as a talisman" for the *Erie* doctrine. Reversed.

CONCURRENCE: (Harlan, J.) Justice Harlan agrees with the result of the Court and its rejection of the outcome determination test. He argues, however, that the Court was wrong in stating that anything arguably procedural is constitutionally placed within the province of the federal government to regulate.

ANALYSIS

This case points a return to the basic rationales of *Erie R. Co. v. Tompkins*, 304 U.S. 64 (1938). First, the Court asserts that one important consideration in determining how a particular question should be classified (substantive or procedural) is the avoidance of "forum shopping" (the practice of choosing one forum, such as federal, in which to file in order to gain the advantages of that forum), which permits jurisdictions to infringe on the substantive law defining powers of each other. Second, the Court seeks to avoid inequitable administration of the laws that would result from allowing jurisdictional considerations to determine substantive rights. Justice Warren, in rejecting the "outcome determination" test, asserts that any rule must be measured ultimately against the Federal Rules Enabling Act and the Constitution.

Continued on next page.

Quicknotes

ARTICLE III, U.S. CONSTITUTION Limits federal judicial power to cases and controversies.

DIVERSITY ACTION An action commenced by a citizen of one state against a citizen of another state or against an alien, involving an amount in controversy set by statute, over which the federal court has jurisdiction.

ENABLING ACT A statute that confers new powers upon a person or entity.

FED. R. CIV. P. 4(D)(1) Governs service of process.

JURISDICTION The authority of a court to hear and declare judgment in respect to a particular matter.

NECESSARY AND PROPER CLAUSE, ACT I, § 8 OF THE CONSTITUTION Enables Congress to make all laws that may be "necessary and proper" to execute its other, enumerated powers.

SUMMARY JUDGMENT Judgment rendered by a court in response to a motion by one of the parties, claiming that the lack of a question of material fact in respect to an issue warrants disposition of the issue without consideration by the jury.

TORT A legal wrong resulting in a breach of duty, which is intentionally or purposefully committed by the wrongdoer.

Walker v. Armco Steel Corp.

Injured carpenter (P) v. Nail manufacturer (D)

446 U.S. 740 (1980)

NATURE OF CASE: Appeal from dismissal of complaint for personal injuries.

FACT SUMMARY: Walker (P) contended that Fed. R. of Civ. P. 3 governed the manner in which an action is commenced in federal court for all purposes, including the tolling of the state statute of limitations.

RULE OF LAW

In diversity actions, Federal Rule of Civil Procedure 3 governs the date from which timing requirements of the federal rules begin to run but does not affect state statutes of limitations.

FACTS: Walker (P), a carpenter, was injured on August 22, 1975, while pounding a Sheffield nail manufactured by Armco Steel Corp. (Armco) (D) into a cement wall. Since there was diversity of citizenship, suit was brought in the United States District Court for the Western District of Oklahoma. The complaint was filed on August 19, 1977, but service of process was not made until December 1, 1977. On January 5, 1978, Armco (D) filed a motion to dismiss the complaint on the ground that the action was barred by the Oklahoma statute of limitations, which stated that an action is not commenced for purposes of the statute of limitations until service of the summons on the defendant. In his reply brief, Walker (P) admitted that his case would be foreclosed in state court but argued that Fed. R. Civ. P. 3 governs the manner in which an action is commenced in federal court for all purposes, including the tolling of the state statute of limitations. Fed. R. Civ. P. 3 states that an action is commenced by filing a complaint with the court. After the Tenth Circuit Court of Appeals affirmed the district court's dismissal of the action as barred by the Oklahoma two-year statute of limitations, Walker (P) appealed.

ISSUE: In diversity actions, does Federal Rule of Civil Procedure 3 affect state statutes of limitations?

HOLDING AND DECISION: (Marshall, J.) No. In diversity actions, Federal Rule of Civil Procedure 3 governs the date from which various timing requirements of the federal rules begin to run but does not affect state statutes of limitations. Rule 3 simply states that a civil action is commenced by filing a complaint with the court. There is no indication that the rule was intended to toll a state statute of limitations, much less that it purported to displace state tolling rules for purposes of state statutes of limitations. In contrast to Rule 3, the Oklahoma statute is a statement of a substantive decision by that state that actual service on and actual notice on the defendant are integral parts of the several policies served by the statute of limitations. Affirmed.

ANALYSIS

The Court in this case applied the rules enunciated in *Erie Railroad Co. v. Tompkins,* 304 U.S. 64 (1938), regarding the application of state law in federal diversity actions. In the *Erie* case, the Court held that "except in matters governed by the Federal Constitution or by Acts of Congress, the law to be applied in any [diversity] case is the law of the State." Id. at 78.

Quicknotes

COMPLAINT The initial pleading commencing litigation that sets forth a claim for relief.

DIVERSITY OF CITIZENSHIP Parties are citizens of different states, or one party is an alien; a factor, along with a statutorily set dollar value of the matter in controversy, that allows a federal district court to exercise its authority to hear a lawsuit based on diversity jurisdiction.

STATUTE OF LIMITATIONS A law prescribing the period in which a legal action may be commenced.

Gasperini v. Center for Humanities, Inc.

Journalist (P) v. Educational publisher (D)

518 U.S. 415 (1996)

NATURE OF CASE: Review of appeal overturning a jury verdict as excessive in action for breach of contract, conversion, and negligence.

FACT SUMMARY: A federal circuit court, hearing a case on diversity jurisdiction, let stand a jury verdict of $450,000 for Gasperini's (P) lost photographic slides; the court of appeals, applying New York law governing excessive damage awards, set aside the verdict.

RULE OF LAW

A federal trial court can apply state law governing the excessiveness or inadequacy of compensation awards without running afoul of the Seventh Amendment's prohibition against re-examination of a fact tried by jury so long as the state standard is applied by the federal trial court judge, and appellate control of the trial court ruling is limited to review for "abuse of discretion."

FACTS: Gasperini (P), a journalist, agreed to supply his original color transparencies to the Center for Humanities, Inc. (Center) (D) for use in an educational videotape. He selected 300 slides; the Center (D) agreed to return the slides, but it could not find them at the end of the project. Gasperini (P) filed suit in the United States District Court for the Southern District of New York, invoking the court's diversity jurisdiction. He alleged several state law claims. The Center (D) conceded liability, and the issue of damages was tried before a jury. The jury awarded Gasperini (P) $450,000 in compensatory damages. The Center (D) attacked the verdict on excessiveness grounds. The district court denied the motion. On appeal, the court of appeals vacated the jury verdict. Applying New York's Civil Practice Law Rules § 5501(c), which permits the ordering of a new trial where an award deviates materially from what is reasonable compensation, the court concluded that evidence at trial was insufficient to determine such a damage award. The appellate court ordered a new trial unless Gasperini (P) accepted an award of $100,000. Gasperini (P) appealed to the United States Supreme Court.

ISSUE: Can a federal trial court apply state law governing the excessiveness or inadequacy of compensation awards without running afoul of the Seventh Amendment's prohibition against re-examining a fact tried by jury?

HOLDING AND DECISION: (Ginsburg, J.) Yes. A federal trial court can apply state law governing the excessiveness or inadequacy of compensation awards without running afoul of the Seventh Amendment's prohibition against re-examination of a fact tried by jury so long as the state standard is applied by the federal trial court judge, and appellate control of the trial court ruling is limited to review for "abuse of discretion." The Seventh Amendment, which governs proceedings in federal court but not in state court, provides that "no fact tried by a jury, shall be otherwise re-examined in any Court of the United States. . . ." When a federal court hears a case under diversity jurisdiction, the court applies state substantive law and federal procedural law. However, classification of a law as substantive or procedural is often difficult. The various circuits have at times set aside awards using "abuse of discretion" as their standard. In such cases, the appellate courts have held that the damages award is no longer a question of fact, but a question of law. However, the federal system and the constraints of the Seventh Amendment must be harmonized with the application of state law. Thus, the district court has the responsibility to apply state laws governing excessive damages awards, and the appellate court must review for abuse of discretion. In this case, the district court should have applied § 5501(c) to determine whether the award deviated materially from reasonableness. The appellate court was constrained to review for abuse of discretion. The judgment of the appellate court is vacated, and that court is instructed to remand so that the trial judge may test the jury's verdict against § 5501(c)'s "deviates materially" standard.

ANALYSIS

The seminal case, *Erie Railroad Co. v. Tompkins,* 304 U.S. 64 (1938), first specified the "substantive" versus "procedural" distinction mentioned in this case. The goal of *Erie* was to prevent forum shopping between state and federal courts. However, Justice Scalia argued that by adopting different standards for appellate review between the state and federal courts, the incentive to forum shop was enhanced. This raises the question, though, as to just how influential a deviation in appellate review standards will be when parties are selecting the lower court forum in which to litigate their claims.

Quicknotes

BREACH OF CONTRACT Unlawful failure by a party to perform its obligations pursuant to contract.

Continued on next page.

CONVERSION Act of depriving an owner of his property without permission or justification.

DIVERSITY JURISDICTION The authority of a federal court to hear and determine cases involving $10,000 or more and in which the parties are citizens of different states, or in which one party is an alien.

NEGLIGENCE Conduct falling below the standard of care that a reasonable person would demonstrate under similar conditions.

SEVENTH AMENDMENT Provides that no fact tried by a jury shall be otherwise re-examined in any court of the United States, other than according to the rules of the common law.

Shady Grove Orthopedic Associates v. Allstate Insurance Co.

Medical association (P) v. Insurance company (D)

559 U.S. 393 (2010)

NATURE OF CASE: Grant of a writ of certiorari.

FACT SUMMARY: Shady Grove Orthopedic Associates (P) sued Allstate Insurance Company (D) for the insurance company's (D) alleged failure to pay interest on overdue insurance payments, on behalf of itself and a class of plaintiffs. The district court dismissed the case on the grounds that New York law prevented a class action lawsuit to recover "penalties," and the Second Circuit Court of Appeals affirmed.

RULE OF LAW

Federal Rule of Civil Procedure 23 preempts state law as to when a class action lawsuit may be filed in federal court.

FACTS: Shady Grove Orthopedic Associates (Shady Grove) (P) provided medical care to Sonia Galvez for her injuries resulting from a car accident. Galvez had an automobile insurance policy from Allstate Insurance Company (Allstate) (D). Shady Grove (P) submitted a claim to Allstate (D) for Galvez's treatment. Allstate's (D) payment to Shady Grove (P) was late, and Allstate (D) refused to pay interest, a charge for which is allowable under New York law. Shady Grove (P) then filed a class action lawsuit in federal court, arguing that Allstate (D) violated New York law by failing to pay interest to policyholders. Allstate (D) moved to dismiss, arguing that under Section 901(b) of the New York Civil Practice Law and Rules, Shady Grove (P) and Galvez could not use a class action lawsuit to collect a statutory penalty unless specifically authorized under the statute, and that such a lawsuit was not specifically authorized by statute. Shady Grove (P) and Galvez argued that § 901(b) did not apply in federal courts because it was a procedural rule and it conflicted with Federal Rule of Civil Procedure 23, which governs class action lawsuits in federal court. The United States District Court for the Eastern District of New York held that Shady Grove's (P) class action claim was not authorized and thus dismissed its claim. The court found that New York insurance laws did not specifically authorize a class action for the recovery of interest, and therefore § 901(b) prevented the filing of the class action. On appeal, Shady Grove (P) argued that the New York law conflicts with Rule 23 and thus was not applicable. The United States Court of Appeals for the Second Circuit disagreed with Shady Grove (P) and affirmed the district court, reasoning that the New York rules of civil procedure did not conflict with Rule 23, and Rule 23 therefore did not control.

ISSUE: Does Federal Rule of Civil Procedure 23 preempt state law as to when a class action lawsuit may be filed in federal court?

HOLDING AND DECISION: (Scalia, J.) Yes. Federal Rule of Civil Procedure 23 preempts state law as to when a class action lawsuit may be filed in federal court. Section 901(b) of the New York rules of civil procedure does not preclude a federal court sitting in diversity from hearing a class action under Rule 23 of the federal rules of civil procedure. If Rule 23 answers the question in dispute, it governs, unless it exceeds its statutory authorization or Congress's rulemaking power. Here, Rule 23 answers the question in dispute—the question being whether Shady Grove's (P) suit may proceed as a class action—and is therefore controlling. The Rules Enabling Act, not *Erie*, 304 U.S. 64 (1938), controls the validity of a federal rule of civil procedure, even if that results in opening the federal courts to class actions that cannot proceed in state court. The concurrence's analysis conflicts with the Court's precedent in *Sibbach v. Wilson & Co.*, 312 U.S. 1 (1941), that the federal rules "really regulate procedure." Reversed and remanded.

CONCURRENCE: (Stevens, J.) Rule 23 applies in this case, but it also must be recognized that in some cases federal courts should apply state procedural rules in diversity cases, because they function as part of the state's definition of substantive rights and remedies.

DISSENT: (Ginsburg, J.) The majority opinion used Rule 23 to override New York's statutory restriction on the availability of damages and consequently turned a $500 case into a $5,000,000 one. It is important to interpret the federal rules with sensitivity to state regulatory policies.

ANALYSIS

Forum shopping is a likely and important consequence of *Shady Grove*. If the federal rules preempt state statutes limiting class actions, as in this case, litigants will likely try to file in federal court. *Shady Grove* may therefore increase the number of class actions brought in federal court and raise strategic considerations about removal for defendants sued in state courts. The plurality recognized this risk, acknowledging "the reality that keeping the federal-court door open to class actions

Continued on next page.

that cannot proceed in state court will produce forum shopping."

Quicknotes

CLASS ACTION A suit commenced by a representative on behalf of an ascertainable group that is too large to appear in court, who shares a commonality of interests, and who will benefit from a successful result.

FORUM SHOPPING Refers to a situation in which one party to an action seeks to have the matter heard and determined by a court or in a jurisdiction that will provide it with the most favorable result.

CHAPTER 10

Finality and Preclusion

Quick Reference Rules of Law

Car Carriers, Inc. v. Ford Motor Company

Transport company (P) v. Major customer (D)

789 F.2d 589 (7th Cir. 1989)

NATURE OF CASE: Appeal from dismissal of suit on grounds of res judicata.

FACT SUMMARY: In 1982, Car Carriers, Inc. (P), an automobile transporter, sued Ford Motor Company (Ford) (D), its major customer, under the Sherman Antitrust Act. The district court dismissed the complaint with prejudice. In 1983, Car Carriers (P) brought a new complaint against Ford (D), utilizing the same basic fact situation, this time for alleged violations of the Racketeer Influenced and Corrupt Organizations Act and the Interstate Commerce Act. The district court dismissed this suit based on res judicata.

RULE OF LAW

Res judicata bars a second lawsuit arising from the same operative set of facts even when an analysis of the rights, duties, and injuries involved in the second lawsuit reveals that they are materially different from those at issue in the first.

FACTS: Car Carriers, Inc. (P), a company that hauled automobiles, alleged that Ford Motor Company (Ford) (D), its major customer, had for many years been entering into conspiracy against trade agreements. In 1982, Car Carriers (P) sued Ford (D) and others under the Sherman Antitrust Act. The district court dismissed the complaint on the grounds that the plaintiff did not suffer the type of harm that antitrust laws were designed to recompense. The court further found that because this defect was non-curable, the claims were dismissed with prejudice. In 1983 Car Carriers (P) brought a new complaint against Ford (D), utilizing the same basic fact situation, this time based on alleged violations of the Racketeer Influenced and the Corrupt Organizations Act and Interstate Commerce Act legislation. The district court dismissed this suit based on res judicata.

ISSUE: Does res judicata bar a second lawsuit arising from the same set of operative facts even when an analysis of the rights, duties, and injuries involved in the second lawsuit reveals that they are materially different from those at issue in the first?

HOLDING AND DECISION: (Ripple, J.) Yes. Res judicata bars a second lawsuit arising from the same operative set of facts even when an analysis of the rights, duties, and injuries involved in the second lawsuit reveals that they are materially different from those at issue in the first. A "cause of action" consists of a single core of operative facts that give rise to a remedy, a test that is decidedly fact oriented. Thus, a mere change in legal theory, as here, does *not* create a new cause of action. Therefore, the prior litigation as to these plaintiffs acts as a bar not only to those issues that were raised and decided in their earlier litigation but also to those issues that could have been raised in that litigation. In this case, plaintiff's Sherman Act, Racketeer Influenced and Corrupt Organizations Act, and Interstate Commerce Act claims essentially all arose from the same set of operative facts. Affirmed.

ANALYSIS

The approach of this court is consistent with the general litigation scheme established by the Federal Rules of Civil Procedure in which litigants have great latitude in joining claims and amending pleadings. Thus, to further the purpose of the Federal Rules, courts have appropriately defined res judicata with sufficient breadth to encourage parties to present all their related claims at one time.

Quicknotes

COMPLAINT The initial pleading commencing litigation that sets forth a claim for relief.

CONSPIRACY Concerted action by two or more persons to accomplish some unlawful purpose.

INTERSTATE COMMERCE Commercial dealings between two parties located in different states or located in one state and accomplished through a point in another state or a foreign country; commercial dealings transacted between two states.

RACKETEER INFLUENCED AND CORRUPT ORGANIZATIONS ACT (RICO) Federal and state statutes enacted for the purpose of prosecuting organized crime.

RES JUDICATA The rule of law a final judgment by a court precludes subsequent litigation between the parties regarding the same cause of action.

Taylor v. Sturgell

FOIA requester (P) v. Federal official (D)

553 U.S. 880 (2008)

NATURE OF CASE: Appeal from affirmance of summary judgment for defendant in action under the Freedom of Information Act.

FACT SUMMARY: Taylor (P) contended his Freedom of Information Act suit seeking records from the Federal Aviation Administration (D) should not have been dismissed on grounds of claim preclusion—on the theory of "virtual representation"—merely because his friend and close associate, Herrick, had filed a similar suit seeking the same records.

RULE OF LAW

A claim may not be precluded under a doctrine of "virtual representation" where a second claimant brings a suit identical to a first claimant and, although the claimants know each other, there is no legal relationship between them and there is no evidence the second claimant controlled, financed, participated in, or even had notice of the earlier suit.

FACTS: Herrick, an antique aircraft enthusiast sought to restore a vintage airplane manufactured by the Fairchild Engine and Airplane Corporation (FEAC). He filed a Freedom of Information Act (FOIA) request asking the Federal Aviation Administration (FAA) (D) for copies of technical documents related to the airplane. The FAA (D) denied his request based on FOIA's exemption for trade secrets. Herrick took an administrative appeal, but when Fairchild Corporation (Fairchild) (D), FEAC's successor, objected to the documents' release, the FAA (D) adhered to its original decision. Herrick then filed a FOIA lawsuit to secure the documents, which was dismissed on summary judgment by the district court and later affirmed by the court of appeals. Less than a month after that suit was resolved, Taylor (P), Herrick's friend and an antique aircraft enthusiast himself, made a FOIA request for the same documents Herrick had unsuccessfully sued to obtain. When the FAA (D) failed to respond, Taylor (P) filed suit in federal district court. Holding the suit barred by claim preclusion, the district court granted summary judgment to the FAA (D) and to Fairchild (D), as intervener in Taylor's (P) action. The court acknowledged Taylor (P) was not a party to Herrick's suit but held a nonparty may be bound by a judgment if she was "virtually represented" by a party. The court of appeals affirmed, announcing a five-factor test for "virtual representation." The first two factors of that test—"identity of interests" and "adequate representation"—are necessary but not sufficient for virtual representation. In addition, at least one of three other factors must be established: "a close relationship between the present party and his putative representative," "substantial participation by the present party in the first case," or "tactical maneuvering on the part of the present party to avoid preclusion by the prior judgment." The court of appeals acknowledged the absence of any indication Taylor (P) participated in, or even had notice of, Herrick's suit. It nonetheless found the "identity of interests," "adequate representation," and "close relationship" factors satisfied because the two men sought release of the same documents, were "close associates," had discussed working together to restore Herrick's plane, had used the same lawyer to pursue their suits, and Herrick had given Taylor (P) documents Herrick had obtained from the FAA (D) during discovery in his suit. Because these conditions sufficed to establish virtual representation, the court left open the question whether Taylor (P) had engaged in tactical maneuvering to avoid preclusion. The United States Supreme Court granted certiorari.

ISSUE: May a claim be precluded under a doctrine of "virtual representation" where a second claimant brings a suit identical to a first claimant and, although the claimants know each other, there is no legal relationship between them and there is no evidence the second claimant controlled, financed, participated in, or even had notice of the earlier suit?

HOLDING AND DECISION: (Ginsburg, J.) No. A claim may not be precluded under a doctrine of "virtual representation" where a second claimant brings a suit identical to a first claimant and, although the claimants know each other, there is no legal relationship between them and there is no evidence the second claimant controlled, financed, participated in, or even had notice of the earlier suit. The preclusive effect of a federal-court judgment is determined by federal common law, subject to due process limitations. Extending the preclusive effect of a judgment to a nonparty runs up against the "deep-rooted historic tradition that everyone should have his own day in court." Indicating the strength of that tradition, this Court has often repeated the general rule that "one is not bound by a judgment in personam in a litigation in which he is not designated a party or to which he has not been made a party by service of process." The rule against nonparty preclusion is subject to exceptions, currently grouped into six categories. First, "[a] person who agrees to be bound by the determination of issues in an action between others is bound in accordance with the

Continued on next page.

[agreement's] terms," Restatement (Second) of Judgments § 40. Second, nonparty preclusion may be based on a pre-existing substantive legal relationship between the person to be bound and a party to the judgment, e.g., assignee and assignor. Third, "in certain limited circumstances," a non-party may be bound by a judgment because she was "adequately represented by someone with the same interests who [wa]s a party" to the suit. Fourth, a non-party is bound by a judgment if he "assume[d] control" over the litigation in which that judgment was rendered. Fifth, a party bound by a judgment may not avoid its preclusive force by relitigating through a proxy. Preclusion is thus in order when a person who did not participate in litigation later brings suit as the designated representative or agent of a person who was a party to the prior adjudication. Sixth, a special statutory scheme otherwise consistent with due process, e.g., bankruptcy proceedings, may "expressly foreclos[e] successive litigation by nonlitigants." Reaching beyond these six categories, the court of appeals recognized a broad "virtual representation" exception to the rule against nonparty preclusion. None of the arguments advanced by that court, the Federal Aviation Administration (FAA) (D), or Fairchild Corporation (Fairchild) (D) justify such an expansive doctrine. The court of appeals purported to ground its doctrine in this Court's statements that, in some circumstances, a person may be bound by a judgment if she was adequately represented by a party to the proceeding yielding that judgment. But the court of appeals' definition of "adequate representation" strayed from the meaning this Court has attributed to that term. Fairchild (D) and the FAA (D) ask the Court to abandon altogether the attempt to delineate discrete grounds and clear rules for nonparty preclusion. Instead, they contend, only an equitable and heavily fact-driven inquiry can account for all the situations in which nonparty preclusion is appropriate. This argument is rejected. First, the balancing test they propose is at odds with the constrained approach advanced by this Court's decisions, which have endeavored to delineate discrete, limited exceptions to the fundamental rule that a litigant is not bound by a judgment to which she was not a party. Second, a party's representation of a nonparty is "adequate" for preclusion purposes only if, at a minimum, (1) the interests of the nonparty and her representative are aligned and (2) either the party understood herself to be acting in a representative capacity or the original court took care to protect the nonparty's interests. Adequate representation may also require (3) notice of the original suit to the persons alleged to have been represented. In the class-action context, these limitations are implemented by Fed. R. Civ. P. 23's procedural safeguards. But an expansive virtual representation doctrine would recognize a common-law kind of class action that would lack these protections. Third, a diffuse balancing approach to non-party preclusion would likely complicate the task of district courts faced in the first instance with preclusion questions. The remaining question is whether the result reached by the courts below can be justified based on one of the six established grounds for nonparty preclusion. With one exception, those grounds plainly have no application here. The FAA (D) and Fairchild (D) argue that Taylor's (P) suit is a collusive attempt to relitigate Herrick's claim. That argument justifies a remand to allow the courts below the opportunity to determine whether the fifth ground for nonparty preclusion—preclusion because a nonparty to earlier litigation has brought suit as an agent of a party bound by the prior adjudication—applies to Taylor's (P) suit. However, courts should be cautious about finding preclusion on the basis of agency. A mere whiff of "tactical maneuvering" will not suffice; instead, principles of agency law indicate preclusion is appropriate only if the putative agent's conduct of the suit is subject to the control of the party who is bound by the prior adjudication. Vacated and remanded.

ANALYSIS

This case presented an issue of first impression in the sense that the Supreme Court had never addressed the doctrine of "virtual representation" adopted (in varying forms) by several circuits and relied upon by the district court and court of appeals below. For example, the Eighth Circuit had developed a seven-factor test for virtual representation, which was adopted by the district court in this case. The Eighth Circuit test requires an "identity of interests" between the person to be bound and a party to the judgment. Six additional factors counsel in favor of virtual representation under the Eighth Circuit's test but are not prerequisites: (1) a "close relationship" between the present party and a party to the judgment alleged to be preclusive; (2) "participation in the prior litigation" by the present party; (3) the present party's "apparent acquiescence" to the preclusive effect of the judgment; (4) "deliberat[e] maneuver[ing]" to avoid the effect of the judgment; (5) adequate representation of the present party by a party to the prior adjudication; and (6) a suit raising a "public law" rather than a "private law" issue. These factors, the court of appeals (D.C. Circuit) in this case observed, "constitute a fluid test with imprecise boundaries" and call for "a broad, case-by-case inquiry." The D.C. Circuit adopted a five-factor test. The Supreme Court resolved these different approaches by rejecting the doctrine of virtual representation altogether, instead relying on well-established principles of due process and claim preclusion.

Continued on next page.

Quicknotes

CLAIM PRECLUSION A procedural rule or order prohibiting the support or opposition to certain claims or defenses.

DUE PROCESS The constitutional mandate requiring the courts to protect and enforce individuals' rights and liberties consistent with prevailing principles of fairness and justice and prohibiting the federal and state governments from such activities that deprive its citizens of life, liberty, or property interest.

INTERVENOR A party, not an initial party to the action, who is admitted to the action in order to assert an interest in the subject matter of a lawsuit.

PARTY Person designated as either the defendant or plaintiff in a lawsuit.

David P. Hoult v. Jennifer Hoult

Father (P) v. Daughter (D)

157 F.3d 29 (1st Cir. 1998)

NATURE OF CASE: Plaintiff's appeal from dismissal of suit on grounds that he was estopped from relitigating issue resolved in earlier lawsuit.

FACT SUMMARY: A father brought defamation suit against his daughter. The daughter claimed the suit should be dismissed on grounds of collateral estoppel.

RULE OF LAW

The doctrine of collateral estoppel precludes relitigation of the central issue in a prior suit.

FACTS: Jennifer Hoult (D) sued David Hoult (her father) (P) for assault, battery and intentional infliction of emotional distress, presenting evidence that he (P) had sexually abused and raped her (D) over a period of many years. The jury found in her (D) favor and awarded damages. Subsequently, the daughter (D) wrote to several professional associations in which she (D) repeated the charge that her father (P) had raped her. The father (P) then brought the present defamation action against the daughter (D). The daughter (D) moved to dismiss the father's (P) complaint on the grounds the jury verdict in her earlier assault action had determined that the father (P) had raped her, thus he (P) should be barred by collateral estoppel from relitigating this finding. The district court granted the motion to dismiss.

ISSUE: Does the doctrine of collateral estoppel preclude relitigation of the central issue in a prior suit?

HOLDING AND DECISION: (Boudin, J.) Yes. The doctrine of collateral estoppel precludes relitigation of the central issue in a prior suit. Even though the jury in the prior suit did not make an explicit finding that David Hoult (P) had raped Jennifer Hoult (D), such finding was a "necessary component of the decision reached" by the prior jury, which had held that Jennifer's father had in many ways sexually abused her. In the daughter's prior suit, the rape charges were pivotal and constituted the "centerpiece" of her case, and both her counsel as well as defense counsel in the prior suit referred to rape. The father's (P) present lawsuit against his daughter (D) simply seeks, in the guise of a defamation action, to retry the central issue in the prior assault case between the same litigants. Affirmed.

ANALYSIS

The court stressed that here the key issue of rape, ultimately a credibility contest between the two opposing parties, was resolved by the jury at the first trial, whose decision about what happened was therefore not open to relitigation.

Quicknotes

ASSAULT AND BATTERY Any unlawful touching of another person without justification or excuse.

COLLATERAL ESTOPPEL A doctrine whereby issues litigated and determined in a prior proceeding are binding upon all subsequent litigation between the parties regarding that issue.

COMPLAINT The initial pleading commencing litigation that sets forth a claim for relief.

DEFAMATION An intentional false publication, communicated publicly in either oral or written form, subjecting a person to scorn, hatred, or ridicule, or injuring him or her in relation to his or her occupation or business.

ESTOPPEL An equitable doctrine precluding a party from asserting a right to the detriment of another whom, justifiably relied on the conduct.

RAPE Unlawful sexual intercourse with a woman by a man by means of fear or force and without her consent.

Jarosz v. Palmer

Individual (P) v. Attorney (D)
Mass. Sup. Jud. Ct., 436 Mass. 526 (2002)

NATURE OF CASE: Appeal from the dismissal of a claim on basis of issue preclusion.

FACT SUMMARY: Jarosz (P) hired Palmer (D), to assist Jarosz (P) and his three partners in the acquisition of a company. Two lawsuits were then filed. The first lawsuit was filed by Jarosz (P) against his partners and the corporation after the partners terminated him as an employee and officer of the company. The company and partners retained Palmer (D) as their attorney. Jarosz (P) moved to disqualify Palmer (D) on the basis of his previous relationship with Palmer (D) in the corporate acquisition. His motion was denied, and the trial judge ruled that Jarosz (P) failed to prove that Palmer (D) had previously represented him individually. Jarosz (P) filed a second lawsuit, this one against Palmer (D) for alleged malpractice. The trial judge ruled that because of the decision denying the motion to disqualify in the first case, issue preclusion prevented Jarosz from asserting that Palmer (D) represented him individually in the business transaction. The trial judge dismissed Jarosz's (P) claim. Jarosz (P) appealed.

RULE OF LAW

The requirement of the doctrine of issue preclusion that the issue decided be "essential to the judgment" necessitates that the issue be essential to the merits of the underlying case.

FACTS: Jarosz (P) and his three partners acquired a company known as Union Products. Jarosz (P) had engaged Palmer (D), an attorney, to assist in the acquisition and financing of the business. When the relationship between Jarosz (P) and his partners soured, Jarosz (P) was terminated as an employee and officer of the company. Jarosz (P) filed suit against his former partners and the company for wrongful termination and breach of fiduciary duty. In that case, Palmer (D) represented the partners and the company. Jarosz (P) moved to disqualify Palmer (D) from representing the partners and the company, on the basis that Palmer (D) had previously represented him individually. The motion was denied on grounds that Jarosz (P) did not establish that an attorney-client relationship existed between himself and Palmer (D) during the acquisition dealings. Thereafter, Jarosz (P) filed this complaint against Palmer (D), alleging breach of contract, breach of fiduciary duty, legal malpractice, and violations of M.G.L. c. 93A. Palmer (D) defended these claims on the grounds that he never represented Jarosz (P) individually. Palmer (D) moved for judgment on the pleadings, arguing that the denial of Jarosz's (P) motion to disqualify in the first lawsuit in another court precluded Jarosz (P) from relitigating the issue in the second. The court granted Palmer's (D) motion, finding that the three requirements for issue preclusion had been met: the issue had been actually litigated, it was the subject of a valid and final judgment, and it was essential to the judge's decision. The court dismissed Jarosz's (P) complaint against Palmer (D). Jarosz (P) appealed the dismissal of his suit against Palmer (D).

ISSUE: Does the requirement of the doctrine of issue preclusion that the issue decided be "essential to the judgment" necessitate that the issue be essential to the merits of the underlying case?

HOLDING AND DECISION: (Cowin, J.) Yes. The requirement of the doctrine of issue preclusion that the issue decided be "essential to the judgment" necessitates that the issue be essential to the merits of the underlying case. Under the doctrine of issue preclusion, when an issue has been "actually litigated and determined by a valid and final judgment, and the determination is essential to the judgment, the determination is conclusive in a subsequent action between the parties whether on the same or different claim." Jarosz (P) claims that the issue was not actually litigated and that it was not essential to the decision. However, the issue of Jarosz's (P) alleged attorney-client relationship with Palmer (D) was actually litigated. The requirement for actual litigation of an issue does not require that a court hold an evidentiary hearing or trial before issue preclusion can apply. The appropriate question is whether there has been an "adversary presentation" and a "consequent judgment" that was not the result of the parties' consent. In the present matter, the issue of Jarosz's (P) attorney-client relationship had been briefed, and there had been a hearing, and the judge made a determination. As a result, the issue had been actually litigated. The denial of the motion to disqualify was not essential to the judgment in the underlying case, however. The requirement that the issue be essential to the judgment necessitates that the issue be essential to the underlying case. The nature of Jarosz's (P) attorney-client relationship with Palmer (D) was clearly not essential to a determination on the merits of his claim against his partner and the company, and the issue was therefore not essential to the judgment. Issue preclusion cannot apply. Reversed and remanded.

Continued on next page.

ANALYSIS

An interesting question is whether issue preclusion will be available when the prior case was terminated by a stipulation of dismissal. A key requirement for application of the doctrine of issue preclusion is that the issue "actually be litigated" and is "essential" to the underlying judgment. When parties stipulate to dismiss a case, nothing has been litigated, and because any claim has more than one element, it will be the rare case that a party can show that an "issue" was essential to that dismissal.

Quicknotes

BREACH OF CONTRACT Unlawful failure by a party to perform its obligations pursuant to contract.

BREACH OF FIDUCIARY DUTY The failure of a fiduciary to observe the standard of care exercised by professionals of similar education and experience.

EVIDENTIARY HEARING Hearing pertaining to the evidence of the case.

ISSUE PRECLUSION When a particular issue has already been litigated, further litigation of the same issue is barred.

LEGAL MALPRACTICE Conduct on the part of an attorney falling below that demonstrated by other attorneys of ordinary skill and competency under the circumstances, resulting in damages.

Parklane Hosiery Co., Inc. v. Shore

Corporation (D) v. Stockholders (P)

439 U.S. 322 (1979)

NATURE OF CASE: Appeal from stockholders' class action.

FACT SUMMARY: Shore (P) and other stockholders brought this action, alleging that Parklane Hosiery Co., Inc. (D) had issued a materially false and misleading proxy statement.

RULE OF LAW

A litigant who was not a party to a prior judgment may use that judgment "offensively" to prevent a defendant from relitigating issues resolved in the earlier proceeding.

FACTS: Shore (P) and other stockholders brought this class action against Parklane Hosiery Co., Inc. (Parklane) (D), alleging that the company had issued a materially false and misleading proxy statement that violated various federal securities laws. Before this action came to trial, the Securities and Exchange Commission (SEC) filed suit against Parklane (D), making the same allegations as Shore. Injunctive relief was requested. The court found that the proxy was false and misleading and entered a declaratory judgment to that effect. The court of appeals affirmed. Shore (P), in the present case, then moved for partial summary judgment against Parklane (D), asserting that it was collaterally estopped from relitigating the issues that had been resolved against it in the action brought by the SEC. The district court denied the motion on the ground that such an application of collateral estoppel would deny Parklane (D) its Seventh Amendment right to jury trial. The court of appeals reversed, holding that a party who has had issues of fact determined against him after a full and fair opportunity to litigate in a nonjury trial is collaterally estopped from obtaining a subsequent jury trial of these same issues of fact. Parklane (D) appealed.

ISSUE: May a litigant who was not a party to a prior judgment use that judgment "offensively" to prevent a defendant from relitigating issues resolved in the earlier proceeding?

HOLDING AND DECISION: (Stewart, J.) Yes. A litigant who was not a party to a prior judgment may use that judgment "offensively" to prevent a defendant from relitigating issues resolved in the earlier proceeding. Unless the application of offensive estoppel would be unfair to the defendant, a trial court has broad discretion to determine when it should be applied. In this case, none of the considerations that would justify a refusal to allow the use of estoppel is present. Since Parklane Hosiery Co., Inc. (Parklane) (D) received a full and fair opportunity to litigate its claims in the Securities and Exchange Commission (SEC) action, the contemporary law of collateral estoppel leads inescapably to the conclusion that Parklane (D) is collaterally estopped from relitigating the question of whether the proxy statements were materially false and misleading. Affirmed.

DISSENT: (Rehnquist, J.) At common law as it existed in 1791, petitioners would have been entitled to have a jury determine the facts in the private action. In 1791, collateral estoppel was permitted only where the parties in the first action were identical to, or in privity with, the parties to the subsequent action. The judge-made doctrine of collateral estoppel cannot contract the right to a jury trial that the defendant would have enjoyed in 1791. Here, the use of collateral estoppel eliminates the right to trial by jury and therefore contravenes the Seventh Amendment. And even if there were no violation of the Seventh Amendment, the use of collateral estoppel here is unfair since the party who is sought to be estopped has not had an opportunity to have the facts of his case determined by a jury. The petitioners were not entitled to a jury trial in the SEC lawsuit.

ANALYSIS

In both the defensive and offensive use of collateral estoppel, the party against whom estoppel is asserted has litigated and lost in an earlier action. Nevertheless, several reasons have been advanced as to why the two situations should be treated differently. First, offensive use of collateral estoppel does not promote judicial economy in the same manner as defensive use does. Defensive estoppel precludes a plaintiff from relitigating identical issues by merely switching adversaries. Second, offensive estoppel may be unfair to a defendant.

Quicknotes

CLASS ACTION SUIT A suit commenced by a representative on behalf of an ascertainable group that is too large to appear in court, who shares a commonality of interests, and who will benefit from a successful result.

DECLARATORY JUDGMENT An adjudication by the courts that grants not relief but is binding over the legal status of the parties involved in the dispute.

Continued on next page.

DEFENSIVE COLLATERAL ESTOPPEL A doctrine that may be invoked by a defendant against a plaintiff, whereby the plaintiff is prohibited from relitigating issues litigated and determined in a prior proceeding against another defendant.

INJUNCTIVE RELIEF A court order issued as a remedy, requiring a person to do, or prohibiting that person from doing, a specific act.

OFFENSIVE COLLATERAL ESTOPPEL A doctrine that may be invoked by a plaintiff whereby a defendant is prohibited from relitigating issues litigated and determined in a prior proceeding against another plaintiff.

PROXY STATEMENT A statement, containing specified information by the Securities and Exchange Commission, in order to provide shareholders with adequate information upon which to make an informed decision regarding the solicitation of their proxies.

SEVENTH AMENDMENT Provides that no fact tried by a jury shall be otherwise re-examined in any court of the United States, other than according to the rules of the common law.

SUMMARY JUDGMENT Judgment rendered by a court in response to a motion by one of the parties, claiming that the lack of a question of material fact in respect to an issue warrants disposition of the issue without consideration by the jury.

Hardy v. Johns-Manville Sales Corp.

Exposed workers (P) v. Asbestos manufacturer (D)

681 F.2d 334 (5th Cir. 1982)

NATURE OF CASE: Appeal of collateral estoppel order in action for damages for personal injury.

FACT SUMMARY: A trial court entered a collateral estoppel order regarding a failure-to-warn basis for products liability, although the jury in the prior action could have based its finding on one of several theories.

RULE OF LAW

Collateral estoppel may be applied only where there is an identity of issues.

FACTS: A class of plaintiffs sued various defendants' products for personal injury related to asbestos exposure. One theory of recovery was products liability based on a failure to warn. The plaintiffs moved for a collateral estoppel order based on a jury finding in a prior case that the same defendants had failed to warn of the danger of asbestos. However, it was unclear from the record of the prior case as to when the jury believed the duty to warn came into being. In the present action, warnings were placed by Johns-Manville Sales Corporation (Johns-Manville) (D) at various times from 1964 through 1969. The district court entered summary adjudication as to the failure-to-warn theory, and Johns-Manville (D) appealed.

ISSUE: May collateral estoppel be applied only where there is an identity of issues?

HOLDING AND DECISION: (Gee, J.) Yes. Collateral estoppel may be applied only where there is an identity of issues. When the prior judgment is ambivalent, the doctrine is not to be utilized. Here, the jury in the prior action could have found that the duty to warn arose any time between 1963 and 1969, when it held the duty to have arisen is unclear from the record. Here, some defendants began issuing warnings as early as 1964. Therefore, it is possible that they fulfilled any duty to warn they may have had. This being so, collateral estoppel was incorrectly applied. Reversed.

ANALYSIS

Most actions involve general verdicts without specific findings by juries. It is difficult to find an identity of issues in such situations. Collateral estoppel is usually more readily available when the prior case contained special interrogatories.

Quicknotes

COLLATERAL ESTOPPEL A doctrine whereby issues litigated and determined in a prior proceeding are binding upon all subsequent litigation between the parties regarding that issue.

DUTY-TO-WARN An obligation owed by an owner or occupier of land to persons who come onto the premises, to inform them of defects or active operations which may cause injury.

INTERROGATORY A method of pretrial discovery in which written questions are provided by one party to another who must respond in writing under oath.

PRODUCT LIABILITY The legal liability of manufacturers and sellers for damages and injuries suffered by buyers, users, and even bystanders because of defects in goods purchased.

B & B Hardware, Inc. v. Hargis Industries, Inc.

Manufacturer (P) v. Manufacturer (D)

135 S. Ct. 1293 (2015)

NATURE OF CASE: Appeal from affirmance of judgment for defendant in trademark infringement action.

FACT SUMMARY: B & B Hardware, Inc. (B & B) (P), the owner of the SEALTIGHT trademark, successfully opposed the registration by Hargis Industries, Inc. (Hargis) (D) of Hargis's (D) trademark, SEALTITE, before the Trademark Trial and Appeal Board (TTAB), which ruled the two marks were confusingly similar. B & B (P), which had also brought a trademark infringement action against Hargis (D) in federal district court, contended the district court should have applied issue preclusion to the TTAB's decision that SEALTITE is confusingly similar to SEALTIGHT.

RULE OF LAW

(1) An agency decision can ground issue preclusion.
(2) There is no categorical reason why trademark registration decisions can never meet the ordinary elements of issue preclusion.

FACTS: B & B Hardware, Inc. (B & B) (P) was the owner of the SEALTIGHT trademark, which it used in connection with metal fasteners in the aerospace industry. Hargis Industries, Inc. (Hargis) (D) sought to register the trademark SEALTITE in connection with metal fasteners used in the construction industry. B & B (P) successfully opposed Hargis's (D) effort to register SEALTITE before the Trademark Trial and Appeal Board (TTAB), which ruled the two marks were confusingly similar. Hargis (D) did not seek judicial review of that decision. While it was opposing Hargis's (D) registration efforts, B & B (P) also instituted a trademark infringement action in federal district court against Hargis (D). In both registration proceedings and infringement litigation, the tribunal asks whether a likelihood of confusion exists between the mark sought to be protected (here, SEALTIGHT) and the other mark (SEALTITE). Before the district court ruled on likelihood of confusion, however, the TTAB announced its decision. B & B (P) argued to the district court Hargis (D) could not contest likelihood of confusion because of the preclusive effect of the TTAB decision. The district court disagreed, reasoning the TTAB is not an Article III court, so its decisions cannot be a basis for issue preclusion. The jury returned a verdict for Hargis (D), finding no likelihood of confusion. The court of appeals affirmed. Although it accepted for the sake of argument agency decisions can ground issue preclusion, it nevertheless affirmed because it found the TTAB uses different factors than the circuit to evaluate likelihood of confusion, because the TTAB placed too much emphasis on the appearance and sound of the two marks, and because Hargis (D) bore the burden of persuasion before the TTAB, while B & B (P) bore it before the district court. The United States Supreme Court granted certiorari.

ISSUE:

(1) Can an agency decision ground issue preclusion?
(2) Is there a categorical reason why trademark registration decisions can never meet the ordinary elements of issue preclusion?

HOLDING AND DECISION: (Alito, J.)

(1) Yes. An agency decision can ground issue preclusion. The Court's cases and the Restatement (Second) of Judgments make clear issue preclusion is not limited to those situations in which the same issue is before two courts. Rather, where a single issue is before a court and an administrative agency, preclusion also often applies. Hargis (D) unconvincingly argues the Lanham Act should not be read as authorizing issue preclusion for fear that doing so might run afoul of the Seventh Amendment and Article III. These fears are unfounded, however. As to the Seventh Amendment, for instance, the Court has already held the right to a jury trial does not negate the issue-preclusive effect of a judgment, even if that judgment was entered by a juryless tribunal. It follows that although the Seventh Amendment creates a jury trial right in suits for trademark damages, Trademark Trial and Appeal Board (TTAB) decisions still can have preclusive effect in such suits.
(2) No. There is no categorical reason why trademark registration decisions can never meet the ordinary elements of issue preclusion. Although many registrations will not satisfy those ordinary elements, this does not mean none will. Issue preclusion will apply where the issues in the two cases are indeed identical and the other rules of collateral estoppel are carefully observed. Here the same likelihood-of-confusion standard applies to both registration and infringement. The fact the TTAB may have erred in applying that standard does not prevent preclusion, since issue preclusion prevents relitigation of wrong decisions just as much as right ones. Also, although the TTAB and district courts use different procedures (most notably, district courts feature live witnesses), such procedural differences by themselves do not

Continued on next page.

defeat issue preclusion. Instead, the correct inquiry regarding procedure should be whether the procedures applied in the first proceeding were fundamentally poor, cursory, or unfair. The fact the TTAB and district courts use different procedures suggests only that sometimes issue preclusion might be inappropriate, not that it always is. Here, there is no categorical reason to doubt the quality, extensiveness, or fairness, of the agency's procedures. In large part they are exactly the same as in federal court. Hargis (D) is also wrong that the stakes for registration are always too low for issue preclusion in later infringement litigation. When registration is opposed, there is good reason to think both sides will take the matter seriously. For these reasons, the court of appeals erred. On remand, the court should apply the following rule: So long as the other ordinary elements of issue preclusion are met, when the usages adjudicated by the TTAB are materially the same as those before the district court, issue preclusion should apply. Reversed and remanded.

DISSENT: (Thomas, J.) The majority incorrectly presumes Congress intended agency decisions to have preclusive effect in this area.

ANALYSIS

When Hargis (D) lost at the Trademark Trial and Appeal Board (TTAB), it had the right to appeal, but it declined to do so. The Court's decision may have the effect of causing losing parties before the TTAB to feel compelled to seek de novo review of the TTAB's decisions in federal court so as to avoid the preclusive effect of the TTAB's decisions. The Court's decision may also have the effect of making the TTAB's actions more important in the eyes of trademark owners, which could cause those proceedings to become more expensive and less streamlined. The same might also be said of proceedings before other agencies where the parties will be concerned with the preclusive effect of those agencies' decisions as a result of the Court's decision in this case.

Quicknotes

ISSUE PRECLUSION When a particular issue has already been litigated, further litigation of the same issue is barred.

TRADEMARK INFRINGEMENT The unauthorized use of another's trademark in such a manner as to cause a likelihood of confusion as to the source of the product or service in connection with which it is utilized.

Federated Department Stores, Inc. v. Moitie

Department store (D) v. Government (P)

452 U.S. 394 (1981)

NATURE OF CASE: Appeal from reversal of dismissal of antitrust action.

FACT SUMMARY: Federated Department Stores, Inc. (D) contended that the doctrine of res judicata barred relitigation of an unappealed adverse judgment where other plaintiffs in similar actions had successfully appealed judgments against them.

RULE OF LAW

Res judicata bars relitigation of an unappealed adverse judgment where other plaintiffs in similar actions against common defendants successfully appealed the judgments against them.

FACTS: In 1976, the Government (P) brought an antitrust action against Federated Department Stores, Inc. (Federated) (D), alleging that it had violated § 1 of the Sherman Act by agreeing to fix the retail price of women's clothing sold in Northern California. Seven parallel civil actions were subsequently filed by private plaintiffs seeking treble damages on behalf of proposed classes of retail purchasers, including that of Moitie (P) *(Moitie I)* in state court and Brown (P) *(Brown I)* in federal district court. Each of these complaints tracked almost verbatim the allegations of the Government's (P) complaint, although the *Moitie I* complaint referred solely to state law. All the actions, including *Moitie I,* were assigned to a single federal judge, who dismissed all the actions because of pleading defects. The plaintiffs in five of the suits appealed that judgment to the federal court of appeals, while the single counsel representing Moitie (P) and Brown (P) chose not to appeal and instead refiled the two actions in state court *(Moitie II* and *Brown II* respectively). Federated (D) removed the new actions to federal district court, where they were dismissed on the grounds of res judicata. However, the court of appeals reversed, such as was obtained by the other five plaintiffs, when their position is closely interwoven with that of the appealing parties. Federated (D) appealed.

ISSUE: Does res judicata bar relitigation of an unappealed adverse judgment where other plaintiffs in similar actions against common defendants successfully appealed the judgments against them?

HOLDING AND DECISION: (Rehnquist, J.) Yes. Res judicata bars relitigation of an unappealed adverse judgment where other plaintiffs in similar actions against common defendants successfully appealed the judgments against them. A final judgment on the merits of an action precludes the parties or their privies from relitigating issues that were, or could have been, raised in that action. A judgment, voidable merely because it is based upon an erroneous view of the law, is not open to collateral attack but can be corrected only by a direct review and not by bringing another action upon the same cause of action. Here, both *Brown I* and *Moitie I* were final judgments on the merits and involved the same claims and the same parties as *Brown II* and *Moitie II.* Both those parties seek to be the windfall beneficiaries on an appellate reversal procured by other independent parties, and it is further apparent that Brown (P) and Moitie (P) made a calculated choice to forgo their appeals. Reversed and remanded.

CONCURRENCE: (Blackmun, J.) *Brown I* is res judicata on Brown's (P) state law claims. Even if the state and federal claims are distinct, Brown's (P) failure to allege the state claims in *Brown I* manifestly bars their allegation in *Brown II.*

DISSENT: (Brennan, J.) The Court today disregards statutory restrictions on federal court jurisdiction and, in the process, confuses rather than clarifies long-established principles of res judicata.

ANALYSIS

The Court, in a footnote, agreed with the court of appeals that at least some of the claims had a sufficient federal character such as would support removal to the federal court. Both the district court and the court of appeals had found that Brown (P) and Moitie (P) had attempted to avoid removal jurisdiction by artfully casting their essentially federal law claims as state-law claims.

Quicknotes

ANTITRUST Body of federal law prohibiting business conduct that constitutes a restraint on trade.

FINAL JUDGMENT A decision by the court settling a dispute between the parties on its merits and which is appealable to a higher court.

JUDGMENT ON THE MERITS A determination of the rights of the parties to litigation based on the presentation evidence, barring the party from initiating the same suit again.

JURISDICTION The authority of a court to hear and declare judgment in respect to a particular matter.

Continued on next page.

PLEADING A statement setting forth the plaintiff's cause of action or the defendant's defenses to the plaintiff's claims.

REMOVAL Petition by a defendant to move the case to another court.

RES JUDICATA The rule of law a final judgment by a court precludes subsequent litigation between the parties regarding the same cause of action.

TREBLE DAMAGES An award of damages triple of the amount awarded by the jury and provided for by statute for violation of certain offenses.

Allen v. McCurry

Policemen (D) v. Criminal defendant (P)

449 U.S. 90 (1980)

NATURE OF CASE: Action for damages for violation of constitutional rights.

FACT SUMMARY: McCurry (P) sought damages from Allen (D) and other policemen for allegedly violating his constitutional rights in seizing the evidence that was introduced at his criminal trial and which resulted in conviction; Allen (D) raised a collateral estoppel defense.

RULE OF LAW

Collateral estoppel can be raised as a defense to a § 1983 suit brought by one convicted of a crime who is precluded from pursuing federal habeas corpus relief.

FACTS: McCurry (P) was convicted in state court after his motion to suppress certain evidence on grounds of unconstitutional search and seizure was denied in part. His conviction was upheld on appeal, and he was unable to pursue federal habeas corpus relief because he did not assert that the state courts had denied him a "full and fair opportunity" to litigate his search and seizure claim. So he brought a suit in federal court under § 1983, seeking damages from Allen (D) and other policemen who had been responsible for seizing the evidence, for an alleged violation of his constitutional rights. Allen (D) raised the state court's partial rejection of McCurry's (P) constitutional claim as a collateral estoppel defense to the § 1983 suit. The district court granted summary judgment for Allen (D), holding that collateral estoppel prevented McCurry (P) from relitigating the search and seizure question already decided against him in the state courts. The court of appeals reversed and remanded, concluding that since federal habeas corpus relief was precluded, the § 1983 suit was McCurry's (P) only route to a federal forum for his constitutional claim.

ISSUE: Can collateral estoppel be raised as a defense to a § 1983 suit brought by one convicted of a crime who is precluded from pursuing federal habeas corpus relief?

HOLDING AND DECISION: (Stewart, J.) Yes. Collateral estoppel can be raised as a defense to a § 1983 suit brought by one convicted of a crime who is precluded from pursuing federal habeas corpus relief. This remains the case even when the party bringing suit cannot pursue federal habeas corpus relief because he does not allege that he lacked a "full and fair" opportunity to litigate his constitutional claim in the state court criminal proceedings against him. Since § 1983 was designed to allow federal relief when state courts were unable or unwilling to protect federal rights, it might well support an exception to res judicata and collateral estoppel where there was not a full and fair opportunity to litigate the constitutional claim or issue in the state court proceeding, but that is the precise general limit on rules of preclusion which already exists. The actual basis of the court of appeals' holding appears to be a generally framed principle that every person asserting a federal right is entitled to one unencumbered opportunity to litigate that right in a federal district court, regardless of the legal posture in which the federal claim arises. However, there is no authority for such a position either in the Constitution or in the language or legislative history of § 1983. The court of appeals erred in holding that McCurry's (P) inability to obtain federal habeas corpus relief upon his Fourth Amendment claim renders the doctrine of collateral estoppel inapplicable to his § 1983 suit. Reversed and remanded.

DISSENT: (Blackmun, J.) Whether or not the doctrine of preclusion is applicable in a § 1983 case should not be determined by simply inquiring whether there was a "full and fair opportunity" to litigate the constitutional claim during the state proceedings. All relevant factors should be considered in each case before concluding that preclusion is warranted.

ANALYSIS

Even before this case was decided, it had been the virtually unanimous view of the court of appeals that § 1983 presented no categorical bar to the application of res judicata and collateral estoppel concepts. However, a few of the courts did suggest that the normal rules of claims preclusion should not apply in one particular instance: where § 1983 plaintiff seeks to litigate in federal court a federal issue which he could have raised but did not raise in an earlier state court suit against the same adverse party. The Supreme Court has yet to decide that issue.

Quicknotes

42 U.S.C. § 1983 Provides that every person who under color of state law subjects or causes to be subjected any citizen of the United States or person within its jurisdiction to be deprived of rights, privileges, and immunities

Continued on next page.

guaranteed by the federal Constitution and laws is liable to the injured party at law or in equity.

COLLATERAL ESTOPPEL A doctrine whereby issues litigated and determined in a prior proceeding are binding upon all subsequent litigation between the parties regarding that issue.

HABEAS CORPUS A proceeding in which a defendant brings a writ to compel a judicial determination of whether he is lawfully being held in custody.

RES JUDICATA The rule of law a final judgment by a court precludes subsequent litigation between the parties regarding the same cause of action.

CHAPTER 11

Aggregate Litigation: It All Comes Together

Quick Reference Rules of Law

	PAGE
1. *Hansberry v. Lee.* There must be adequate representation of the members of a class action or the judgment is not binding on the parties not adequately represented.	*166*
2. *Phillips Petroleum Co. v. Shutts.* (1) A class-action defendant has standing to challenge the jurisdiction of the class-certifying court over all class members where most of the members have no connections to the state in which the court sits, notwithstanding the rule that generally a party may assert only its own rights and has no standing to assert the rights of its adversary for the purpose of defeating a judgment in favor of the adversary. (2) In a class action, a court satisfies due process requirements and properly asserts personal jurisdiction over absent class members and their claims by having those members provided with notice, an opportunity to appear in person or by counsel, an opportunity to opt out of the class, and adequate representation, rather than requiring the absent members to affirmatively opt in to the class.	*168*
3. *Wal-Mart Stores, Inc. v. Dukes.* (1) A class consisting of more than one million women employed by a single employer nationwide cannot be certified as a class if they do not meet the "commonality" threshold for class certification under Federal Rule of Civil Procedure 23(a)(2) because they cannot demonstrate all class members were subject to the same discriminatory employment policy. (2) Claims for monetary relief may not be certified under Federal Rule of Civil Procedure 23(b)(2) where the monetary relief is not incidental to the injunctive or declaratory relief.	*171*
4. *Martin v. Wilks.* A consent decree mandating affirmative action does not have preclusive effect upon a subsequent challenge to those programs brought by persons not parties to the prior action.	*173*

Hansberry v. Lee

Purchaser of real property (D) v. Landowner (P)

311 U.S. 32 (1940)

NATURE OF CASE: A class action to enforce a racially restrictive covenant.

FACT SUMMARY: Lee (P) sought to enjoin a sale of land to the Hansberrys (D) on the grounds that the sale violates a racially restrictive covenant.

RULE OF LAW

There must be adequate representation of the members of a class action or the judgment is not binding on the parties not adequately represented.

FACTS: The Hansberrys (D), a Black family, purchased land from a party who had signed a restrictive covenant forbidding the sale of the land to Blacks. Lee (P), one of the parties who signed the covenant, sought to have the sale enjoined because it breached the covenant. Lee (P) contended that the validity of the covenant was established in a prior case in which one of the parties was a class of landowners involved with the covenant. To be valid, 95 percent of the landowners had to sign the covenant, and the trial court in the prior case held that 95 percent of the landowners had signed the covenant. That case was appealed, and the Illinois Supreme Court upheld the decision, even though they found that 95 percent of the landowners had not signed the covenant, but the court held that since it was a class action, all members of the class would be bound by the decision of the court. The Hansberrys (D) claimed that they and the party selling the house were not bound by the res judicata effect of the prior decision, as they were not parties to the litigation. The lower court held that the decision of the Illinois Supreme Court would have to be challenged directly in order that it be set aside or reversed. Otherwise, their decision was still binding. The case was appealed to the United States Supreme Court.

ISSUE: Must there be adequate representation of the members of a class action to make the judgment binding on the parties not adequately represented?

HOLDING AND DECISION: (Stone, J.) Yes. There must be adequate representation of the members of a class action or the judgment is not binding on the parties not adequately represented. It is not necessary that all members of a class be present as parties to the litigation in order to be bound by the judgment if they are adequately represented by parties who are present. In regular cases, to be bound by the judgment, the party must receive notice and an opportunity to be heard. If due process isn't afforded the individual, then the judgment is not binding. The class action is an exception to the general rule. Because of the numbers involved in class actions, it is enough if the party is adequately represented by a member of the class with a similar interest. The Hansberrys (D) weren't adequately represented by the class of landowners. Their interests were not similar enough to even be considered members of the same class. Lee (P) and the landowners were trying to restrict Blacks from buying any of the land, and the Hansberrys (D) were a Black family attempting to purchase land. When there is such a conflicting interest between members of a class, there is most likely not adequate representation of one of the members of the class. There must be a similarity of interest before there can even be a class. Since there was no similarity of interests between Lee (P) and the Hansberrys (D), the Hansberrys (D) could not be considered a member of the class so the prior judgment was not binding on the Hansberrys (D). The Hansberrys (D) were not afforded due process because of the lack of adequate representation. Reversed.

ANALYSIS

Rule 23(c)(3) requires that the court describe those whom the court finds to be members of the class. The court is to note those to whom notice was provided and those who had not requested exclusion. These members are considered members of the class and are bound by the decision of the court whether it is in their favor or not. The federal rules allow a member of the class to request exclusion from the class, and that party will not be bound by the decision of the court. Since a party must receive notice of the class action before he can request exclusion from the class, the court must determine if a party received sufficient notice of the action or if sufficient effort was made to notify him of the action. The rules state if the court finds that the party did have sufficient notice and was considered a member of the class, he is bound by the decision.

Quicknotes

CLASS ACTION SUIT A suit commenced by a representative on behalf of an ascertainable group that is too large to appear in court, who shares a commonality of interests, and who will benefit from a successful result.

COVENANT A written promise to do, or to refrain from doing, a particular activity.

Continued on next page.

DUE PROCESS CLAUSE Clauses, found in the Fifth and Fourteenth Amendments to the United States Constitution, providing that no person shall be deprived of "life, liberty, or property, without due process of law."

ENJOIN The ordering of a party to cease the conduct of a specific activity.

RES JUDICATA rule of law that a final judgment by a court precludes subsequent litigation between the parties regarding the same cause of action.

Phillips Petroleum Co. v. Shutts

Oil land lessee (D) v. Royalty owner (P)

472 U.S. 797 (1985)

NATURE OF CASE: Appeal from a state's highest court's affirmance of an award of damages in a class action for interest on suspended royalty payments by a lessee of land producing natural gas.

FACT SUMMARY: In a class action brought against it, Phillips Petroleum Co. (D) contended that Kansas courts lacked jurisdiction over out-of-state class members (P) where those members (P) had not affirmatively opted in to the class and otherwise did not have minimum contacts with Kansas.

RULE OF LAW

(1) A class-action defendant has standing to challenge the jurisdiction of the class-certifying court over all class members where most of the members have no connections to the state in which the court sits, notwithstanding the rule that generally a party may assert only its own rights and has no standing to assert the rights of its adversary for the purpose of defeating a judgment in favor of the adversary.

(2) In a class action, a court satisfies due process requirements and properly asserts personal jurisdiction over absent class members and their claims by having those members provided with notice, an opportunity to appear in person or by counsel, an opportunity to opt out of the class, and adequate representation, rather than requiring the absent members to affirmatively opt in to the class.

FACTS: A class-action lawsuit was filed in Kansas state court on behalf of around 33,000 royalty owners (P) seeking interest payments on delayed royalty payments against Phillips Petroleum Co. (Phillips) (D), an oil company that leased land in 11 states from which it extracted natural gas that it sold in interstate commerce. The class members (P) resided in all U.S. states, the District of Columbia, and foreign countries. The class was certified over Phillips's (D) objections. Notice of the lawsuit was sent by first-class mail to each class member (P) with an explanation that each class member would be bound unless the member "opted out" of the suit, along with other information about the action and the representative plaintiffs. Of the roughly 28,000 members (P) who opted in, fewer than 1,000 resided in Kansas. Moreover, only one quarter of one percent of the gas leases at issue were on Kansas land. At the end of the trial, damages were awarded against Phillips (D) at interest rates under Kansas law, but the court did not determine whether any difference existed between the laws of Kansas and other states, or whether another state's laws should be applied to non-Kansas plaintiffs or to royalties from leases in states other than Kansas. On appeal to the Kansas Supreme Court, Phillips (D) claimed that the trial court lacked personal jurisdiction over absent class members (P), and that the "opt-out" notice to absent class members (P), which forced them to return the request for exclusion to avoid the suit, was insufficient to bind class members (P) who were not residents of Kansas or who did not possess "minimum contacts" with Kansas. Second, Phillips (D) claimed that Kansas courts could not apply Kansas law to every claim in the dispute, and that the trial court should have looked to the laws of each state where the leases were located to determine, on the basis of conflict of laws principles, whether interest on the suspended royalties was recoverable and at what rate. The Supreme Court of Kansas rejected both these claims and affirmed. Phillips (D) appealed to the United States Supreme Court, arguing that the Due Process Clause prevented the Kansas courts from exercising jurisdiction over the class members (P) that had no contacts with Kansas. Phillips (D) also argued that the Due Process Clause and the Full Faith and Credit Clause of Article IV of the United States Constitution prohibited the application of Kansas law to all the transactions between Phillips (D) and the class members (P). The United States Supreme Court granted certiorari.

ISSUE:

(1) Does a class-action defendant have standing to challenge the jurisdiction of the class-certifying court over all class members where most of the members have no connections to the state in which the court sits, notwithstanding the rule that generally a party may assert only its own rights and has no standing to assert the rights of its adversary for the purpose of defeating a judgment in favor of the adversary?

(2) In a class action, does a court satisfy due process requirements and properly assert personal jurisdiction over absent class members and their claims by having those members provided with notice, an opportunity to appear in person or by counsel, an opportunity to opt out of the class, and adequate representation, rather than requiring the absent members to affirmatively opt in to the class?

Continued on next page.

HOLDING AND DECISION: (Rehnquist, J.)

(1) Yes. A class-action defendant has standing to challenge the jurisdiction of the class-certifying court over all class members where most of the members have no connections to the state in which the court sits, notwithstanding the rule that generally a party may assert only its own rights and has no standing to assert the rights of its adversary for the purpose of defeating a judgment in favor of the adversary. Although it is true that one of the prudential limits on Article III standing is that a litigant must normally assert his own legal interests rather than those of third parties, and that Phillips Petroleum Co.'s (Phillips's) (D) interests are not aligned with those of the class (P), Phillips (D) is seeking to vindicate its own interests. If it is decided that Kansas does not have jurisdiction over the class (P), Phillips (D), as a class-action defendant, will be bound by the Kansas court's decree but none of the class members (P) will be bound thereby. Thus, there would be the potential for Phillips (D) to face numerous later individual suits by these class members (P) because a judgment issued without proper personal jurisdiction over an absent party is not entitled to full faith and credit elsewhere and so has no res judicata effect as to that party. And the only way a class-action defendant like Phillips (D) can assure itself of this binding effect of the judgment is to ascertain that the forum court has jurisdiction over every class member (P) whose claim it seeks to adjudicate, sufficient to support a defense of res judicata in a later suit for damages by class members (P). Because Phillips (D) would be immediately injured if the class-action judgment were to become final without binding the class (P), such injury is sufficient to confer standing on Phillips (D) to raise the jurisdictional issue. Judgment for Phillips (D) as to this issue.

(2) Yes. In a class action, a court satisfies due process requirements and properly asserts personal jurisdiction over absent class members and their claims by having those members provided with notice, an opportunity to appear in person or by counsel, an opportunity to opt out of the class, and adequate representation, rather than requiring the absent members to affirmatively opt in to the class. Phillips's (D) essential argument is that absent an out-of-state class member's (P) affirmative consent to opt into the class, the court lacks jurisdiction over that member (P), and that the opt-out election does not constitute such consent. Effectively, Phillips (D) would require that out-of-state class member plaintiffs (P) (about 97 percent of the class) have "minimum contacts" with Kansas to the same extent that due process requires that out-of-state defendants have minimum contacts with a jurisdiction before that jurisdiction can exercise personal jurisdiction over those defendants. The "minimum contacts" test of *International Shoe Co. v. Washington*, 326 U.S. 310 (1945), recognizes that due process demands that a defendant should not be subjected to the expense and uncertainty of defending in an alien forum unless the defendant has sufficient contact with the forum that would make it reasonable that he or she would reasonably expect to "being hauled" into court there. However, Phillips's (D) argument that out-of-state plaintiffs are similarly situated jurisdictionally—and require the same due process protections—as out-of-state defendants is unpersuasive. A class-action plaintiff is in nowhere nearly as perilous a position as a civil defendant. In contrast to an out-of-state defendant, a class-action plaintiff need not travel, need not retain counsel, need not engage in discovery (which can be extensive and costly), need not face potential damages upon losing the suit, and need not face potential liability for court costs and attorney's fees. It is precisely because the burdens on an out-of-state defendant are potentially great that the minimum contacts requirement and due process notions of fair play prevent a forum state from unfairly imposing such burdens. On the other hand, the class-action plaintiff can sit back and do nothing; from the class-action plaintiff's view, the action resembles a quasi-administrative proceeding conducted by a judge. The court must certify the class, after conducting numerous inquiries designed to protect absent members, so the danger of improper inclusion and inadequate representation in a class is minimal, since the court and named plaintiff protect the absent members' interests. Moreover, the court continues to be solicitous of, and to guard, such interests. Because an out-of-state class-action plaintiff does not face the potential burdens faced by an out-of-state civil defendant, less protection is required for the class-action member under the Due Process Clause than for the out-of-state defendant. Thus, a forum state may exercise jurisdiction over the claim of an absent class-action plaintiff even though that plaintiff may not possess the minimum contacts with the forum that would support personal jurisdiction over a defendant. If the forum state wishes to bind an absent plaintiff concerning a claim for money damages or similar relief at law, it must provide minimal procedural due process protection. Here, such minimal protections were provided when each plaintiff was notified and given the opportunity to "opt out" of the suit in a reasonable time, with guarantees of adequate representation. This was all due process required. Therefore, the Kansas courts properly exercised jurisdiction over the out-of-state class-action

Continued on next page.

members (P). The Kansas Supreme Court's judgment is affirmed insofar as it upheld such jurisdiction. Judgment for the class-action members (P) as to this issue. Affirmed in part, reversed in part, and remanded.

ANALYSIS

The Court's holding as to jurisdiction over out-of-state class-action plaintiffs was limited to those class actions that seek to bind known plaintiffs concerning claims wholly or predominately for money judgments; it did not extend to other types of class actions, such as those seeking equitable relief. Nor did the Court's discussion of personal jurisdiction address class actions where the jurisdiction is asserted against a defendant class.

Quicknotes

CLASS ACTION A suit commenced by a representative on behalf of an ascertainable group that is too large to appear in court, who share a commonality of interests, and who will benefit from a successful result.

DUE PROCESS CLAUSE Clauses, found in the Fifth and Fourteenth Amendments to the United States Constitution, providing that no person shall be deprived of "life, liberty, or property, without due process of law."

Wal-Mart Stores, Inc. v. Dukes

Retail giant (D) v. Female employees (P)

564 U.S. 338 (2011)

NATURE OF CASE: Class action based on gender discrimination.

FACT SUMMARY: A small group of women filed a gender discrimination claim against Wal-Mart Stores, Inc. (D). A class was certified, and the original small group of women who filed the claims wanted to represent the class. The class was the largest in history.

RULE OF LAW

(1) A class consisting of more than one million women employed by a single employer nationwide cannot be certified as a class if they do not meet the "commonality" threshold for class certification under Fed. R. Civ. P. 23(a)(2) because they cannot demonstrate all class members were subject to the same discriminatory employment policy.

(2) Claims for monetary relief may not be certified under Fed. R. Civ. P. 23(b)(2) where the monetary relief is not incidental to the injunctive or declaratory relief.

FACTS: Betty Dukes (P), a Wal-Mart Stores, Inc. (Wal-Mart) (D) "greeter" at a Pittsburg, California, store, and five other women filed a class-action lawsuit in which they alleged that the company's nationwide policies resulted in lower pay for women than men in comparable positions and longer wait for management promotions than men. The U.S. District Court for the Northern District of California certified the class, finding Plaintiffs satisfied the requirements of Fed. R. Civ. P. 23(a)(2) and 23(b)(2). The certified class was estimated to include more than 1.5 million women including all women employed by Wal-Mart (D) nationwide at any time after December 26, 1998, making this the largest class action lawsuit in U.S. history. Wal-Mart (D) argued that the court should require employees to file on an individual basis, contending that class actions of this size—formed under Fed. R. Civ. P. 23(b) of the federal rules of civil procedure—are inherently unmanageable and unduly costly. The United States Court of Appeals for the Ninth Circuit upheld the class certification three times.

ISSUE:

(1) Can a class consisting of more than one million women employed by a single employer nationwide be certified as a class if they do not meet the "commonality" threshold for class certification under Fed. R. Civ. P. 23(a)(2) because they cannot demonstrate all class members were subject to the same discriminatory employment policy?

(2) May claims for monetary relief be certified under Fed. R. Civ. P. 23(b)(2) where the monetary relief is not incidental to the injunctive or declaratory relief?

HOLDING AND DECISION: (Scalia, J.)

(1) No. A class consisting of more than one million women employed by a single employer nationwide cannot be certified as a class if they do not meet the "commonality" threshold for class certification under Fed. R. Civ. P. 23(a)(2) because they cannot demonstrate all class members were subject to the same discriminatory employment policy. The class action is "an exception to the usual rule that litigation is conducted by and on behalf of the individual named parties only." In order to justify a departure from that rule, "a class representative must be part of the class and 'possess the same interest and suffer the same injury' as the class members." Rule 23(a) ensures that the named plaintiffs are appropriate representatives of the class whose claims they wish to litigate. The Rule's four requirements—numerosity, commonality, typicality, and adequate representation—effectively "limit the class claims to those fairly encompassed by the named plaintiff's claims." The second of the Rule's four requirements, "proof of commonality," necessarily overlaps with the group's argument that Wal-Mart Stores, Inc. (Wal-Mart) (D) engages in a pattern or practice of discrimination. Under Title VII, the central inquiry involves the reason for a particular employment decision, and the plaintiffs wish to sue for millions of employment decisions at once. Without something holding together the alleged reasons for those employment decisions, it would be impossible to say that examination of all the class members' claims will produce a common answer to the crucial discrimination question. The testimony of the plaintiffs' social science expert who claimed that Wal-Mart's (D) culture was susceptible to gender bias is unpersuasive. The testimony is useless to the question of whether the plaintiffs could prove a general policy of discrimination. Also rejected, is the use of aggregate statistical analyses and the mere existence of gender disparities in pay, promotion, or representation to meet the commonality burden. Instead, to show commonality, a plaintiff would at least need to demonstrate store-by-store disparities. Third, affidavits from 120 individuals, or one out of every 12,500 class members, did not constitute "significant proof" that Wal-Mart (D) operates under a

Continued on next page.

general policy of discrimination. The members of the plaintiffs' group held many different jobs, at different levels of Wal-Mart's (D) hierarchy, for variable lengths of time, in 3,400 stores, across 50 states, with many different supervisors (male and female), subject to a variety of regional policies that all differed. Some thrived while others did not. They have little in common but their sex and this lawsuit.

(2) No. Claims for monetary relief may not be certified under Fed. R. Civ. P. 23(b)(2) where the monetary relief is not incidental to the injunctive or declaratory relief. After satisfying the elements of Rule 23(a), the proposed class must satisfy at least one of the three requirements listed in Rule 23(b). The plaintiffs sought certification under Rule 23(b)(2), which applies when "the party opposing the class has acted or refused to act on grounds that apply generally to the class, so that final injunctive relief or corresponding declaratory relief is appropriate respecting the class as a whole." But Rule 23(b)(2) applies only when a single injunction or declaratory judgment would provide relief to each member of the class. It does not authorize class certification when each individual class member would be entitled to a *different* injunction or declaratory judgment against the defendant. Similarly, it does not authorize class certification when each class member would be entitled to an individualized award of monetary damages. The "predominance test" established by the Ninth Circuit, which permitted the certification of claims for monetary damages so long as claims for injunctive relief "predominated" over the claims for monetary damages, is rejected. Rather, the "incidental damages" test, which permits certification of claims for monetary relief as long as relief "flow[s] directly from liability to the class as a whole," which "should not require additional hearings," is more appropriate. The adoption of a bright-line rule prohibiting all money damages from ever being certified under Rule 23(b)(2) is not considered here. Reversed.

CONCURRENCE AND DISSENT: (Ginsburg, J.) The class should not have been certified under Fed. R. Civ. P. 23(b)(2), because the plaintiffs, alleging discrimination in violation of Title VII, seek monetary relief that is not merely incidental to any injunctive or declaratory relief that might be available. But a class of this type may be certifiable under Rule 23(b)(3), if the plaintiffs show that common class questions "predominate" over issues affecting individuals, such as qualification for, and the amount of, back pay or compensatory damages, and that a class action is "superior" to other modes of adjudication. Whether the class the plaintiffs describe meets the specific requirements of Rule 23(b)(3) is not before the Court, and that matter should be reserved for consideration and decision on remand. But the majority disqualifies the class under 23(a)(2), holding that the plaintiffs cannot cross the "commonality" line, and by doing so imports into the Rule 23(a) determination concerns properly addressed in a Rule 23(b)(3) assessment. The majority errs in importing a "dissimilarities" notion suited to Rule 23(b)(3) into the Rule 23(a) commonality inquiry.

ANALYSIS

This is a landmark case that was thoroughly analyzed in the media when it was released. Many criticized the decision as inappropriately and unfairly raising the bar for certification to the detriment of those with valid Title VII claims. District courts will now be required to scrutinize closely all alleged common questions of law and fact to determine if the proposed common questions generate common answers that are apt to drive resolution in each case. It will not be sufficient for plaintiffs to allege a "general policy" without proving the existence of the policy and its impact on each class member.

Quicknotes

CLASS ACTION A suit commenced by a representative on behalf of an ascertainable group that is too large to appear in court, who shares a commonality of interests, and who will benefit from a successful result.

CLASS CERTIFICATION Certification by a court's granting of a motion to allow individual litigants to join as one plaintiff in a class action against the defendant.

Martin v. Wilks

Municipality (D) v. White firefighters (P)

490 U.S. 755 (1989)

NATURE OF CASE: Review of order reinstating reverse discrimination action.

FACT SUMMARY: In a reverse discrimination action, it was contended that an earlier consent decree mandating certain affirmative action procedures barred a subsequent reverse discrimination action by parties not involved in the prior action.

RULE OF LAW

A consent decree mandating affirmative action does not have preclusive effect upon a subsequent challenge to those programs brought by persons not parties to the prior action.

FACTS: Several Black firefighters brought a discrimination action against the City of Birmingham, Alabama (D). The suit was settled by way of a consent decree wherein certain affirmative action programs were mandated. Subsequently, several White firefighters (P) brought suit, contending that the affirmative action programs constituted reverse discrimination in violation of federal civil rights laws. The district court dismissed, holding that the prior judgment had preclusive effect as to the validity of the programs. The Eleventh Circuit Court of Appeals reversed. The United States Supreme Court granted review.

ISSUE: Does a consent decree mandating affirmative action have preclusive effect upon a subsequent challenge to those programs brought by persons not parties to the prior action?

HOLDING AND DECISION: (Rehnquist, C.J.) No. A consent decree mandating affirmative action does not have preclusive effect upon a subsequent challenge to those programs brought by persons not parties to the prior action. It is a principle of general application in Anglo-American jurisprudence that one is not bound by a judgment in personam in which he was not a party. This rule is part of our deep-seated tradition that everyone should have his own day in court. However, the argument is made here that because the plaintiffs in this action had notice of the prior action and could have intervened, they cannot now complain of the prior judgment. This is incorrect. Fed. R. Civ. P. 24, which deals with intervention, is cast in permissive, not compulsory, terms. Rule 19, dealing with joinder, can be compulsory. Where Rule 19 is not invoked to join a nonconsenting party, as was not done here, a judgment cannot bind the nonparty. Affirmed.

DISSENT: (Stevens, J.) The Court has crafted a rule that in essence allows nonparties to appeal a final judgment an indeterminate time after it is entered.

ANALYSIS

This decision and several others handed down the same year provoked a reaction in the civil rights community. Congress eventually passed the Civil Rights Restoration Act, which was vetoed in 1990 but signed in 1991. The rule of this case was legislatively overruled.

Quicknotes

AFFIRMATIVE ACTION A form of benign discrimination designed to remedy existing discrimination by favoring one group over another.

COLLATERAL ATTACK A proceeding initiated in order to challenge the integrity of a previous judgment.

CONSENT DECREE A decree issued by a court of equity ratifying an agreement between the parties to a lawsuit; an agreement by a defendant to cease illegal activity.

FED. R. CIV. P. 19 Governs compulsory party joinder.

FED. R. CIV. P. 24 Establishes intervention requirements.

JOINDER The joining of claims or parties in one lawsuit.

Glossary

Common Latin Words and Phrases Encountered in the Law

A FORTIORI: Because one fact exists or has been proven, therefore a second fact that is related to the first fact must also exist.

A PRIORI: From the cause to the effect. A term of logic used to denote that when one generally accepted truth is shown to be a cause, another particular effect must necessarily follow.

AB INITIO: From the beginning; a condition that has existed throughout, as in a marriage that was void ab initio.

ACTUS REUS: The wrongful act; in criminal law, such action sufficient to trigger criminal liability.

AD VALOREM: According to value; an ad valorem tax is imposed upon an item located within the taxing jurisdiction calculated by the value of such item.

AMICUS CURIAE: Friend of the court. Its most common usage takes the form of an amicus curiae brief, filed by a person who is not a party to an action but is nonetheless allowed to offer an argument supporting his legal interests.

ARGUENDO: In arguing. A statement, possibly hypothetical, made for the purpose of argument is one made arguendo.

BILL QUIA TIMET: A bill to quiet title (establish ownership) to real property.

BONA FIDE: True, honest, or genuine. May refer to a person's legal position based on good faith or lacking notice of fraud (such as a bona fide purchaser for value) or to the authenticity of a particular document (such as a bona fide last will and testament).

CAUSA MORTIS: With approaching death in mind. A gift causa mortis is a gift given by a party who feels certain that death is imminent.

CAVEAT EMPTOR: Let the buyer beware. This maxim is reflected in the rule of law that a buyer purchases at his own risk because it is his responsibility to examine, judge, test, and otherwise inspect what he is buying.

CERTIORARI: A writ of review. Petitions for review of a case by the United States Supreme Court are most often done by means of a writ of certiorari.

CONTRA: On the other hand. Opposite. Contrary to.

CORAM NOBIS: Before us; writs of error directed to the court that originally rendered the judgment.

CORAM VOBIS: Before you; writs of error directed by an appellate court to a lower court to correct a factual error.

CORPUS DELICTI: The body of the crime; the requisite elements of a crime amounting to objective proof that a crime has been committed.

CUM TESTAMENTO ANNEXO, ADMINISTRATOR (ADMINISTRATOR C.T.A.): With will annexed; an administrator c.t.a. settles an estate pursuant to a will in which he or she is not appointed.

DE BONIS NON, ADMINISTRATOR (ADMINISTRATOR D.B.N.): Of goods not administered; an administrator d.b.n. settles a partially settled estate.

DE FACTO: In fact; in reality; actually. Existing in fact but not officially approved or engendered.

DE JURE: By right; lawful. Describes a condition that is legitimate "as a matter of law," in contrast to the term "de facto," which connotes something existing in fact but not legally sanctioned or authorized. For example, de facto segregation refers to segregation brought about by housing patterns, etc., whereas de jure segregation refers to segregation created by law.

DE MINIMUS: Of minimal importance; insignificant; a trifle; not worth bothering about.

DE NOVO: Anew; a second time; afresh. A trial de novo is a new trial held at the appellate level as if the case originated there and the trial at a lower level had not taken place.

DICTA: Generally used as an abbreviated form of obiter dicta, a term describing those portions of a judicial opinion incidental or not necessary to resolution of the specific question before the court. Such nonessential statements and remarks are not considered to be binding precedent.

DUCES TECUM: Refers to a particular type of writ or subpoena requesting a party or organization to produce certain documents in their possession.

EN BANC: Full bench. Where a court sits with all justices present rather than the usual quorum.

EX PARTE: For one side or one party only. An ex parte proceeding is one undertaken for the benefit of only one party, without notice to, or an appearance by, an adverse party.

EX POST FACTO: After the fact. An ex post facto law is a law that retroactively changes the consequences of a prior act.

EX REL.: Abbreviated form of the term "ex relatione," meaning upon relation or information. When the state brings an action in which it has no interest against an individual at the instigation of one who has a private interest in the matter.

FORUM NON CONVENIENS: Inconvenient forum. Although a court may have jurisdiction over the case, the action should be tried in a more conveniently located court, one to which parties and witnesses may more easily travel, for example.

GUARDIAN AD LITEM: A guardian appointed by the court to represent a minor or incompetent person in a legal action.

HABEAS CORPUS: You have the body. The modern writ of habeas corpus is a writ directing that a person (body) being detained (such as a prisoner) be brought before the court so that the legality of his detention can be judicially ascertained.

IN CAMERA: In private, in chambers. When a hearing is held before a judge in his or her chambers or when all spectators are excluded from the courtroom.

IN FORMA PAUPERIS: In the manner of a pauper. A party who proceeds in forma pauperis because of his poverty is one who is allowed to bring suit without } liability for costs.

INFRA: Below, under. A word referring the reader to a later part of a book. (The opposite of supra.)

IN LOCO PARENTIS: In the place of a parent.

IN PARI DELICTO: Equally wrong; a court of equity will not grant requested relief to an applicant who is in pari delicto, or as much at fault in the transactions giving rise to the controversy as is the opponent of the applicant.

IN PARI MATERIA: On like subject matter or upon the same matter. Statutes relating to the same person or things are said to be in pari materia. It is a general rule of statutory construction that such statutes should be construed together, i.e., looked at as if they together constituted one law.

IN PERSONAM: Against the person. Jurisdiction over the person of an individual.

IN RE: In the matter of. Used to designate a proceeding involving an estate or other property.

IN REM: A term that signifies an action against the res, or thing. An action in rem is basically one that is taken directly against property, as distinguished from an action in personam, i.e., against the person.

INTER ALIA: Among other things. Used to show that the whole of a statement, pleading, list, statute, etc., has not been set forth in its entirety.

INTER PARTES: Between the parties. May refer to contracts, conveyances, or other transactions having legal significance.

INTER VIVOS: Between the living. An inter vivos gift is a gift made by a living grantor, as distinguished from bequests contained in a will, which pass upon the death of the testator.

IPSO FACTO: By the mere fact itself.

JUS: Law or the entire body of law.

LEX LOCI: The law of the place; the notion that the rights of parties to a legal proceeding are governed by the law of the place where those rights arose.

MALUM IN SE: Evil or wrong in and of itself; inherently wrong. This term describes an act that is wrong by its very nature, as opposed to one which would not be wrong but for the fact that there is a specific legal prohibition against it (malum prohibitum).

MALUM PROHIBITUM: Wrong because prohibited, but not inherently evil. Used to describe something that is wrong because it is expressly forbidden by law but that is not in and of itself evil, e.g., speeding.

MANDAMUS: We command. A writ directing an official to take a certain action.

MENS REA: A guilty mind; a criminal intent. A term used to signify the mental state that accompanies a crime or other prohibited act. Some crimes require only a general mens rea (general intent to do the prohibited act), but others, like assault with intent to murder, require the existence of a specific mens rea.

MODUS OPERANDI: Method of operating; generally refers to the manner or style of a criminal in committing crimes, admissible in appropriate cases as evidence of the identity of a defendant.

NEXUS: A connection to.

NISI PRIUS: A court of first impression. A nisi prius court is one where issues of fact are tried before a judge or jury.

N.O.V. (NON OBSTANTE VEREDICTO): Notwithstanding the verdict. A judgment n.o.v. is a judgment given in favor of one party despite the fact that a verdict was returned in favor of the other party, the justification being that the verdict either had no reasonable support in fact or was contrary to law.

NUNC PRO TUNC: Now for then. This phrase refers to actions that may be taken and will then have full retroactive effect.

PENDENTE LITE: Pending the suit; pending litigation underway.

PER CAPITA: By head; beneficiaries of an estate, if they take in equal shares, take per capita.

PER CURIAM: By the court; signifies an opinion ostensibly written "by the whole court" and with no identified author.

PER SE: By itself, in itself; inherently.

PER STIRPES: By representation. Used primarily in the law of wills to describe the method of distribution where a person, generally because of death, is unable to take that which is left to him by the will of another, and therefore his heirs divide such property between them rather than take under the will individually.

PRIMA FACIE: On its face, at first sight. A prima facie case is one that is sufficient on its face, meaning that the evidence supporting it is adequate to establish the case until contradicted or overcome by other evidence.

PRO TANTO: For so much; as far as it goes. Often used in eminent domain cases when a property owner receives partial payment for his land without prejudice to his right to bring suit for the full amount he claims his land to be worth.

QUANTUM MERUIT: As much as he deserves. Refers to recovery based on the doctrine of unjust enrichment in those cases in which a party has rendered valuable services or furnished materials that were accepted and enjoyed by another under circumstances that would reasonably notify the recipient that the rendering party expected to be paid. In essence, the law implies a contract to pay the reasonable value of the services or materials furnished.

QUASI: Almost like; as if; nearly. This term is essentially used to signify that one subject or thing is almost analogous to another but that material differences between them do exist. For example, a quasi-criminal proceeding is one that is not strictly criminal but shares enough of the same characteristics to require some of the same safeguards (e.g., procedural due process must be followed in a parole hearing).

QUID PRO QUO: Something for something. In contract law, the consideration, something of value, passed between the parties to render the contract binding.

RES GESTAE: Things done. In evidence law, this principle justifies the admission of a statement that would otherwise be hearsay when it is made so closely to the event in question as to be said to be a part of it, or with such spontaneity as not to have the possibility of falsehood.

RES IPSA LOQUITUR: The thing speaks for itself. This doctrine gives rise to a rebuttable presumption of negligence when the instrumentality causing the injury was within the exclusive control of the defendant, and the injury was one that does not normally occur unless a person has been negligent.

RES JUDICATA: A matter adjudged. Doctrine which provides that once a court of competent jurisdiction has rendered a final judgment or decree on the merits, that judgment or decree is conclusive upon the parties to the case and prevents them from engaging in any other litigation on the points and issues determined therein.

RESPONDEAT SUPERIOR: Let the master reply. This doctrine holds the master liable for the wrongful acts of his servant (or the principal for his agent) in those cases in which the servant (or agent) was acting within the scope of his authority at the time of the injury.

STARE DECISIS: To stand by or adhere to that which has been decided. The common law doctrine of stare decisis attempts to give security and certainty to the law by following the policy that once a principle of law as applicable to a certain set of facts has been set forth in a decision, it forms a precedent that will subsequently be followed, even though a different decision might be made were it the first time the question had arisen. Of course, stare decisis is not an inviolable principle and is departed from in instances where there is good cause (e.g., considerations of public policy led the Supreme Court to disregard prior decisions sanctioning segregation).

SUPRA: Above. A word referring a reader to an earlier part of a book. (The opposite of infra.)

ULTRA VIRES: Beyond the power. This phrase is most commonly used to refer to actions taken by a corporation that are beyond the power or legal authority of the corporation.

Addendum of French Derivatives

CHATTEL: Tangible personal property.

CY PRES: Doctrine permitting courts to apply trust funds to purposes not expressed in the trust but necessary to carry out the settlor's intent.

IN PAIS: Not pursuant to legal proceedings.

PER AUTRE VIE: For another's life; during another's life. In property law, an estate may be granted that will terminate upon the death of someone other than the grantee.

PROFIT A PRENDRE: A license to remove minerals or other produce from land.

VOIR DIRE: Process of questioning jurors as to their predispositions about the case or parties to a proceeding in order to identify those jurors displaying bias or prejudice.